LAKEFRONT AIRPORT
Philip Marshall

Copyright © 2013 by Phillip Marshall
All rights reserved. This book or any portion thereof
may not be reproduced or used in any manner whatsoever
without the express written permission of the publisher
except for the use of brief quotations in a book review.

Printed in the United States of America

Second Printing, 2013

ISBN 978-1481859653

Veritas vos liberabit

PROLOGUE

Never Amounted to Shit

Between radar sweeps and perilous night swells of the Gulf of Mexico, the leading importer of recreational goods from South America kept the twin-engine Piper Seneca on course with sharp eyes and steady hands. Through a windscreen streaked with moisture, Brophy Wales raced to beat the approaching cold front against a forty knot headwind that was kicking up whitecaps just twenty feet below. Instant death would be the first hint of narcolepsy.

Aft of the cockpit bulkhead, fifteen wrapped bales moved slightly with each bump around a makeshift fifty-five gallon auxiliary fuel tank in the space normally occupied by passenger seats. A locator antenna was attached to each two-kilo bale.

For the past five hours, Wales had flown the second leg of his journey by the seat of his pants with all lights out to keep his night vision perfect. Finally, dawn cracked against florescent orange of high cirrus to the east above drilling rig derricks that glistened like Christmas trees on the horizon.

Though he flew with hollow bones of a bird, time was gaining on the former airline pilot. He sat forty pounds heavier than optimum weight for a six-foot man of forty-three. The black hair he combed over the thin spot on his crown was going gray. Crow's feet framed intense bloodshot brown eyes that began to burn with the energy-sapping sunrise. His belly growled with hunger. He could pee for thirty minutes.

Wales was blessed and cursed with a photographic memory. A slideshow had perpetually clicked in his head during the marathon cruise from Colombia. Again, he visualized his drop plan with worries about those damn intangibles that could fluke him into a federal penitentiary. Click. He ran through a plan for contingencies that he could imagine and trusted his cunning for the ones he could not. Click. His tanks held ninety minutes of fuel. Click. In an hour and a half, he would either be on his way home or on his way to the big house.

The air traffic radar he was currently eluding was a remote antenna for Houston Center, located just south of beautiful downtown Leesville, Louisiana. It had swept all night, but nary a blip reflected from the Seneca. The radar had begun to pick up Petroleum Helicopter's fleet of Bell 212s as they lifted from drilling rigs of the massive oil patch with crews of exhausted roughnecks and roustabouts heading home from seven-day hitches. Leesville bounced their blips to Houston Center, where they painted on the screens of ten air traffic controllers. The targets all squawked the code for Visual Flight Rules on electronic transponders, solely an advisory to the controllers, who had no real need to identify or talk with the pilots. The controllers simply ignored the dozen PHI targets offshore on the lower portion of the round green screen. Their main concerns were the business planes on instrument flight plans they worked in and out of Houma, Lafayette and Morgan City. There certainly was no alarm when another target appeared seventy-five miles south of Grand Isle within a dozen targets, all squawking 1200.

Wales turned to the right seat. "Damn son...ya gonna sleep all day, too?" Wales yanked the yoke aft, jolting Camille Mouton from a Jamaican beach to the harsh morning light of the sky-filled windscreen. Gravity paralyzed him to the seatback and he nearly wet his Levis.

"Goddamn...You bastard." Mouton pulled himself up groggily and looked out of his side window to see the turbulent Gulf water below as the plane climbed. "On course?"

"Course this...We're gonna find out right now." Wales leveled off at 1,400 feet, high enough to ping the radar and to pick up navigation signals from the station at Grand Isle. He pulled the throttles back to eighty knots and dialed 1200 into the transponder. To the controllers at Houston Center, it was obviously another PHI chopper. He centered Grand Isle with his navigation needle as the Distance Measuring Equipment lit up seventy-two miles. Wales lifted his eyebrows to his lethargic co-pilot. "Easy money."

Posing as a Petroleum Helicopter, he flew directly over the PHI heliport just south of Morgan City at 1,400 feet, pulled both throttles to idle until he reset power fifty feet above the swamp a mile west of Louisiana Highway 1. Calmly, he waited for the pre-arranged site to appear. After twenty seconds, he spotted the narrow, cypress-lined bayou and rolled the Seneca into a smooth forty-degree bank below the treetops. As the plane roared up the deserted waterway, egrets and redfish dove for cover. Wales scanned the surface for the pirogue anchored at the mouth of a small lake, the signal that the coast was clear. Mouton crawled back over the cargo and fuel tank, popped open the lower entry door and pulled the first bale into position.

Three men below manned their own flat-bottomed skiffs. Each was equipped with a fishing pole, handheld radios, a receiver to locate the transmitter on every bale, a Mac 10 semi-automatic machine gun and enough ammunition to hold off the Lafourche Parish Sheriff Department for days. God help any Cajun boy who might innocently wander upon the men, who had been there since three a.m.

Wales pulled his handheld radio. "Twenty?" He let go of the mike key and instantly got his answer.

"Twenty-one clear," said the man in the boat on the bayou side of the pirogue.

"Thirty?"

"Thirty-two clear," said the man in the boat on the west shore of the lake.

"Forty?" Wales banked left along the shore of the four-mile wide lake.

"Forty-three clear."

Wales signaled Mouton to kick the first package into moist, warm air. He continued circling the lake as his co-pilot kicked another fourteen times on cue. They circled back once more to count the bales aloud and confirm that all packs were within easy recovery range. As the boats converged for pickup, Wales pushed the throttles to the firewall and the Seneca shot west, flying a hundred feet above the swamp for ten miles before spiraling to 1,000 feet to check for tails. A leisurely cruise north around the west of Baton Rouge preceded a smooth landing at the uncontrolled 3,000-foot strip at New Roads, Louisiana.

As the plane rolled to a stop, a Chevy van appeared with a young brunette at the wheel. After Wales enjoyed a divine bladder release in the gravel parking lot, she drove the smuggler south to Baton Rouge. Firing up his new Toyota Corolla, Camille Mouton lit a Camel, inhaled deeply, and headed north to St. Francisville for several well-earned days of solitude and ganja.

Back on Highway 1, an unmarked panel truck approached the small Cajun town of Golden Meadow. In the rear were the booty, the boats, the guns and all the damning evidence a prosecutor could dream up. Three men in the cab reminded each other that the speed limit change from fifty-five to thirty was well hidden behind the Welcome to Golden Meadow sign. All looked straight ahead as they passed directly by the local heat's radar gun and slid through town. Strictly obeying all traffic laws, they made their way to Baton Rouge.

Following thirty sleepless hours, a three-hour nap in his own bed was enough to revive Wales. Ever cognizant of police tails, he drove his Mercedes out to his warehouse near Ryan Airport with one eye constantly fixed in the rearview while the other scanned aggressively for local, state and federal heat. His meanders spent little time upon main roads and would usually include a U-turn or two.

The panel truck showed up on schedule at high noon and Wales waited inside the aluminum prefab warehouse to crank the chain rope that opened the cargo door and the truck and his three men slowly nosed in.

At noon plus five, a yellow Ryder truck with two men arrived. Wales directed them to back up to the panel truck for the transfer. Wales' men slung out the fifteen packages from behind three pirogues while Wales held a Mac 10 in the ready-for-any-surprise position. A stocky man from the Ryder received and threw the booty behind a leather living room set and a king-size bed. Wales ordered them all back into their respective cabs. He walked around to the driver of the Ryder to receive a duffel bag and disappeared between the trucks.

Wales would not miss this opportunity. Of all the sound effects he had perfected, nothing unnerved more in this line of work than the po-lice siren. And so he began, ever so faintly, on the whoo-whoo-whoo warning that puts the fear of God in people engaged in offenses that bring major slammer time. He increased the wail slightly and gave the order in a feigned panic. "Okay... Get lost!" He pushed the volume to the max and stepped quickly out of the way. Never in the history of the planet have two trucks disappeared faster.

Wales closed the cargo door briskly and quickly unzipped the canvas duffel. His grin grew as he gazed at his first payoff from the Cartel: 10,000 pictures of Benjamin Franklin.

In total darkness, blood circulated through the listless bag of water and bones that contained the defeated, seasick soul of the Gulf Viking's new deckhand. The lower bunk Randolph Chapman occupied in the ocean-going tug creaked harshly within a symphony of rolls and blasts that had miraculously lulled him to sleep an hour earlier. This latest awakening delivered anxiety with each new breath.

The blasts were the intersection of fifteen-foot swells and the starboard bow of the 101-foot Viking as she pulled an empty barge against the approaching cold front through deep blue Gulf of Mexico waters. The creaks were the slight yield that the tug allowed in heavy seas. The slide... the slide was new. Chapman wearily reached for the light switch. In dim light, he spotted a disc moving upon the polished teak floor before it disappeared beneath his bunk.

With another bow blast, the disc reappeared to the far wall. A ten degree roll to port completed the triangular course of the disc now positively identified as a copper penny. He turned out the light and tried, in vain, to picture his future.

It was just three months earlier that the deckhand had drifted through the chancellor's stirring orientation speech: "If… you don't cut it here at USL, the work gloves are out there waiting for you in the Gulf." That guy… was right, Chapman now painfully realized. In a blink, his brief campus stint had vaporized within a vortex of probation letters, loose women and an oasis of Wild Turkey.

A continuous loop echoed a thousand voices of warning: "Out there," the chancellor had intoned, pointing south, "unskilled laborers are referred to simply as hands." He held palms skyward. "If you don't use your head," he added, tapping his own noggin, "statistics show that you will probably be a lifer out there, swinging sledgehammers on a greasy drilling rig or tugboat until your miserable death." That final red flag went unheeded.

Grim reality had found him in the open Gulf, three feet below the waterline. His primitive calendar to mark miserable days in frigid December waters with a motley crew of parolees and refugees were pieces of duct tape stuck to the bottom of the upper bunk. Deliriously, he realized that his one semester at USL made him, by far, the most educated fellow on this bobbing bucket… just before the next dry heave over the plastic garbage bag that slid upon the teak below. He made promises he couldn't keep to heaven above, but there were no answers and no connection.

A stronger, more troubling voice shared the echo within his throbbing head. It was his father's familiar refrain of prognostication: "If… you don't straighten up, you'll never amount to shit." He…was also right. "Keep this up and you'll find yourself facedown in a gutter." As the Viking lurched into Christmas, he had the visual of the old man heading the family dinner table, waving a glass of gin, waxing infinite justification: "I told him to join the Navy. I told him to study. But he just sat around dreamin', waiting for something to fall from the god-damn sky."

His eyes rolled back and he was blessed with unconsciousness until the sky itself seemed to fall with a forward catapult, brief flight and hard teak landing at three a.m. Chapman could hear the Cajun captain yell for all hands on deck and wearily pulled his slicker over Levis, flannel shirt and the fresh knot on his forehead. He surmised through rants of French-Cajunese that the Viking's towline had snapped and the barge was adrift in heavy seas.

Chapman and his fellow deckhand Quan, a Vietnamese refugee with a vocabulary of one worthless phrase, scrambled down the bow-hole to fetch a new ten-inch diameter, 300-pound line. They wrestled it up narrow metal stairs to the deck while captain kept the Viking in pursuit with a searchlight on the barge. Gasping for breath, Chapman and Quan dragged the massive coil to the dark stern in a cold, driving rain. They removed the icy, severed line from the winch hub and managed to heave it overboard. Frozen hands fed the new line out like a monster Anaconda onto the stern deck.

The captain moved to the upper stern's aft-facing throttles. He could see that the barge was drifting dangerously toward a populated area of drilling rigs as rain poured from his nose and chin. With new line secured and the barge within reach, he quickly went through his options for line-catcher. The new hand seemed athletic. He yelled for him.

"Yes sir?" Chapman's nose was runny and red from the cold.

"Look, I'm gonna back da boat up to da barge, and I want you to jump on it."

"Okay."

"Make sure you jump when da barge is below you and moving downward."

"Okay."

"If you go in, we'll throw you a ring."

"Okay."

He slowly looked up at the new hand, unable to recall his name. *He ain't so bright, dis boy...*

Chapman stood balanced on the stern, all flood lights pointed on him and the barge. He began timing the swells over the roar of the engines. Except for the split-second that they were level, the barge's bow and the Viking's stern were at an impossible distance. *Shit.* Unless he timed the jump just right, the hammerheads would soon feast on that rare deckhand catch.

The propellers gurgled with massive power changes. A hard reverse changed the sea from black ink to white foam. Behind the captain, the Viking's crew gathered in great anticipation. Something bad was probably going to happen and goddamn if they were gonna miss it. The toothless cook ventured out from the galley. Even the old diesel engineer had stumbled up from the engine room, reeking of Old Grand Daddy, and fired up his fifty-third Pall Mall of the day despite forty knots of crosswind. Quan stood right behind his partner, ready with a lifeline and words of encouragement. "Makie no difference."

The captain maneuvered the stern to the barge's bow with doubts that he would be able to spot Chapman in the dark rough water if he went in. With another swell, the barge came down as the tug scissored up. One, two...and the new hand was airborne.

A sudden swell sent the barge skyward and Chapman could only extend his arms as he slammed into the barge with hands just above the bow. Miraculously, his death grip held as he looked back for the stern deck; but the captain feared a massive collision and had retreated downwind. Chapman eyed his white tennis shoes dangling twenty feet above the open Gulf. He managed to smile at the unexpected peace he felt from the powerful sea below while rain tapped tranquility upon his slicker. He was done. Yet the old refrain played on.

The bastard was right…Never amounted to shit.

1. Bird Strikes

A soul is timeless, same at seven and seventy. Cancel aches, pains, mirrors, and the soul would be void of humanity. At seven, Brophy Wales had seen a silver Lockheed Lodestar depart from Lakefront Airport. As the plane disappeared into the wild blue, his solid premonition was that one day he would hold that plane in his hands.

To-day was one day. After his first year on the Cartel run, Wales easily had enough to pay cash for the best airliner of the late 1930s. He was a kid again in the cockpit within a classic technological masterpiece. The cabin held remnants of departed souls from the era of Bogart, Garbo, and Roosevelt as Wilbur Wright's Cyclones roared strongly to 17,000 feet. At cruise, while co-pilot Mouton snored, Wales plotted his course to Las Cruces knowing that he had finally found the perfect airplane. He pictured Howard Hughes flying this very Model 18 Lodestar around the globe to set the world record that eclipsed Wiley Post's record by half. In this very... seat.

Once on the ground at Las Cruces, polished silver made a grand entrance as aviators of all ages watched the tail-dragger, with big radials grumbling, taxi to the west hangar. The airport manager was delighted to top off its tanks, and returned the favor by offering the pilots his personal Impala for ground transportation. Mouton drove Wales to a new contact on the outskirts of town and parked on the street outside of a prefab aluminum building. Wales waddled in front of Mouton to the door.

"Okay, switch off the light."

A thin man dangled a Lucky from his lips. He reached for the switch. "Lights are off."

"Light this off." Wales hit the small button on the outside of the nightvision goggles and the battery quietly whirred. Through the dull greenish tint he could clearly see Camille groping around like a blind man at a desk ten feet away. Wales walked right up to him and put his hand on his shoulder. "Can you see me, Mouton?"

"I can't see a goddamn thing."

"Thing this, Mouton, you as ugly in the dark as you are in broad daylight." Wales scanned the room. A pencil sat on the far desk and he saw it in perfect detail. He watched smoke drift upward from his contact's filter-less cigarette, the ratty moustache behind it and the gun charts on the wall. Everything. The goggles magnified available light 50,000 times. To test new super-powers, Wales tiptoed around Mouton and crouched covertly behind him.

"How much?" he asked. As his voice drifted up from below, Wales saw the two men adjust their heads. He threw the pencil over Camille's head and watched it bounce first on the eraser to the point. They both moved their heads toward the sound.

"Six thousand." The contact's voice was raspy. A naked ink girl swung from a vine on his muscular forearm.

"Six this...I'll give you 40,000 cash for ten." The guy nearly grinned before he realized that Wales could see him. His back straightened as he added numbers in his head. Wales could see adrenaline flowing.

"You want all ten?" His eyes danced in darkness.

"Did I stutter? All ten, 40,000 cash in the next two minutes... and I'm walkin' out the door."

"You got it my friend." A police siren could be heard faintly. It seemed to be getting closer... and closer. It was getting louder... and louder. They must be in the damn parking lot. The contact opened the door and moved frantically toward the window in the front room to scan... an absolutely empty lot, except for his Ford pickup and the Impala parked on the street. What tha fuck...? The siren miraculously stopped. Bewildered, he turned around to see the lights were back on as Wales counted out stacks of bills on his desk.

Wales took instant possession of two boxes with five sets of goggles apiece and stepped out into the crisp New Mexico day. He placed them carefully into the trunk. The Chevy listed to the right as he parked his beefy frame next to his wheelman before Camille gunned it out of sight within the aforementioned two minutes.

The contact rushed back to the pile of cash full of mistrust until he confirmed 400 pictures of Ben Franklin. He pumped his fist. "Yessss."

A bronco kick to the head spun stars through his darkness. Another to the stomach kicked out his ribs and ruptured lungs. One good bloodshot eye opened. The room swirled uncontrollably. A newfangled digital clock radio blinked 5:00 AM as Al Green sang of Love and Happiness on WTIX.

Auburn hair piled the pillow beside him, a huge stuffed bear on the shelf behind. How did this happen? All of yesterday, he had promised himself... promised...that immediately after teaching his groundschool class, he would drive the SS straight home and go straight to bed. But...but...but...after class, his student Tom Gorman made an offer he couldn't refuse for just one nightcap. He began to retrace.

Groundschool ended at nine-thirty... a nightcap of bird at Bart's... a couple of gals from LSU...a redhead.... He cut his eyes to his companion. Musta been charming again. Back in the car... driving... driving to... oh shit! Not the French Quarter! Flames... flames... waterfall... big flaming waterfall... Pat O' fucking Brien's... uh-oh... Hurricanes! How many? One... shit... two. The locals' bar... courtyard bar... piano bar... Ed-dee the thimble man... chain-smoking. Back on Bourbon to... candles... candles... Lafitte's... and more bird. How many...? Two... three...Oh shit.... Walking... stumbling... not the... the fuckin'... Dungeon. I'm a dead man. Who put this fire hose in my ear? Where the fuck is... here?

Painfully, he lifted himself toward the window across the bed hoping to see the only easy way out. He begged for fog... fog and drew back the curtain with trembling hand. A low, thick cloud would provide ample justification to cancel his first airborne traffic report, due in forty-eight minutes. Through one half-mast eye he spotted the SS parked on the lawn under a monster live oak, twenty feet from the driveway, two feet from the front door. That musta been real funny. He saw clear darkness to a million stars. "Damn!" His head pounded like a marching band as he slid down the wall.

The hair spoke. "It's a mayhn." She pulled the dangle, slid a hand to his hamstring and mumbled between suctions. "You're not leaving any time soon."

He crashed on top of her and made eye contact. "Hey... you're cute." He pulled the covers south to inspect her as she giggled, full freckled breasts bouncing. "Very nice. Very, very nice... ma'am."

She pressed warmth to his chest in the first light of dawn. Pain subsided and, for a few seconds, there was no pain at all. Each hand held a cheek, while tongues met through alcohol fumes. "You, my man, are turning me on."

"Ditto for you." He tried to catch his breath. "May I ask a question?"

"You better not ask my name, Randolph Chapman."

"Why is there a car parked in the middle of your yard?" He stared at her in mock seriousness and glanced toward the window.

Her eyes followed. An open smile rushed her face as memory resurfaced. "Oh my God!" She jumped up to push the curtain aside. "My mama's gonna shoot you."

"Mama? You took me to your mama's house?" Head beneath her undercarriage, he popped her behind.

"Ouwwah...hey."

"Pardon me ma'am...What's the address here? I gotta be at Lakefront in twenty."

"Lakefront Airport? So, you are a pilot."

"Let's have it, lady. Don't make me call the po-lice."

"Well flyboy, you're one block off St. Charles and Napoleon."

"Holy Mac-a-roni!" He sprang from bed to an initially cold shower. "Mind if I use your toothbrush?"

"I'm sure." She yelled from the bedroom.

Rand toweled off and gathered his clothing items, yard-sale style. "Hairbrush?"

She sat up amused and pointed to her dresser top. "Right there."

He scurried to retrieve Ray-Bans on the dresser top, collected and stuffed a pile of crumpled dollars and fifty coins into his Levis, made a pass with the brush and recited a checklist aloud: "Wallet... watch... spectacles... testicles." He touched all of the above to confirm and shot her a grin. "I'll call you."

Finding keys still inserted in the ignition, he turned the V way... down and carefully backed the old girl onto and out of the driveway. A green streetcar clanged next to him as he accelerated up the elegance of oak-lined St. Charles Avenue, nearly deserted at this hour, to the I-10 on-ramp, floored an eastward sprint, flying across the Industrial Canal to the exit on Downman Road. At five to six, he passed his lonely apartment and two minutes later, squealed into the parking lot at Aero Services.

Ollie, Aero's head lineman, methodically untied the chain from under the wing of the radio station's Cessna 172 as Rand approached with a familiar, unsteady gait. "Whoooohhhhhheeee. Nick o' time, same clothes as yes-te-dey." The lineman missed very little. "Womens, I'm sure. Death o' you. Tide t'day." Shaking his short Afro in disbelief, he let loose the piercing laugh that echoed perpetually between hangers. "Weeeoooooaahhaaaaa...Two minutes ta spare, weeeeooooohaa."

Rand smirked, shook his head, jumped into the Cessna's left seat, pulled the cool dual-channel headset over his mop, hit the master switch and hoped not to puke. In his right ear, he could hear Jim Anderson, the WWL news anchor, begin to read the six o'clock headlines.

"Clear prop," Rand yelled. The propeller took one slow rotation before the engine fired up. Prop wash immediately closed the pilot's door under the high wing. As he taxied toward the runway, Ollie ran up with a cup of hot coffee. Rand opened his side window, accepted the java, placed it in the plastic holder, blew him a kiss and closed the window. The traffic watch jingle was just beginning as he made the taxiway corner. He quickly picked up the mike with trembling hand.

"Lakefront Tower, this is Eight-Seven Whiskey Lima ready for takeoff on Three-Six Left."

"Roger, Whiskey Lima, you are cleared for immediate takeoff," squawked the controller in his left ear. "Runnin' a little late this mornin', I see."

"Yeah, it ain't pretty." Rand pushed the throttle to the stop and the engine ran at maximum RPM. The oil pressure was in the green band and the oil temperature was… close enough. At seventy knots, Rand pulled the yoke and the single-engine plane popped from terra firma.

"And now high above the city, we call on the soaring Rand Chapman with today's first airborne traffic report," announced Steve Sasso, the morning talk show host, from the station's French Quarter studio. Rand heard the introduction as Lake Pontchartrain slid a mere fifty feet under the left wing, in a 45-degree bank.

"Morning Steve, it's a great day for flying. I haven't seen any major problems on the expressways leading into the Big Easy this morning. The Industrial Canal overpass is in great shape and the I-10 is clear from New Orleans East to the downtown area. Now, the I-10 coming in from Metairie could be tricky with the rising sun in everyone's face, so be careful approaching from the west. The causeway from the Northshore is open and traffic is flowing smoothly." I hope… "From high above the city"…a hundred feet…"this is Rand Chapman for Skywitness Traffic."

"Thanks Rand. Now back to the news desk and Jim Anderson."

The Cessna climbed to altitude and Rand had fifteen minutes before his next report. After clearing his flight path with the Moisant Tower controllers at New Orleans International, he headed west to see how well he'd done on the first report. Thankfully, he spotted no disasters. Popping the plastic lid off his coffee, he raised the cup to the gods and took a short sip. The dead feeling in his gut resurfaced and his hands were in steady tremble. Got… to slow down.

In a cloudless sky, he hawked the traffic crossing the twenty-four mile causeway that split Lake Pontchartrain and winged over the I-10 to the aging Huey P. Long Bridge before circling back over Algiers. On the West Bank Expressway, he watched the traffic slowly intensify, as if someone had kicked a red-ant pile. Soon, one of those cars was going to collide with another and unfortunate ants would be jammed behind, unable to see the cause of the delay. Rand would pinpoint the accident or breakdown, determine the severity, and report it to the thousands of properly tuned ants.

"The temperature in New Orleans will reach close to a hundred degrees again today, so the heat is on," Rand heard through his right ear as the traffic jingle began. "And now... back up to the eye in the sky, our man Rand."

The Greater New Orleans Bridge, always a trouble spot, came into view below. "Well Steve, here we go again on the G-N-O. I am approaching the bridge from the West Bank and see some sort of a breakdown." He descended to 1,000 feet for a better look. "It seems the driver has abandoned his green pickup midway across the bridge in the westbound lane that we all know is really eastbound." He could hear Sasso laugh at the running joke; thanks to a radical bend in the Mississippi, the West Bank is actually east of the city. "I hope we don't have another jumper here, Steve, we all know what that does for our traffic situation. People, if you're gonna jump, please don't do it at rush hour." Another laugh from Sasso. "Okay, here's a new one. Seems as if this particular truck has lost a wheel and the driver is rolling it back toward his vehicle. People, don't forget to tighten your nuts before coming to work today. How many times do I have to tell you? The Causeway looked clear a few minutes ago and I'm heading east now for my next report featuring more fun and games from high above downtown... Rand Chapman reporting for Skywitness traffic."

"Rand, it sounds like you got your nuts tightened pretty good today."

"You know it, Steve."

Chapman pulled off the heavy headset and checked his Seiko. He had fourteen minutes before the next report. His coffee was gone and he relapsed into a setback. Tonight... dammit... I'm going home to sleep... sleep... sleep. He flew above St. Charles to spot the house, big oak and the small yard that recently had a four-wheel trespasser before a bank down Napoleon past Tipitina's to the levee, down Tchoupitoulas into the CBD, across Poydras and Canal to the French Quarter. Street cleaners scrubbed drink spillage and vomit from the narrow pavement of Bourbon Street below. Rand found Pat O'Brien's on St. Peter, and pinpointed the fountain in the back courtyard. Someone had put out the flame. Deeper into the Quarter on Bourbon, he spotted Lafitte's Blacksmith Shop, the candle-lit smuggler's den from the 1700s named for the notorious pirate. Rand tipped his wing to the bartenders there, who intimately knew Mr. Chapman's beverage: a bucket of Wild Turkey, a splash of Seven. Barkeep p-p-please, another word... with the bird.

Rand banked to the 60-degree mark and rolled out on an easterly heading. He passed over Chalmette, site of the 1815 Battle of New Orleans where 2,000

Redcoats were mowed down in the last British-American clash: Ironically, it was Lafitte who had informed Andrew Jackson about the planned invasion. Present-day Chalmette is known locally as Yatville. Where y'at dawlin'? In this brand of Brooklynese, oil is a man's name and Earl is the stuff that goes in an engine. Dredges and workboats appeared through his propeller in the Industrial Canal under the I-10 high-rise bridge that connects Jacksonville to Los Angeles. Rand pulled back the throttle as he approached Lakefront's airspace.

"Lakefront tower, this is Eight Seven Whiskey Lima approaching from downtown to check the I-10 high-rise at 1,500, over."

"Roger, Whiskey Lima, approved", replied the tower controller, spotting him with huge binoculars.

Another complete circle of the city was finished. He fished for a Marlboro Light and, after a momentary panic, found the last of the pack hidden behind the foil wrapper. He lit the correct end and took a long pull that lightened his head and released tightness in his chest. On the second drag, a white dot ahead enlarged as the Cessna caught up with a slower plane over City Park. It was the competition. Ah-toney!

Decked out in J.C. Penney, Anthony Romano cultivated an image of the great Eye-talian lover. Formerly an aggravating local TV reporter, he'd been exiled to traffic detail after finally pissing off the right/wrong people. After just enough flying lessons to be dangerous, he was assigned to a 1948 vintage canvass-winged Piper Cub. Tony was on a direct radio to the producer of 620's Morning Show, a forty-three-year-old divorcee with dyed red hair and synthetic eyelashes. One of her daily chores was to decline his incessant overtures.

"Lunch?"

"Not today."

"Dinner?"

"Not gonna happen, Tony."

Romano continued to press her bravely from a safe altitude, oblivious to the white Cessna below. Rand was in plain view as he inched up to a hundred feet beneath the Cub. He ascended just below Tony's left wing and could see lips flapping beneath a black mustache and Ray-Bans.

Rand clicked 620 into his right ear in time to catch the station's slightly different jingle. The morning host, Mike Wilson, introduced Tony. "It's six-forty and time to check in with Tony and traffic... A-tony!"

"Yeah, Mike, it's funny. You were talking about having dinner at Commander's. I was there last night and didn't see you."

"That's cause I saw you first Tony."

"……….Oh…..haha. Haahaaahhahhahhhahhhahhah…" The fifty-year-old voice reeked of chain-smoker.

"Uh, Tony…how's the traffic doin' up there?"

"Oh, ha ha, the traffic is doing great today, no accidents or breakdowns to report. The I-10 coming in from the west is slow because of the sun shining brightly on some dirty windshields. It'd be a good idea to clean off your windshields."

"I'll try to remember to do that on my lunch hour Tony, thanks."

"Well Mike, you know…" The producer cut him off.

Rand's eyes burned and yet, suddenly there was peace and… silence. He was entering his apartment and could see his bed. He smiled contently just as his head fell to… the side and woke him. The engine noise returned. Shit. Ten minutes of sleep would bring sanity, but that would be a risky stunt at 1,500 feet in an autopilot-less airplane. Nine o'clock seemed one fine star away. He desperately needed adrenaline activation. This familiar problem had remedy. He had developed… ways.

Rand reached blindly beneath the right seat for a roll from his stash, but there was none. Dammit. The toilet paper trick had provided boredom relief when he first began flying traffic watch with State Trooper Charlie Chapman, no relation, New Orleans' pioneer traffic reporter. Before each flight, Charlie, in full trooper garb, would run up to the plane grinning like a schoolboy with two rolls of TP, swiped from the men's room under his shirt and badge. After a few reports, they'd climb up to 3,000 feet, open the side window and launch the rolls that would unfurl gloriously. The objective was to make a coordinated three-sixty to cut the floating target with the wing. But thanks to Tony, WWL discovered that Rand could do the reports and fly the plane. Charlie missed the free flying lessons and Rand had recently degenerated into blasting butt-wipe with spinning propeller, causing New Orleanians to wonder why paper bits occasionally snowed from above.

Rand took a devilish peer east to the railroad track across the marsh, hoping to see one of his favorite sights: A train approaching the city. In an abundant repertoire of buzzes, his favorite was to strafe the tracks, landing light ablaze. To the sleepy engineer, he looked like a damn-fast ghost train from the next lifetime. Usually, when he got to the engine, it spewed sparks and was nearly stopped, confirming success. But today: no train. Shit. Falling asleep would not be cool. Hmmm. There was… some-thin'…

He altered his pattern to cut across Ochsner Hospital at the river and banked toward the Huey P., where Tony was scheduled to give his next report in two minutes. Rand scanned the sky in a slow climb to 3,000 feet. Just at level-off, he spotted the big, fat target circling the bridge a thousand feet below. Rand switched over to 620.

"...just coming over the Huey P. Long Bridge, Mike, looks as if there is a dump truck taking up both lanes coming into Metairie at a snail's pace."

Rand's windscreen filled up with Piper Cub. He realized if things didn't go just right, the goof just might panic and fly right into him. *Maybe I shouldn't.*

"Ya know Mike, it would really be a great idea if somebody would outlaw..."

The Cub turned west in a shallow bank as Tony blabbed. Rand was a screaming eagle from above with airspeed needle fused to the red line. *I got plenty o' speed.* Rand's prop dipped twenty feet behind the Cub's rudder at twice the velocity.

"...traffic on the bridge will be slow for awhile..." Tony casually peered through his propeller in search of profound adjectives. He banked slightly to get a better look at the bridge, just missing sight of the Cessna torpedo, thirty feet below. Loving the broadcast of his voice, he pictured faithful listeners absorbing his eloquent description of dump truck.

Without warning, lightning struck A-tony like electrodes attached to both testicles. A bright set of white wings illuminated out of nowhere, just feet in front of him, and his brain screamed instant midair collision. "Shiiiiit!" He could not have calculated that Rand had already passed through his altitude and the dangerous part was over.

Romano knee-jerked the stick hard left to the stops, a perfect air show entry to a snap roll. Tony's yoke felt disconnected from the plane as the wings yanked past ninety degrees, a chainsaw slice downward, acceleration faster than the Zephyr at Pontchartrain Beach. "Holy... fuckkk!"

The Cub yawed into a tight spin as the altimeter swiftly descended: 1500...1300...1000...900....

Tony's windscreen filled with a twirling steel bridge. Inverted dirt from the floor hit the roof, along with Tony's clipboard, pen and pencil set, and the brown pleather shoes that he had placed on the backseat just after liftoff. One of his shoes popped his dyed-black, curly head. "Fuuuccckkkk" came out sounding "Fuu-thump-uccckkk" while he hung from seatbelt.

Back in the studio, Mike Wilson sat up abruptly in his chair, semi-perturbed at the language going out over 30,000 watts. "Tony! Are you OK?"

Rand's excess airspeed from the high dive began to die at 3,000 feet. He kicked left rudder to locate the Cub. Listening to Tony's gut-wrenching screams over the air, he instantly regretted the prank. It was painfully apparent that the Cub was in serious trouble, heading straight for the Huey P. in a spinning dive. Oh... shit. It was now his testicles' turn to ache. The next six seconds seemed an hour. A fine mess. He switched quickly over to approach frequency and pushed the transmission button to tell him to pull the power off until, at that exact instant, A-tony panic-kicked a hard right rudder. The Cub recovered at 500 feet above the mighty river.

Rand's heart pumped outrageously. Finally... son. Cold sweat blasted his face as it flushed to crimson. He took a gigantic breath. It was way too early for this to be funny.

Tony leveled the airplane; shocked, bewildered, confused, as warm urine reached his socks to announce the wetting of his polyester pants. He could barely hear Mike Wilson yelling; the on-air transmission terminated as he tried to focus on the suddenly much-closer wetlands. As 620 went to commercial, Rand tried to recover from his self-inflicted near-heart attack. Depart the scene... fast.

Rand pushed the throttle up and redlined the RPM over to the G-N-O for the next report. Shit. He tried to collect his scattered thoughts as the traffic jingle began. "Hey, Steve...been flying over the GNO for a few minutes, trying to see what's the problem here... but it might be just over-congestion. The previous accident has been cleared and no one has thrown a wheel in over an hour." He barely caught his breath. "The I-10 from the east is backed up to Downman Road, but once you cross the overpass, it's clear sailing to the Vieux Carre exit. The I-10 coming from the west is stop and go and the backup is at the 17th Street-Canal interchange, as usual. Haven't been over to the Huey P. for a while, but the last time I checked, there was just slow traffic and the backup was to the Highway 90 exit." And nearly a gaping hole through the eastbound lane caused by a plummeting I-talian in a 1948 Piper Cub, he didn't add. "The Westbank expressway is slow moving again and the backup is to the round hotel. You guys down there know what I'm talking about... For Skywitness Traffic this is Rand Chapman, high above the Big Easy."

"Thanks Rando, back to the news desk and Jim Anderson...Jim?"

Curiosity shot his hand back to the radio dial and he spun 620 into the headset. At forty after, Wilson made the report himself with no mention of Tony. His info was obviously copied from Rand's report.

The final hour saw a steady decline in traffic and by the last report at nine a.m. the expressways and bridges flowed smoothly. Rand headed into a short left pattern for Runway Two-Seven. He let the Cessna roll to the end and exited the 3,000-foot strip just a short distance from the ramp and tie-down area. He found the usual spot and the usual black man holding the usual rope and brought the plane to rest over the usual cable.

Ollie immediately tied the right wing down and Rand jumped out to tie the left. While Rand knotted, Ollie squatted to secure the lower tail hook. He looked up at Rand with raised eyebrow. "Tony came back early t'day..."

"Really. Why?"

"You don't know?" Ollie watched closely.

"Why should I know?" A slight lip movement.

Under the Aero hat, Ollie's eyes lit up with confirmation. "I knew it!"

"What?"

"I knew you dit it! Look like he saw a big ol' ghost! Came on in, ditn't say nothin to no botty, jus' stumble to iz car. Whhhoooohhhheee, wha' you dit? He hat no blut in iz face. Whhhhooooooooeeeeeee. Mizta Bernstein be askin, wha' happen to dat man? I says I ditn't know... but I know... Oooohhhhhhh... wwwweeeeeeeaaahha."

"Wha...?"

"Dat man hat wet his briches. I tied dat Cub down mysef. He jus' hat one brown shu. Ooooooeeeee, I sez to mysef, I know who dit dat."

Rand pulled the coffee cup from the backseat, crossed the ramp to the lobby and fished out a dollar. He hit F2 on the food simulator panel and was rewarded with a Twinkie from the door below. C6 machine coffee would wash down the sugar bomb. Ahhh... breakfast. He ascended stairs with hands in mild tremble. A dozen birds chirped in his ears as he pushed through the glass door to the plush lobby of the Lakefront Flying Club, his employer for over a year.

The flight school's stereo was tuned to a light rock station. A petite Cajunette worked the phone behind a glass case filled with flight computers, whiz wheels, navigation charts, calculators, watches, sunglasses and sundry supplies for instant pilots. Beth Talley surveyed Rand as he crossed thick beige carpet. Her left eyebrow shot toward her dark hairline as a small smile rode from her lips to the deep chocolate eyes that circled his outfit. She hung up the beige receiver.

"Nice shirt."

"Oh thanks. Got this at a two-for-one sale...looks just like the one I had on yesterday." His eyes were a disaster.

She sniffed across the counter. "Yeah, but this one smells like alcohol and smoke." Beth pointed at the schedule board. "You got a student at nine-thirty, a new guy. At ten-thirty it's Chris Tyson. And Jan Cloar called this morning and wanted to know if you could fly a plane over to Abita Springs and start the lesson from over there with her..." She looked up. Nothing. "At two-thirty it's T.G., which brings you up to traffic watch from four till six. And, hey guess what...? It's Thursday, you don't have to teach ground school, but Walt Sampson called this mornin' and wants you to call him about a night lesson."

"That's it? Hey, no midnight cruise down the Mississippi?"

"You might wanna go change your shirt at some point in the day."

"Yes, dear."

She looked out the window. "There's your nine-thirty."

By noon, Rand had five point seven hours of flight time logged, and furthermore, had sucked down two Twinkies and five cups of C6. Flying alone at 1,000 feet, he peered through his spinning propeller to the green pine forest of the Northshore, where his next student and trophy wife of a prominent surgeon waited. He wished for the strength of adrenaline as the Warrior's wings rode beneath him and her engine purred sweetly. He recalled the stormy night on the Viking and the burst of adrenaline that had propelled him instantly to the bow of that barge. He allowed himself a wry smile with the recall of the shocked faces of the motley crew as he stood and yelled for Quan to throw the damn line. "Come on...throw it!" God, he was glad to be out of the oilfield, but perpetual celebration of the reversal of fortune was collecting a major toll.

The Abita airport was a rectangle cut within the thick pine forest. Hundred-foot southern pines surrounded a short north-south paved landing strip. Rand radioed on the unicom frequency of 122.8 that he was five miles south for a straight-in landing to runway Three-Four. He touched down between the white-painted numbers and made the perpendicular taxi halfway down the runway and continued onto the ramp area, where twenty small airplanes were tied down. He spotted the red convertible in the clamshell parking lot, a blonde driver behind dark Hollywood sunglasses. Rand whipped the plane around and shut down the engine thirty feet from the car. He popped the door open. "Hey girl...what's up?"

"Come on, leyt's goh dew lunych!" She waved casually.

"What... no flying lesson?" The sun cooked the top of the Warrior as the heat wave continued. Sweat slid down his nose as he leaned across the co-pilot's seat to the opened door.

"Leyt's practice raydio cawls." Her accent dripped magnolia and julep. A pained expression cried, are you... so... stuypid?

Radio calls...uh-oh. He unfastened his belt and climbed out onto the wing, from skillet to flame.

Harvey Hudson, the hayseed airport manager/custodian who resided at the palatial doublewide adjacent to the strip, moseyed dangerously close to direct sunlight within the hangar, accompanied by his sleepy southern Bloodhound.

Two sets of brown eyes slid over to the BMW. The primate whistled through his teeth, because he could. Nothin' unusual about seein' somethin' unusual 'round here....

Rand found himself in the convertible's right seat with a feeling that he was about to be the student. They sailed down the gravel road, kicking up rocks before a controlled tire-screeching skid onto the main paved highway.

Jan's garb was a sleeveless, button-less, braless cotton shirt and super-shorts above bare feet. She cut her eyes to confirm that Rand watched what danced beneath. Peryfect. "Looyk in the bayackseat. I goyt ya somethin'."

"A present...?" Rand spotted a D.H. Holmes bag in the backseat. "For me?" A piece of puny fabric had a price tag of eighty dollars. "What's this? A bikini...eighty bucks? Whoa. Hell, I need to go into the bikini business." Men's swimming trunks were at the bottom of the bag.

"Yoy lyike it? I just goyt iyt thyis morniyn." She found the on-ramp to the I-12 and pushed the Beemer easily up to eighty, flying through heavy intoxicating pollen of the forest. "Try yours on."

"Uh, Jan? Where we goin' swimmin'?"

"Oh, we're goin' wahderskiyin'."

"Hell, I should have known. What's the matter with me?"

"Heyre, leyt me see myine." She leaned forward to grab her shirt just below the collar, casually raised it above the windshield into eighty mph of relative wind and released. Bosom swayed beneath a defiant smile of freedom as Rand neck-swiveled to see the discarded shirt dance happily over asphalt. She unzipped her pants and let them fall to the floorboard.

"Now here's somethin' ya don't see everyday...a woman flying down the I-12, buck naked." Nipples stood erect. "You aren't trying to get me shot, are you Jan?" Hey good news... hangover's gone.

"Heyhh, puht yur syuit oyon!"

"Well, why the hell not...?" He dug into the bag as she made the exit just west of Causeway Boulevard. Fortunately, the roads were deserted in the heat of mid-day as humidity hung like a wet rug. Rand's heart sank as a pickup approached from the opposite direction. Miraculously, the cowboy hat passed without noticing... the naked driver. After two hard rights and a left, Jan wheeled into an abandoned road and backed up on gravel for a hundred yards before braking hard to a stop. A dust cloud of the car's wake hovered over them for a second before Rand could see through the fog...a red ski boat, in the water, tied to the dock. There were only two other boats in the private cove, surrounded by giant cypress.

"We'yre heyre." Jan inhaled the natural setting. She nonchalantly popped off the price tag and tossed it to the dirt before slipping into the bikini. Rand pulled his Levis off as her view was obstructed momentarily by the pullover cotton shirt. She waited patiently and watched him casually thread his right foot through the trunks. Her tongue moved out to glisten in bright sunlight. "Lyet's goh."

Rand recognized the cove as one he'd been to many times as a kid. The cricket's screams through cypress and the swamp-water aroma delivered a familiar anxious tingle as he sensed the ever-present moccasins, cottonmouths and mysterious creatures that infested the Tchefuncte River. He also remembered that many people knew him and her around here and that secrets are not kept well in small Louisiana towns. He was in dangerous territory, but strangely, felt no fear.

Jan cranked the engine. Fully fueled, they launched out of the cove on vacant, glass-smooth water. Rand watched their wake hit the brown Tchefuncte riverbank under royal blue sky, inhaling crisp fresh air that delivered bittersweet memories of carefree adolescence. Don't go there... He slouched back on the aft bench seat to watch Jan's hair fly, her Gucci shades sparkling in the sunlight. Her firm body was motionless as she sat atop her dream world on the driver's seat. At twenty-seven, she refused to waste her great-body years pushing strollers and shooting the breeze with neighbors. She refused to purchase guilt and was perfectly willing to give gossips potent material. If they only knew. A big smile jumped onto her face and she turned to Rand. "Wanna go swyimmin?"

"Do I have a choice?" Rand yelled over thirty knots of wind in his face.

"Iye doynt thiynk so." She smiled and shook her head. "Wanna beyer?" She reached into the cooler. They shot up a mile-long straightaway just two bends from the country club.

In the banquet room of the Covington Country Club overlooking the river, the garden club luncheon had just begun. This juicy picture of confirmation would surely quicken hearts with envy disguised as outrage, shifting the agenda from magnolias and dogwood to yummy scandalous fornication and that whore, Jan Cloar. But that delightful possibility was averted when Jan wheeled up a bayou and turned into a secluded cove. The garden club ladies methodically moved on to azaleas, their restless eyes peering out to still water and moss-drenched oaks on the opposite bank.

Jan dropped anchor, killed the engine and pushed in a cassette. Elton John pierced silence with Funeral for a Friend. "Now I know where you get your good touch with the airplane." Rand smiled. "You handle a nice boat, ma'am."

"Thaynks." She reached for a Heineken. "I thoyht yew cud use a lyittle bryeak from ayirplaynes for awyile." An egret glided in and greased the water, landing just upstream.

He sipped beer. "Yeah, thanks, this is great. Nice day." Cypress knees sprang from muddy banks. Rand gazed up into the moss-covered branches and over to Jan. She was truly beautiful, clenched to youth. Her eyes begged as Rand stood. The boat listed softly to port as he approached to remove her sunglasses.

Two hours later, he taxied up to the Aero ramp. Tom Gorman and Beth were seated on the bench under the lobby overhang. T.G. shook his head, arms folded below shit-eating grin and aviator Ray-Bans.

"Hey T.G. Ya ready, big guy?"

Beth headed toward the Warrior, log in hand. "I need to get the Hobbs reading before T.G. starts his lesson." She jumped the wing and looked in.

Rand could only watch. Think fast man.

Her eyes popped out of her dark face. "What ya ben doin' Chapman...? There's only point five elapsed from the Hobbs. You been givin' a dif'rent kine of stick time...all sunburned an everythin'." She smiled like a fifth-grader.

"Hey, we needed to go over a few ground school items." Sweat trickled down to his chin. "Radio calls and all."

"Yeah, I can jus' imagin'. More like calls of tha wild. Yak yak yak...."

"Don't you have work to do? C'mon T.G. Let's fly."

Tom Gorman loved to fly. There was just one minor problem: Flying solo scared the hell out of him. As they climbed east out of Lakefront's airspace, Rand put his head back on the seat, on standby for when dragons might leap from the swamp below. A mighty slumber took him to deep peace, and an occasional snore, while T.G. inhaled the miracle of flight.

Forty minutes later, eyes still closed, Rand sensed that weird, electric energy of wakeful consciousness that only surfaced with daytime slumber. He was a bag of water, bones, muscle, blood and organs. He was conscious of the awesome vehicle that contained his soul. He felt blood circulate at a perfect pressure and temperature and asked again silently: Who... did this? He was acutely aware of his location upon a tiny sphere that swirled with living organisms inside an incomprehensible vacuum where few could define a sensible purpose. Hurricanes, floods, tornadoes, earthquakes. Wars erupt over flawed interpretations of an afterlife. Human beings, all different, yet all alike, filled with hate, mistrust and prejudice, kill and mutilate neighbors by the thousands... millions. Families argue empty issues as the world spins through a million miles of empty space. Over-population...epidemic disease... pollution. His head swirled. With eyes shut, he touched his left arm and felt tiny hair follicles, amazed that he had control over his own limbs in an aimless drift through time. Isolation, his nemesis, began to feast. He opened his eyes as his body realigned 3,000 feet above the wetlands. He was back.

"How's it goin' my brother?"

"You're the best instructor around."

Rand pulled his seat up to see the huge white Michoud hangar ten miles east of Lakefront where booster rockets were built for NASA during the Gemini and Apollo days. "Had enough for today?"

"I have."

"Great. Let's head back. I got traffic watch in thirty." Rand turned with a sly smile. "So what happened to you last night?"

"Ah...not much. I got the babe home but nothing seemed to work after that. Woke up half-naked with wicked headaches." Tommy grinned back at Rand. "Man, you were blasted."

"Yeah. Didn't feel too hot this morning."

"I bet. Uhhhh, so who's this gal across the lake?"

"Well, mother, I don't like to kiss and tell."

"Beth says she's married and you're gonna get your ass shot off."

"Anything's possible." Rand peered at the runway through spinning propeller.

"You better watch out, boy, before we have to bury your ass."

No shit. "Okay."

T.G. rolled his eyes to the back of his head.

The Warrior was one of several planes taxiing across the field as Reni DuVette parked her new Mustang close to the Aero Services entrance. Sun-streaked sandy hair cascaded to mid-back as she pulled the lobby door, Times-Picayune Classifieds in hand. Her entrance drew three corporate pilots to long, tanned legs, shaped by daily three mile runs, a mini-dress that ceased conversation, a flat athletic tummy, a C-cup bosom sway that terminated all pure thought.

Pale blue eyes scanned the lobby to the terrified eyes of the receptionist behind a chest-high counter. "Hi, I'm here for the interview."

Dawn Boudreaux, suddenly in defense of her Airport Babe reign, tried to suck in ten pounds and the temptation to point Reni to the nearest swamp. "Yeah, upstairs. Ask for Mr. Bernstein."

As she ascended stairs, every male in the lobby below exchanged a silent message: Je-sus Christ...did you see that...!

Reni knocked lightly on the door marked General Manager under Jeffery G. Bernstein. After getting a "come in," she stuck her head around the door with a playful smile and short wave. "Hi!"

Bernstein, a recent transplant from Aero's Teterboro, New Jersey office with orders to turn a profit, was not prepared for what was about to transpire. As Reni sashayed toward the desk, his eyes became lightning rods in a world-class electrical storm. He could not select one focal point, amping-out between full lips, crystal-blue eyes and gravity-defying initial instruments of temptation. He sprung to his feet, begging for the four inches that would bring his curly black hair above her nose level. "Have a seat," he cleared his throat.

"Thanks, I'm Reni DuVette. I'm here for the receptionist position that was in the paper. She took the adjacent seat while Bernstein nearly missed his. I called a little while ago." Hel-looo…? She waved the Picayune.

He swallowed hard. "Oh sure…Do you have a resume?" Or not. His chest pounded and his composure decomposed.

"No sir. I've never held a job before. I just finished my first semester at UNO and I'm going to take the next semester off."

A long silence hid the chaos that stormed within. The wife… the kids… the house… will just have to… go! "Have you spent any time around an airport?"

"Nossir." Her neck, throat, ears, seemed to call him.

You're… hired! "Well, your…uh, the receptionist position entails quite a bit of responsibility. Whenever a plane comes in, you ask the pilots what services they require, such as fuel, catering, maintenance, cleaning and so forth." His eyes parked on full lips. "We are called an FBO, which stands for fixed base operator. Our main source of income is fuel. We are a gas station first and foremost." He gestured toward the picture window behind him. "These business jets have an option to come here to Aero or go over to Eagle or to Wedells. If they get good service here, they will likely come back again and again." Bernstein used superhuman strength to swivel his chair to look outside while wishing for double-hair coverage on his crown. "See that Learjet? It comes here twice a week from Los Angeles. We fill his empty tanks to the top. That Saberliner jets in every other day from Teterboro. A huge bank out of Manhattan owns the airplane. We pumped 1,000 gallons in her and sold $300 worth of catering to them today."

"Would I be fueling the airplane?"

"Absolutely not. We have linemen around here for that. They do all the fueling." He pointed out to a stocky black man walking toward the building, grinning. "There's Ollie, our head lineman." Bernstein's eyes narrowed. If that guy only knew what he's worth. "The receptionist just takes the order and hands it over to one of the linemen. He takes care of the rest. Same with catering, you just take the order and phone it in."

"What are the hours?"

Overtime... "Normally, it's a seven to five job with an hour for lunch, but big events are our forte, and during Super Bowl or Sugar Bowl and Mardi Gras we work around the clock."

"Well, this place is interesting."

"The position pays two-fifty an hour, time and a half for overtime."

"Oh. I had an offer yesterday at five an hour in the CBD. But thank you for the interview." She stood and Bernstein's eyes slalomed north from yams... to trailer... to... "Five dollars an hour it is." What tha hell did I just say? "And the job is yours..." What tha... hell did I just say? This could... would trigger a major revolt. He quickly calculated a raise for his remaining girls and the numbers came up short. What the hell... did I just say?

"Really?" She sat down.

"I'll have to clear it with New York but I have been trying to create a new position." What the hell... did I just say? " How do you spell your name? R-e-n-n-y?"

"No, it's R-e-n-i." She watched him print before reciting her phone number.

"I'll call you tomorrow." He offered a slight smile. "I believe you will enjoy working out here." What the hell did I just...

Reni surveyed her new domain descending back into a charged field of strangers as chatter dropped to a hush. A wavy blond head followed her from the corner of the room. Rand absorbed a sharp jolt as his eyes widened. This... is gonna cause major problems... will need... serious maintenance. The smoke he was attempting to light dropped to the floor. He smiled wryly as she sashayed out the door. Serious... maintenance. Reni had left the building.

"Oh sweet Lawd. Where did you get dat dress? You look like a prostitute."

"Oh mama, there's nothing wrong with this dress. I got it at Town and Country on the Avenue, a ninety-year-old lady sold it to me." Reni picked up a green apple from the kitchen counter. "Where's daddy?"

"Daddy? Why, what have you done?"

"Nothing. I just need to talk to him about taking a job at the airport."

"Oh dear Say-via. People go to da airport an' neva come back. Dey go wit suitcases an passports an' dey neva come back. No granchidren... no..."

"Don't be silly, mama."

"Your great Uncle Buddy went to da airport once and we neva seen him a-gain."

"This isn't World War II, mama and I'm not leaving Nawlins. It's just a job out at Lakefront."

"Lakefront? Oh dat's different. I thought you were talkin about Moisant." TV images of Pakistan and Beirut dissolved. "Dat's jus' where dem small planes land, huh baby? Dat's where Aunt Rose met dat nice mechanic." Wasn't he the one that tol' us about all dem crazy pilots and drinkin an partyin' and chasin' wom..."LAKEFRONT! You can't work at Lakefront! Don't ever go dare again Reni, I'm warnin' ya, dem pilots out dare are heathen womanizers an' hell raysas. You stay far away from Lakefront Airport!"

2. Miracle Number One

A late September cold front pushed the last dragon breath of summer into the Gulf just in time for Aero's annual crawfish boil. The thermometer at Lakefront tower, three miles east of the picnic site, read seventy-five degrees with unlimited visibility as airport employees and company clients began to gather on the shores of Lake Pontchartrain. Soaring high above, the bright red dot in the sky was the flying club's new Grumman Tiger, where T.G. practiced maneuvers while Rand evaporated last night's bird in deep slumber. T.G. absorbed the stupendous view of royal blue sky against the plane's fire engine red cowling as the Tiger flew smoothly with unlimited views of the Big Easy south to English Turn and north to the higher ground of Mississippi. As his instructor snored, T.G. made coordinated lazy eights around a shell barge below.

Rand slowly found consciousness. The weeklong lump in his gut greeted him and he smirked away the uneasy feeling as he transitioned back to 4,000 feet above the watery planet. He could not stop thinking about Reni. And he had plenty of company. For the past month, every pilot, every mechanic, every CEO, every mailman who had spotted her behind Jeffrey Bernstein's counter suddenly had business at Aero Services. An oilman with a Beech Duke landed a lunch date. A New Orleans motorcycle cop worked the account with two dinner dates and spent numerous shifts looking for suspicious characters around Lakefront Airport. Lurking tactically in his office, Jeffrey Bernstein noted the spike in business. The brainchild of his lower head had added 10,000 bucks to the coffers this month with increased business from corporate jets.

Rand's strategy was to style himself as the graceful dolphin amongst sharks, serpents and snakes. While other suitors paraded up to bat, Rand refused to join the lineup of desperados. Instead, he let his eyes send Reni a subliminal message while placing routine fuel orders: One day. Occasionally, he slipped in a smile that said someday. The ingenious plan was driving him nuts. And now, one day had turned into to-day.

In the meantime, Rand needed a distraction from uneasy impatience. All he lacked was adrenaline. And he had developed... ways. Through the Tiger's sliding overhead glass canopy he spotted a bass boat below. "Okay Tommy, I got it a sec." The throttle was pulled to idle and the 180-horse Lycoming growled no longer.

Tommy's euphoria faded with slowing propeller and that look. He felt his ass lighten with a negative gravity inducing yoke push. "Uh-oh. Here we go."

Rand sliced a 90-degree right bank as the engine kitty-whined with increased airspeed in a tight, spiraling descent. He moved the sun to his tail, a birds-of-prey trick that casts perfect light on a blinded victim.

Two fishermen were catching trout, drum and a buzz. They heard an irritating insect in the distance as they passed a twisted cigarette. The buzz intensified as the anglers searched the sky, swiveling their heads until at last they spotted a red flare blast from the morning sun, out of control and heading straight for...

Poles, hooks, lines and sinkers seesawed into the water as they hit the deck. At the last possible second, Rand had pulled the plane back up to 1,000 feet as T.G. howled with insane relief that the sweet Lord had answered his continuous pleads of the past forty-three and a half seconds.

Sleepy Lakeshore Drive began to stir with activity as Ollie rolled the first keg of Dixie into position under a giant oak. Fifty pounds of crawfish boiled in a ten-gallon pot, new potatoes in another as the waft of Zatarain's bubbled into sunshine. Two large Bose speakers pushed out Clifton Chenier's zydeco as the first batch of steaming mudbugs were poured onto the Picayune-covered picnic table. All heads slowly turned toward the sound of a redlined Tiger streaking insanely at fifteen feet above smooth, brackish water. A-Tony sprayed his Dixie.

"Goddammit!" Gordon, the chief instructor yelled. "Who the hell is in the Tiger today, Beth?"

All heads turned to the Cajunette so they would know which bastard to flog. A small grin came to her face.

"One Randolph Chapman."

Everyone laughed, except Gordon.

Half an hour later, Rand and T.G. rolled up in Tommy's Mercedes. "Gordon's gonna kill you boys!" hooted fellow flight instructors. Rand's gut sank slightly when he spotted Tony. A-Tony! His eyes flitted past Jan Cloar and four or five of his other students before landing on... and there she was, pouring a plastic cup of brew. He noted the position and immediately began to formulate a plan of attack. Mick Jagger pulsed Time...time... is on my side... yes it is...

"Chapman!" Gordon barked. "Was that you in the Tiger?"

"Yeah, sorry, man, I was landing on Nine. Didn't want to overshoot," he deadpanned.

"I don't imagine you did."

Everyone laughed, including Gordon.

Rand darted eyes behind Ray-Bans. Reni stood next to Ollie, who laughed loudest of all. She smiled with Rand's glance and noticed that again, he pretended to be looking for someone else. Give... it up.

Thinking he was invisible, Rand circled around the kegs to casually walk up to the objective. "Ollie, aren't you supposed to be at work?" He teased. "You know you don't get any days off."

"Whhoooeee. No sir. Mizda Bernstein says I can takes the rest o' tha day owff. He goot ta me. Treat me jus lie whitefolk! Whoooooeeee....Reni, you stay fa fa away fro dis boy. He always crazy."

"Thanks for the endorsement," Rand grinned. He casually looked her way. "Reni...right?" He stopped breathing.

"That's what they call me." She gazed directly into his eyes and held out a soft palm. He took it lightly, a bird in hand. "Nice to see you, Rand." Ollie bolted for the bucket of Popeye's.

"You look lovely today, ma'am." A chill pinged up his neck as a breeze ruffled her hair. The musk was overkill. His palm began a sweat and he gently let her hand go. "Cocktail? What ya drinkin' there?"

"A Dixie. C'mon, let's get you somethin'." They walked slowly together toward the makeshift bar. "Great day, huh?"

He spotted a Wild Turkey. "Yeah, and it just got nicer." Rand packed a plastic cup with ice. No more flying today. He poured three fingers and splashed it with Seven. Reni topped off her beer. Boz Scaggs began through the Bose.

"Wanna dance?"

"Sure."

Hope they never end this song
This could take us all night long

Bird in hand, Rand followed Reni to a herd of dancers, slid his empty hand to her waist. She meshed softly with his pull; her hair against his cheek. He tried to remain calm as his chest warmed to her press. Reni sipped beer and checked the crowd that seemed to be tracking positions. The musk made him lightheaded. He inhaled her. As she drank, Rand got a reward for the angle. Her low-cut shift had shifted and the view was brilliant. He became weak as a kitty. God is great. He closed his eyes. So did she.

Love, look what you've done to me
Never thought I'd fall again so easily…

"You are lovely," he whispered.
"So are you", she whispered.
"When ya gonna take me out…woman?"
"You name it…man."
"Tonight?"
"Tomorrow."
"Tomorrow it is." Rand gave her a light brush on the lips. "Sorry, I couldn't help myself."
"It's okay, I like it."

More couples began dancing. A game of croquet started. Fueled by beer and bird, the party kicked up a notch. Reni began to decline all dance requests from motorcycle cops, airplane owners, CEOs as she found comfort in constant touch with Rand. Game over.

Rand and Reni mingled through the crowd and came across Chris Cullins, a guy Rand knew from high school on the northshore. Chris graduated two years before Rand. They shook hands. "Chris…?" Their eyes were exactly level.

"Rand Chapman… The last time I saw you…you were streaking down the football field for a touchdown against Hammond at Homecoming a few years back… Now I see a Tiger streaking down the lakefront and somebody said it was you." He took a long circle of Reni.

"Oh… You were there? Yeah, that makes sense." His chest expanded with mention of his football days. And right in front of… "Chris, meet Reni, she's the Ramp Director at Aero."

"Hey, everybody knows Reni." He took her hand anyway. "Somebody… told me you were flying out here. Oh yeah, Dr. Cloar said his wife took some lessons from you."

Whoa boy. "Hey, she's a pretty good pilot, I'd say. So what are you up to these days?" He eyed Jan chatting forty feet away. "What are you flying?"

"I'm still on the Merlin... with Hotchkiss."

"Hotchkiss?"

"Oh...you don't know Hotchkiss? He's a piece of work."

Reni popped in. "He's got a girl in every town...type."

Chris laughed. "Well if ya wanna call em' girls. Goes ugly an hour before early, it's less work for him." They all laughed. "He's a great pilot though... I've learned a ton from him."

"Where do you guys fly?" Reni took the words from Rand's mouth. He smiled at her. She smiled back.

"We fly for C.F. Benson, the dredging company, so just about anywhere there is water or a channel that needs to be dredged. We go to Washington, DC a lot, cause the Corps of Engineers is based there and we get a lot of contracts through them. We just got back yesterday from Mexico City." He looked at Rand.

Mexico City...? Washington. "Really?" was all Rand could muster.

"But, I'm ready to move on... to my own gig." Chris glanced toward Reni's dress and back to Rand, who didn't miss eyes on the move. "Matter of fact, I landed a Cheyenne job in Houston."

"Really?"

"So you're gonna quit Hotchkiss?" Reni asked, puzzled at Rand.

"Yeah, but don't say anything quite yet... Hey, there's Curt!" Curt was the captain of a ten-seat King Air for Schwegmann's grocery. Apparently, they had something to discuss and walked away.

Reni looked deep into Rand's eyes. He looked so innocent. She wanted to kiss him for some reason. "Whata ya thinkin'?"

"Did yooooou... hear that?"

"What?"

"If Chris leaves for Houston... That leaves the Merlin job vacant...and..."

"Ooohhh...That's where you went... I was wondering about you. All you said for a few minutes was 'Really?'."

"Really?" He smiled.

Chris returned. "You should jump on the Merlin carpet. Kiss is a great pilot and you'll learn a ton from him."

"Really?"

The party broke up at sunset and everybody drove home drunk through the Big Easy, the city that care forgot.

Streetlights of Downman Road danced on the polished hood while Mick and the boys began Shattered. Rand approached the lakeshore and wheeled for the on-ramp to the Simon Bridge over the canal. He glanced back toward Aero, hoping to catch a glimpse of the Merlin, but was distracted spectacularly with an orange moonrise over the field. Across the canal, he took the first right back to Lakeshore Drive and the SS pulled herself into the parking area to face the airport. His hand hit the electric window switch to allow warm, sweet air to circulate his soul. Five airplanes in the landing pattern flashed strobes against the twilight. Judging from the calm of the Pontchartrain, the world was at peace.

He had a vision. It was going to happen. He pictured Reni dabbing lipstick, brushing out her hair. He closed his eyes for a moment. And the moment was gone.

The light in front of Reni's house burned just like she'd promised as Rand parked on the street. His hands were damp; the gut anxiety reminded him of an opening kickoff. He knocked gently.

George DuVette pulled the door open. "You must be Rand. Come on in." He held out his thick hand and pulled him warmly into his home. Rand basked in the friendly welcome from the tall man with thick gray hair. "I hear you every morning driving to work. Sasso really likes you, doesn't he?"

"I guess. He's a pilot, you know. I've flown his Comanche with him a couple o' times. He's a nice guy." Rand's heels clanked on the hardwood floor. He liked the feel of the old house. Three bronze horses galloped in the statue that was centered on the rectangular cedar coffee table. The Holy Bible lay next to a lamp between sofas on the end table. Jesus Christ hung on a crucifix on the dining room wall. A family portrait obviously taken several years ago indicated Reni was the youngest in the family. Her three brothers wore pleasant expressions, while she smiled happily.

"Great house. Comfortable."

"Thanks. We've been here thirty years. The boys are gone now, but they visit a lot...Reni!" He called to the hallway.

"Just a second, Daddy!" Her voice was behind at least one closed door.

Mrs. DuVette came in from the kitchen; a royal blue dress matched her eyes. She was Reni's build. "You must be Randolph." She looked straight into his eyes and offered her hand. "You certainly are a tall young man."

"Very nice to meet you, Mrs. DuVette."

"So you're a pilot, I hear." She smiled slightly.

"Yes ma'am."

"Do you know a mechanic out dare?" Smile went bye-bye.

"Yes ma'am, I know quite a few mechanics." What the...

"Okay. That'll be enough of the third degree." Reni slid from the hallway into the living room. A short black evening dress with spaghetti straps hung loosely over bosom sway. Blonde locks pulled back and brushed away allowed a hormonal binocular treat. Except for a muted lipstick, she wore no makeup.

Rand's jaw dislodged from upper lip. Jeeezus! He felt locomotion within new silky trousers. Whoa boy! Shut your mouth... get a pure thought in your head...! "Wow...look at you," he managed.

"Hi Rand. You've met my folks?" She took her dad's hand and peered at her mother, slightly raising both eyebrows. Be...good.

"You look gorgeous, sweetie." George saw everlasting beauty. "I love the new dress."

"Thanks, Daddy. Come on, Rand. Let's hit the road." She gazed at him. "Hey, nice jacket. I've never seen you duded up before. Nice tie, too." Nice lips...and...

Mrs. DuVette suggested an early evening as they stepped out onto the driveway and George called goodnight. Rand opened Reni's door and floated around the back of the car as she unlatched his door from the inside and pushed it toward him a little. Nice touch.

"Mama didn't work you over too hard, did she?" Reni patted his forearm.

"Naw. She was fine. Hey, your dad's a great guy."

"He's my buddy...watch that pothole!"

"Ten degrees right." Rand guided the wheels around the ubiquitous New Orleans road hazard.

"Did ya hear about the Merlin job?"

"Naw, I hear nothing." He smiled. "Guess I'll be a single-engine guy for awhile."

"There will be more chances."

"I ain't complaining."

Tonight was no time for experiments. He wheeled directly up St. Charles Avenue to oak-infested Washington Avenue and a smooth stop at the valet for Commander's Palace. The maitre d' greeted and escorted the couple through the former mansion that had been converted to a series of small, elegant dining rooms. A dozen busboys and waiters hovered above white linen tables of the first room where every last male snuck a discreet peek at Reni's transit to the wooden stairway. They were seated upstairs at a small table next to a picture window; a 200-year-old oak was strategically lit in the St. Augustine lawn below. Reni ordered Cabernet over the tinkle of fine china and Rand, a double bird. Within a minute, their drinks arrived and Rand ordered alligator tail appetizer and turtle soup. Reni selected the pheasant entrée and Rand asked the waiter to bring him what he, the waiter, would order.

"Thanks for taking me here, Rand. I love this place."

"Yeah, me too." He took her hand and a deep breath.

His hand felt strong in hers. "I gotta ask you, Rand. Why in the world do you call your car the SS?"

He laughed softly. "She's my modern day horse. Every car should have a name." He took a sip. "One night we were out partying in a monster rain storm, ya know, thunderstorms and lightning and all. The wind was howling out of the north as we rolled down Lakeshore and water from the Pontchartrain was blowing onto the road." His second sip of bird delivered euphoria. "Even with my wipers on, I could barely see two feet."

"Yeah?" Reni focused on his lips as he spoke.

"The puddles turned into deep water as waves formed and rolled across the hood. And the engine quit."

"Oops." A sip of wine.

"Half my ground school class was jammed in the car and we were stranded in this fuckin...sorry, freaking...flood. I couldn't see anything except waves and my headlights were underwater." Another sip. "Everybody got real quiet for a few seconds as hail banged on the roof and water started coming in the windows. We were so screwed."

She smiled.

"So I just had a feeling...and hit the ignition again. She miraculously fired right up and sailed for high ground, pushing a huge wake in front of us. On queue, we all sang along as Ride Captain Ride blared on the FM. It was too perfect." He grinned. "From then on, the ol' girl has been the SS, you know, sailing ship. You may have noticed the nautical flag on the starboard side. We sailed straight to the drive-thru at the Daiquiri Factory."

"My mother was just talking about that place yesterday. She can't believe that you can order daiquiris from a drive-thru. She says New Orleans is the only place in the world that would allow that."

The waiter had hovered covertly around the table. "Another wine ma'am?"

"Oh yes. Please." She lifted her eyebrows playfully. Cabernet began to massage her shoulders. "Why aren't you in school?"

"Uh-oh." He took her hand. "I already graduated."

"From where?"

"OFU."

"OFU?"

"Oil Field University. The grad school of hard knocks."

"The rigs? I hear it's hard out there."

"Wasn't much easy about the place."

"How long were you out there?"

"Two and a half years."

"You're kidding."

"And six months before that on an ocean-going tug."

"So you never went to college?"

"One semester at USL. It wasn't for me."

"Why?"

"It was prison."

"So you quit?"

"I was a bird in a cage. One day, while some Sixties burnout with muttonchop sideburns and earth shoes droned on melodramatically about some place I'm sure he'd never been, I just couldn't take it anymore. I walked out and headed for Morgan City."

"Who's in Morgan City?"

"A guy in a bar had told me a company was hiring deckhands. So I drove over and talked the personnel man into hiring me. He kept looking at me as if I was a wuss or something. I told him just to hire me; that I wouldn't let him down. It took me a half-hour to convince him."

"And he hired you?"

"Yeah, but it wasn't exactly the Love Boat that I had envisioned. I was the only guy out there who wasn't a refugee, an ex-con or a coonass." Another sip. "But I scored a roughneck job on a drilling rig and things got a lot better."

"What's a roughneck do?"

"Mostly deals with drilling. The hole is drilled by a Hughes bit about so big." He held out his hands about a foot apart. "Its diamond tipped and a rotor in the rig floor turns while this gnarly lubricant is pumped into the pipe. We drilled in thirty-foot joints until it got to the rig floor and we would spin another to the last one with a huge pneumatic tool and heavy tongs." Rand sipped bird. "When the bit wore out, we'd have to pull out the entire string to change it. Sometimes we would be twenty thousand feet deep."

"That deep?"

"Oh yeah... it would take up the entire twelve-hour shift. I'd go straight to bed and sleep for eleven hours after one of those days."

"I hear there's a lot of fights and tough guys out there."

"There was a lot of blood out there. Mostly from people getting fingers and hands cut off."

"You? Did you ever get hurt?" Reni looked him over.

"Yeah, couple of times..." He held up his right hand. "This is a plastic hand... the first one got chopped off."

"What!!" She reached over quickly and saw veins. "Dang you, boy."

"Actually, I just broke a small bone in this hand. No big deal. A guy I worked with got his hand between the pipe and the strand at the wrong time... and thousands of pounds of pipe landed right on his wrist. It was the nastiest bone crunch I've ever heard... and blood squirted everywhere. Wadn't pretty."

"Gross. Does everybody at Lakefront know you worked out there? I had no idea."

"Naw. A few. Glad to be out of the oil patch, girl."

"How did you start flying?"

"Well, we worked seven on and seven off out there, and one day I drove past the Lafayette airport with a thousand bucks in my pocket. I took a flying lesson and knew that's all I wanted to do. Hey, this...is the joke."

"What joke?"

"How do you know that you're on a date with a pilot?"

"I don't know."

"Well, he takes you to dinner and after an hour he says, 'Hey, enough about me. Let's talk about aviation.' Sorry." She laughed and Rand was manic. "What about you? You're not in school."

"I was at UNO for a semester. I didn't know what to study so my dad advised to take a year off to see the real world." She looked around. "I'm beginning to see his point."

Fresh coffee and Bananas Foster finished them off. Rand tipped as if his checking account wasn't two grand in the red and held her hand as they proceeded out onto Washington in the warm night. He handed the valet his ticket and they were alone on the quiet corner under giant oaks.

"That was great. Thank you." She slid her hand around his back and into his right hand.

"The pleasure was mine, madam." He got his left hand behind her soft neck and gently pressed his lips to hers.

Rand wheeled the SS into a spot on St. Philip and they walked two blocks to the candle-lit Lafitte's. A man played the piano as patrons, stools pulled up to the grand, sang along. Between numbers, a trumpet echoed through soothing humidity, wrought-iron balconies and red bricks of the Quarter.

In the gentle breeze of the open-air bar, candles twinkled at each table against exposed brick. Reni was comfortable holding his hand and kisses warmed with each sip.

At midnight, they made a drunkenly exit to the SS. Rand talked to the car at each red light. "Whoa boy!" The light changed to green and, "Gettie up!" She had never laughed harder as Rand pulled into her driveway. He wisely decided not to pull the ol' car in the front yard gag. They stood away from the porch light. He took her in his arms, jacket long retired in the backseat. "Well good-night ma'am." A small peck.

"Thanks for taking me out." A warm kiss, a nibble to his lower lip. She felt safe in these arms. "I'll see you tomorrow." Reni pulled back to look into his eyes. "You will acknowledge me now that your waiting game is over?"

"Waiting game...?" Rand looked innocently into her eyes but it was his that betrayed. Busted. "Yes ma'am."

No buzzes were needed on Monday's traffic watch as adrenaline flowed in Rand with the sweet musk of Reni on his hands. He finished traffic watch and made his way up the stairs into the flying club with Twinkie and C6 in hand. The phone rang and Beth motioned it was for Rand. "Yel-low?"

"Rand? This is Ken Hotchkiss."

"It is?" What tha...? He held his breath.

"Could you come over here? I'd like to talk to ya." The voice sounded like a General. "When can you be here?" George Patton barked.

"Twenty...thirty minutes." Rand stood at attention.

"See ya then." The line went dead.

Rand held up the phone; his face flushed. "I may be a little late for Wilson at ten. Tell him to watch the thunderstorm tape till I get back." Blue eyes danced.

"What is it Chapman? Who was that?" Beth smiled without a clue.

"What are you? The po-lice?" He bolted for Shelly Arms, shaved and put on his new blue jacket, gray slacks and the tie he wore with Reni. Fifteen minutes later he passed the receptionist at the Aero East hangar with game face on. She whistled approval. He knocked on the open door and Hotchkiss looked up from behind the desk and stood.

"Come on in, young man." Six inches shorter than Rand, Hotchkiss had ordered his hair cut short. The dab of Brillcream held the slight crop in a rooster hold. A tight belly rested between calloused hands. His dark brown eyes pierced.

Rand was certain that this man was aware of everything. No time for bullshit. "Hello sir, I'm Rand Chapman."

"Ken Hotchkiss. Sit down." He pointed to the metal chair. "I hear you might want to work for me."

"Yessir."

"Tell me...What is the PCA, and what does it mean to you?" He looked into Rand's eyes as a small red flush appeared upon youthful face.

Rand's mind took off, not expecting this type of question. He felt anxiety and tried hard to mask it. Fuck…PCA…that was on the commercial written test a couple of years ago…hey…I know that one…. "Let's see…that's the Positive Control Area…starts at 18,000 feet. All planes in it have to set altimeters at twenty-nine ninety-two. Uhhh, got to be on an IFR flight plan with an altitude reporting transponder. Personally, I've never been that high…unfortunately."

"Is that at or above 18,000?" Hotchkiss sat expressionless, though the eyes were locked on Rand's.

"Yes. At eighteen or above eighteen." That was a guess.

"Where does it stop?"

His heart thumped hard. His brain searched. "Stop…? Hell, I don't know."

"Hell…I don't either." Hotchkiss laughed. "Chris tells me that you're from across the lake. I live over in Slidell."

"Yeah? I used to play football against Salmon and Slidell High."

"Look Rand, I have a fourteen-hundred local wheels-up time on Thursday over to Houston and back. Report at thirteen hundred and I'll show you how to stock the airplane with adult beverages, use the coffee maker and fill the ice. I'll file the flight plan. How's that sound?"

"That sounds great. I'll be here." Whoa.

"And if all goes well on Thursday, there's a Mexico City overnight next Monday. You got a passport?"

Rand sank. "Uhhh, no."

"Go get yourself one. Mexico doesn't require one, but you're gonna need it eventually." He sat back in his chair, exhaled a tension-filled breath, grabbed a tin of Copenhagen, pinched a big portion of the black stuff under his lower front teeth, spotted a Styrofoam coffee cup and set it in front of him on the desk. "I tried to call you Sunday night for this trip. You need an answer phone."

Chris walked in. "Hey, Rand."

"Hey guy! Thanks for puttin' a good word in for me. I appreciate it."

"No problem. You may not be thanking me when you find out what a horse's ass you're working for." They all laughed. Good humor is always based on truth.

Rand felt like the third wheel. "Where ya headin', all dolled up?"

"Ken here called me for this trip to D.C. today. It'll be my last hurrah with him. I don't need to be in Houston till next Tuesday."

"Plus, he's got a great piece of ass in D.C. He's a horny bastard." Hotchkiss smiled and lightly spit into the cup.

"Me? Ya should see the account Rand was working at the party."

"That's what's wrong with you young shits. Always chasin' pussy." Another spit. Hotchkiss spotted the beeper on Chris' belt. "Pass the torch."

Chris unhooked the device from his belt and handed it to Rand. "This is required anatomy of a corporate jock."

Beneath a clear blue sky, Rand sailed merrily across the Pontchartrain Causeway to the Northshore. The day was a beautiful thing. Finally, all the miserable time on the Viking and the rigs were beginning to bear fruit. The days of being beat to hell in a single-engine plane in 90-degree heat and turbulence for a thousand bucks a month would soon be history. His new machine was a powerful, air-conditioned, pressurized turbo-prop that zoomed above the planet at 340 knots. He would climb above the haze at 3,000 feet per minute, stay in fancy hotels around the world—at an unheard-of salary of forty grand a year. Get out. The Houston turn was this afternoon.

Lulled into reverie by the clip-clop of Causeway beneath his wheels, he allowed his eyes to close for a moment as Dust in the Wind came on the FM. The ballad took him back to another defining moment: his break away from the Viking. After a particularly grueling two-week hitch, he'd walked into Progress Marine Drilling in Morgan City and thirty minutes later, he'd walked out with a job on one of the company's twenty offshore drilling rigs at three times his deckhand salary. His new position was called a roughneck, whatever the hell that is, he wondered at the time. Driving home in his VW Bug, he heard Dust in the Wind for the first time on the radio and it spoke directly to him.

I close my eyes
Only for a moment
And the moment's gone...

Everything could change in a moment. Suddenly, a path had cleared to finance his dream of flying airplanes. He activated an escape plan from the oilfield although his co-workers would cast serious doubt: "Once you put on the gloves... they ain't comin' off..." Like hell. Now, as the song replayed for him over the Pontchartrain, Rand felt the same uncertain energy.

Dust in the wind
All we are is dust in the wind...

Rand surfed a wave of positive energy as the Causeway ended in Mandeville. Eight miles north, he felt his chest tighten slightly with a left onto Tchefuncte Drive. Slowing to 25 mph, he wound his way through middle-class estates of the quiet neighborhood deep in the pine forest. His gut rode rolling hills for two miles before a dive as he spotted the curved drive and the red brick house beyond it, surrounded by oak, dogwood, and magnolia. The familiar squeak of a humidity-swollen front door announced his entrance into the foyer. His heart quickened. So many times growing up he had hesitated here before braving the living room, knowing the old man waited, tanked on gin. Is it the rare good drunk, or the usual angry rant? Usually, it was bad things that greeted him just about...

And there she was, a deer in the headlights, a far-away look in her eyes. "Hi mom!"

It was nearly noon, yet Judy Chapman still wore her faded blue nightgown. Ringed by deep charcoal circles, her eyes stared vacantly through unkempt, graying hair. She mumbled through parched lips. "Oh my god... Why are you here...?" Her hand went to the back of her neck. "I'm a burden and... you should be working." She fidgeted with a strand of hair and turned toward the picture window. "I'm worthless to everyone...please go back to work...you have work to do."

Rand approached slowly. "Mom?" He had seen this most his life, but it always ripped his gut to see her this way. There were never tears but she looked wrung out. He watched her turn to pace barefooted, heart rate at a gallop. The back of her neck was aglow with red blotches from incessant rubs. Familiar tension returned to Rand's throat. Her pain was excessive and there was never a damn thing he could do about it.

"Why are you here?" she asked again.

"I landed a great job flying a turboprop. I need to get my birth certificate for a passport." He naturally raised his voice so she could hear above her inner roar.

"Oh my God, those crash all the time. Maybe you should go back to college and finish... Oh, I don't know." She wrung out her hands, fingers twisted till the tips were white. "At least you'll be something more than me...a big burden on everyone."

Rand found an empty glass in the cupboard and filled it with tap water. "Here, your mouth seems dry. Are you taking your medicine?" Judy gulped the water down and drifted into the master bedroom as Rand followed her to the small file cabinet against the wall. He noticed several gift-wrapped packages set out neatly on twin beds.

"Whose presents are these?"

"These are for Earl. It's his birthday. He wanted me to give him a big party...but he changed his mind. Now he wants to stay with his friends at Guzzo's. They're throwing him a big party." Her eyes darted back and forth.

"It's dad's birthday?" Ironically, Rand looked over a paper that certified that he was alive. "I completely forgot." He slipped it into back pocket as his mom stared into the dresser mirror. "Is he coming to get you?"

"Oh no...I'm not invited to that party."

"Hey mom, give me Dr. Blackwell's number. I think he needs to see you."

"I have an appointment tomorrow."

"What time?"

"Uhh...sometime in the morning." She could not remember that Blackwell had been on vacation for a month.

"Look, I have a flight to Houston in two hours. I'll call you as soon as I get back tonight. Okay?" He checked his watch. No time.

"Uh huh." She followed him to the front door.

"I love you mom. I'll call you. Okay?" He held her by both shoulders. Her body was weak. He wanted to shake her.

"Goodbye Rand." She gazed blankly into space.

As late afternoon approached, Phil Donahue interviewed a transvestite prostitute who complained about his/her father's disapproval. Judy walked past the TV set to the bedroom in a deep trance. This is it. She found the mirror and stared into haze. The gray hair told her that she'd spent enough time on this rock of humiliation. Her hands trembled as she found the pills that she'd accumulated for the lethal dose. She filled the glass and methodically took four at a time. After the thirteenth dose, she crawled in bed and pulled the covers to her chin. She looked at the presents neatly arranged on the opposite single bed, took the receiver off the hook and, through chaos, prayed that her Father would meet her today. She closed her eyes for the final time; the textured ceiling above turned to white fuzz. Happy birthday Earl...I know this is the best present I could ever give you... Daddy... I'm coming home... God...please forgive me, but I can't take it anymore. Please watch over my children.

Judy lost consciousness. The lights went out at four-forty-one in the afternoon. The silence of the quiet home echoed through blood flow in her ears. A scarlet red Cardinal chirped from the pine outside the window. Her life began to drain away swiftly.

Runway Three Six Left received the Merlin at sunset. Hotchkiss went straight for his car and Rand went straight to the Benson office to phone home. It was busy. Thank God. She's okay. Or... is she? He felt a strange sense of urgency. He dialed the neighbor across the street from memory. Jean Mortenson answered.

"Jeanie, this is Rand."

"Hey Rand, haven't seen you in awhile, but we hear you on the radio all the time. What's up, sweetie?"

"Well, it's probably nothing, but I was over to see my mom today and she...uhh...wasn't feeling so well. I'm a little concerned. Would you mind going over and seeing that she's okay?"

"Of course Rand."

"Her line is busy now, but I'm hoping that she's talkin' to the doctor or somethin'."

Jean had just started the dinner process. "Sure, I'll walk over."

"Thanks a million. I'll call you in a few."

"Not to worry, Rand. She's fine."

"Thank God. Was she in bed?"

"Yeah, lying on her back, sleeping like a baby."

On her back? She doesn't sleep on her back. It hit him hard and fast. "Jean...I need you to go over and wake her up. I got a real bad feeling."

"Are you sure... you want me to wake her?"

"God yes, Jean. Please."

Ten minutes later, Rand finally got a ring on Judy's line. Jean was hysterical. "She's not breathing Rand...She's not breathing...! Oh my God...I'm sooo sorry...oh my God!"

Rand slumped over the desk. He slugged himself, hard. You ignored every red flag. You... let her die. He heard Jean continue to scream, now at someone. "Jean...Jeanie! Who's there?"

"Paramedics. Oh my God...they're thumping her chest." She moved the phone away from her mouth. "Oh God...it's too late...oh my God." Her voice trailed away and he could hear the metal stretcher click into locks.

Rand's energy died. His head fell to the desktop. Peace... I hope she finds peace finally... God, give her the peace she couldn't find here. He heard Jean come back on the line.

"Rand! They're taking her to St. Tammany."

"Is she still alive?"

"I doubt...uh...I don't think so."

"I'll be there as soon as I can, Jean." He hung up and stared unfocused while he struggled to comprehend what had just happened.

Reni moved to the doorframe with a smile that instantly transformed to a mirror of enormous pain and bewilderment. "Rand...?"

As if in a deep vacuum, he answered automatically as both messenger and receiver. Tears streamed his cheeks. "My mom just killed herself."

Rand raced onto the freeway and sped westbound toward the Causeway. He backed his foot to the bridge's posted limit of 55 mph as the clip-clop carried him across in a stunned stupor. Just this morning, on this very spot, he'd thought he was on top of the world. Clip-clop...clip-clop. He stared straight ahead and saw a crossover approach at mile four. He pulled in, walked to the rail and peered into the gray Pontchartrain. My God. Water returned him to his near-deather on the Viking. He knelt down on the oil-stained pavement. Dear God... I need a miracle here....

3. Uncle El Gordo

A large brown leather chair conformed to the rear end of Pablo in his mountain fortress above Medellin, Columbia. The Cartel leader listened with amusement and quiet admiration as his main link to the U.S. fondled nightvision goggles while he explained in fluent Spanish how they and the Lodestar had perfected his operation.

"Bonito...Muy bonito, Gordo." Pablo constantly scrutinized to determine if betrayal was possible. The Cartel had agreed that they would definitely waste Wales one day. The question was when, not if... and the when question was voted on after each operation. Pablo's bad gut was reason enough and Wales was keenly aware of his position.

The three Cartel leaders were invincible. Pablo, Jorge Ortiz and Carlos Vilez were happy to donate millions to the community and were widely viewed as the Godfathers of Medellin. One judge had attempted a case against them, but quickly retreated after his eleven-year-old daughter was found decapitated in the trunk of his car with a note that indicated she would be the first of his four children to meet this fate. The case was instantly withdrawn. Sitting on $15 billion, the Cartel basically ran the local government, guarded by a 1,000-man, heavily armed force. Seventy-five of these guards were now scattered below the 10,000-square-foot palace at the summit of the highest hill in the state, replete with harem.

"So what do you do with all the money?" Pablo narrowed his focus beneath wiry black hair.

"It is stacked away. I'm washing in Miami. A Mercedes dealer."

"You will have many cars then."

"I move airplanes the same as automobiles." Though he spoke with a strange twang, Wales had command of the Spanish language. But El Gordo's explanation that this facility was due to a superior memory needed to be constantly explored. Time to retest.

Pablo stood to open a cabinet in the mahogany wall. "Gordo, do you remember who this is?" He handed Wales a wallet-sized, black and white photograph of a little girl.

"Yes."

He had shown him the exact same picture precisely fourteen months and twenty-two days earlier. "What do you remember about this picture?"

Wales glanced briefly at the image before he steadied his eyes on Pablo.

"Her name is Lucia and she was seven-and-a-half when the photo was taken. She was killed twelve days before her ninth birthday in a boating accident off the north coast of Anquilla in a squall after the boom hit her across the head and threw her into the choppy water. Her father sailed the boat around and picked her up within minutes, but she had died from the strike to the head. She lived with her family in Barranquilla and she was your first aunt. She died in 1954." Wales' body remained still as he recited. Did I forget anything? No.

Pablo again was painfully cognizant that this was a superior human sitting in front of him. "How is your new plane running?"

"Perfecto. Just like it was when they took it out of the box forty years ago. She flies like a dream." Wales was accustomed to these awkward interviews with Pablo.

"What will be your route to Louisiana?"

"Same as last time. One stop in the Yucatan and then straight across the Gulf at wavetops."

"Last time you stayed in Mexico an extra day, no?" Two traveling guards had camped a mile from the DeSoto Ranch on his previous visit.

"Si, I wanted to get a better day for the weather. I was sure you knew because of the men that were camping just north of the ranch. I found out about them as soon as I landed there. I was hoping that they worked for you. One skinny with a moustache and one skinny without, but with pock marks on his face."

"What is this potmarks?"

Wales had never heard the Spanish equivalent, so he had pronounced it in English. "You know, like acne scars from his childhood perhaps."

"Oh yes, that is the man that was there. Bueno." Pablo worked to his feet and Wales rose with him. "You leave tonight?"

"Tonight's the night."

"Bueno. And your co-piloto?"
"Waiting in Mexico."
"Perfecto."

The green coastline of Mexico rotated beneath the nose of the Merlin as Rand spotted foreign soil for the first time. His eyes drew starboard to the chrome spinner of the propeller against verdant hills of the countryside. Ahead was a giant bowl of milk, surrounded by mountains.

"Under all that muck lays beautiful downtown Mexico City." Ken Hotchkiss looked over to his new co-pilot and laughed. "It's a real beauty. Every approach in here is on instruments, because of the smog of nineteen million people with no pollution controls. Makes the tree-huggers look damn smart." He pulled out the approach chart for runway Five Right and began to brief. "The airport is 7,300 feet above sea level, so the altitude at the outer marker is way up at 8,800. You gotta train your brain to land at high altitudes." He removed a detailed airport diagram from the thick Jeppson binder and pointed to the two long runways. "And remember, these are parallel runways. Five Left will be off to the left of us when we break out of the smog. Last year, Western drove a DC-10 down to the wrong runway, killing a bunch of folks."

"Oh yeah, I remember that. Weren't there construction workers on the runway?"

"Yeah, a crew was working on Five Right and Western was cleared to land on Five Left. But when the plane cleared the murk, the first thing they saw was Five Right and they drove straight into the workers on the closed runway. Ruined their whole day." Hotchkiss spit Copenhagen into his Styrofoam cup and let out a high pressure sigh. He slowed to 210 knots for the final approach, whistling Up the Lazy River with both hands on the yoke.

Rand tried to get his bearings. He couldn't see through the white haze and felt disoriented in a foreign country in a strange airplane. His job was to work the radios. It seemed a simple enough task.

"Nobemba Nie Fie Ate Bravo Chalie, tur let headin zero nie zero, clear to atety ate hunred an clear for ILS Runwa Fie Rite approch, contat towa on one one ate point fie," said the voice on the speaker in rapid-fire bursts of Spanglish.

Rand tried to decode the transmission as Hotchkiss calmly replied for him. "Roger, Nine-Five-Eight Bravo Charlie, cleared for the ILS and going to tower."

Ken rolled into thirty-five degrees of left bank. The windscreen was gray drapes at the outer marker. Hotchkiss called out 8,800 feet and began whistling Stormy Weather. Rand cross-checked his altimeter and picked up the microphone.

"Mexico City Tower, the Merlin Nine-Five-Eight Bravo Charlie at the marker inbound." The tower did not acknowledge. Shit.

"Try again," advised Hotchkiss between chirps. "Landing gear down."

An unintelligible squawk of Spanish came over the speaker. As they breached the smog, Rand saw smoke billowing from a sea of tin-roofed shacks, all rusted and discolored. What kind of hellhole is this? The sea of roofs ended abruptly at a long, rubber-stained runway. Still with no landing clearance, Rand quickly hit the mike key as an impoverished urban landscape slid beneath his window. "Nine-Five-Eight Bravo Charlie, landing on Five Right Mexico City."

"Ro-yer, I say...agin." This time, the controller spoke in English. "Cleared to land."

"Das too bad about dat pilot's mama, baby. Ya tink he's doin' okay?"

"I don't know, Mama." Reni sighed. "He's on a trip now with his new company, the one with a Merlin."

"An he left his mama layed up all alone in da hospital...? Don't he love his mama, for Jesus' sake?"

"He was at her bedside all weekend, mama. He can't just stop workin', he's got bills to pay an all."

"Oh my Gawd! Ya see what happens when babies grow up? Jus forget about who raised ya an go on wit your own life. Probably neva been in a church."

"That's not true. They're Presbyterians."

"Oh sweet Jesus! Not dem people."

"I'm sure they're good people, mama. Look at how nice Rand is."

"His mama tried to axe herself. And what's his daddy like, dawlin'? Dat's what ya got ta look at. Probably a big drinker, like mos dem Presbyterians."

Reni gulped down the last of her orange juice. "I gotta go to work, mama."

"You seein' dat pilot tonight?"

"I just told you...he's in Mexico."

"Mexico! Oh Lawd Jesus! Only gangstas and drug dealas go to Mexico..."

Rand and Hotchkiss reeled from a dozen near-crashes in a beat-up Mexican taxi as the driver, hand welded to horn, finally finished his personal Grand Prix and screeched to a halt in front of the El Presidente Hotel. Two uniformed doormen sprang to open the cab door and ushered the pilots into the luxurious lobby. The walls and stairways were finished with rich mahogany; an enormous crystal chandelier was suspended above. Rand reached his room to find that his clothes had already been tucked into drawers and hung in the closet.

Alone for the first time since he rose from his own bed at sunrise, Rand's ears rang with screaming Garretts as he drew the curtain back over headlights and blaring horns. Mexico City rush hour was at full steam as the sun set into gray haze. Whipped after an average of three hours of sleep in the past four days, he lay down upon the bedspread with thoughts of a nap until memories of the hospital raided him. He quickly jumped to feet, moved to the shower, dressed and headed downstairs.

Except for three Asian businessmen, the bar in the hotel lobby was a morgue. Rand scanned the liquor bottles lined up on the shelf. Tequila was dominant. Three shots of Hornitos returned energy, courage and brilliance.

The doormen graciously swung doors open to the Zona Rosa's trendy bars and restaurants. A half-dozen blocks later, Rand stumbled into Rosie Disco with lungs full of monoxide. His mouth was dry as he squeezed through an energetic crowd to flag the bartender. He fished out a Marlboro Light. A lighter appeared from nowhere. Donna Summer moaned Love to Love You Baby as Rand followed from lacquered nails to olive-skinned forearm to full breasts and lustrous black hair. He leaned over to the flame. "Thanks."

"Americano?" She wore red lipstick.

An army of testosterone charged his unit. "Yes...ah, si." He'd never seen a Latin quite like this before. "I sure hope you speak English. Cause if you don't, we're gonna have to move along..."

"Oh yes, I speak English, but not perfectly." She looked into his eyes.

The short walk from the hotel had left him depleted. He felt a wave of exhaustion approaching. The fatigue of the day...of the week...had begun to catch up. He wished he could just lie in the fetal position and pillow his weary head within her ample bosom and sleep until the middle of next week. Deliriously, he debated whether it would be appropriate to ask her if this was possible as the wave hit him with full force. He was going down... right in the middle of the Zona fucking Rosa... and she was the only thing between his face and the grungy floor.

Suddenly, he was blessed with situational awareness. He spotted the bartender in slo-mo. Magically, Rand guided his tongue. "Dos tequillas por favor." He held up the international signal for the number two. Ten point three seconds later, two shot glasses landed on the bar, filled with liquid gold.

"A shot?"

"Si, why not?" This Americano had just stepped off the street and into the Rosie as if he owned the place. He stood head and shoulders above the crowd with toned arms, blond hair and intense blue eyes. Perhaps he is from Hollywood. She picked up the silver salt shaker and licked the back of her hand. "Salud." She drained the glass and quickly sucked a lime slice. She laughed as Rand went through the exact routine.

"Dos mas!" he called to the bartender, raising an eyebrow at her in a universal gesture: Can you hang with me?

"Aye yi..." She rolled her eyes. "Okay, mister." The ritual was repeated. "Where do you come from?"

Rand hated discos, but had learned to communicate effectively with short bursts of information shouted directly into the receiver's ear. "New Orleans," he yelled over Barry White.

"Oh yes, I know of New Orleans. It was home of the great pirate Lafitte."

"Lafitte? How do you know that?"

"We have schools here in Mexico also, mister." Her smile revealed straight teeth of pearls. Her eyes danced with educated amusement. "Of course, I also know about the war in 1812 against the British and of the Spanish domination before that in the 1700s." She liked his eyes. "What brings a man from New Orleans to Mexico City?"

"I'm a spy for the CIA, I came here to get you," Rand deadpanned. He was surprised at the sober expression that crossed her face for an instant. He laughed. And through the haze: A Wild Turkey on the label behind the bar. Well... well. Rand ordered up a bird. She wisely down-shifted to Tecate.

"Salud. Me llama Luz. My name is Luz. Can you dance?" Rand held her warm hand that pulled him through the crowd to the rear of the dance floor. A fresh bird followed in his trailing right hand.

Luz moved seductively as Rand twirled her beneath his arm and caught her gently on the back end, drink still as a retriever on hunt. She laughed hard at his imitation of Travolta and the famous point-and-shoot.

Five blinks later, his head was reduced to a skull, the moisture sucked out with alcohol evaporation from dry, high altitude. His eyes throbbed and his back ached. The assailant was the dreaded tequila, no doubt. He now began on the usual questions on time and space, and the identity of the face under the pile of hair next to him. This time it was jet black.

Luz had studied the lump in her bed impatiently for an hour. She had just turned her back on him before his breathing changed and he let out a strangulated moan. She quickly rolled over to face him.

"Bueno." Luz whispered while his reddened eyes surveyed dark nipples, as if for the first time.

"Bueno?" His face was mashed to pillow.

"Good, like good morning. Buenos dias. Comprende?"

"Oh...si, comprende." Blood audibly rushed his head and he could barely keep his right eye open. "Buenos dias muy bonita amigo."

"Amiga." She smiled as she corrected.

"Oh, si, amiga. I forgot already." His eyes scanned the room: stucco walls, oil paintings, ceramic vases filled with fresh flowers. An AM radio played a Spanish tune. "How are you?"

"Muy bien. Are you hungry?"

"Negative."

"What is this...negative?"

"Just silly pilot talk." Rand's own breath gagged him. "Hey girl, you got a toothbrush?"

"If you want a toothbrush, I will bring you a toothbrush." She stood, giving Rand a clear view of her fineness. "I will be right back." She threw on a silk robe.

Rand found his feet despite the tribal drum in his head. Naked, he proceeded to the far window. The street below was damp, the cars raced and honked as the mist and smog refreshed his memory. Hole-E-Shit. The vision of the Merlin cruising at altitude with an empty right seat smacked him. Thinned blood blitzed his heart. He could not remember a departure time and he could be miles from the hotel. A cold panic slimed him as he went to his pile of clothes and hurriedly began to dress.

Luz came back with a fully pasted toothbrush and was walloped by the sudden getaway mode. "What is happening?"

"This is not good. I gotta get my ass back to the hotel before they leave me." His mouth was dry.

"Who? I thought you were the piloto."

"Well, I am actually the co-piloto and El Capitan could easily leave my ass here in Mexico." Rand took the toothbrush and moved into the small bathroom next to the bed. He brushed, spit, and caught a glimpse of his face in the mirror. Deep dark circles under his eyes announced his state clearly. He was running on empty.

"Aye yi...what time is your flight?"

"I don't know. I think it was later today but now I'm not sure."

"You know, Señor, we have this thing in Mexico, we call it el telefono. You pick it up, dial a few numbers and the darn thing rings at the other end. If someone is there, they pick it up and you can say anything you like. You can even ask questions like: 'Hello sir, what time does my flight leave today?'"

Rand smiled. "And you have one of these telefonos?"

"Oh yes, I do mister. It is right under that bookshelf."

"I'm sure I can use your assistance with this."

After a call to a directory service and another to the hotel, Luz handed the phone over to Rand. He asked in English for Hotchkiss' room. A great sigh of relief came over him as he heard Ken pick up.

"Señor Chapman, que pasa?" He was out of breath but in a great mood. "Have you had breakfast?" Rand's anxiety dissipated as Hotchkiss outlined the steps to an early evening departure over female moans. Rand realized that some sort of bodily performance was in progress.

"We are not leaving until five tonight, ma'am." Rand grinned. "Sure as hell should have made sure yesterday." He looked down at cleavage. "Are you working today?"

"I am to be there by ten o'clock."

"Ain't that a shame. Guess I should head for the hotel and get a little more sleep."

She looked hard into his eyes. "But you know, this is Mexico. And if a Señorita does not feel like going to work one day, she does not go. Today, I think I will stay home and rest. And today I will have lunch with a new friend. But first, we must go back to sleeping."

After a sound three hours, Luz rose to boil water on the gas stove. Rand watched curiously from her bed. She was independent and determined, as if she had expected that they would dance and laugh and she would drag him to her flat to make love with windows open. She poured coffee, added thick cream, a truckload of sugar, walked back to the bed, handed over the mug and dropped her robe.

"Como esta?" Luz let her hair lose and crawled back under the covers. She kissed his mouth.

"I've had worse days." He sipped the thick coffee. "Whoa girl!" He looked at the mug. "Good God, I could run back to New Orleans today. Who needs an airplane?"

"You are quite loco, no?" Luz again kissed him. "You know Señor, I know quite a bit about your New Orleans. I think it is my favorite city in Estados Unidos." She sipped from the mug. "My favorite thing is the pirate Jean Lafitte."

"Lafitte? Yeah, mine too. It's my favorite bar."

"What is this...bar?"

"It is on Bourbon Street, but not right in the turista section. It's called the back of the Quarter, the French Quarter. You have heard of the French Quarter?"

"Yes, I have heard of the French Quarter, but I do not know what you are talking about, a bar." She kissed his eyes shut. "This Jean Lafitte I know saved

New Orleans in the battle against the British, no? Against the red coats when they tried to attack the city in 1815. He was a thorn in the side of Americans until he helped defend the city for the green coats, yes?"

"Green coats?" Rand looked at her. "You mean the gringos?"

"Of course, that is what the Mexicans call the Americanos, yes. They called the soldiers green coats and the Americans thought they were saying gringos. But of course that was a different war, no?"

"If you say so. How do you know so much about Lafitte?"

"My father has a very good amigo from the Estados. He is like an uncle to me. He tells many stories from the America. He is also a pilot. And he also lives in Louisiana."

"Really? What's his name?"

"He calls himself El Gordo. I do not know his real name."

"Uncle El Gordo. Now there's one ya don't hear everyday. So, how fat is he?"

"He is not very fat, but he has a cerveza belly, a beer belly, although he does not drink alcohol. He is always laughing and having a good time."

"So when do you see...Uncle El Gordo?"

"He comes to our farm in the south."

Farm? "In the south? South of what?"

"Yes, my family has a farm down in the Yucatan, around the Ciudad de Merida. You know Merida? Anyway, he has his own plane and he and my father fly together. Sometimes Gordo will stay with us for a week or two."

"You're kidding. You own a farm...in Merida?" Rand sat up and looked hard at the smooth-skinned, prettier-by-the- second wealthy girl. "Blow me down."

"No Señor, I do not own a farm, my father owns the farm."

"And what do we grow on this farm?"

"Oh well, let's see. We have cattle and we have the goats and the chickens and we have cane fields on the... what we call the norte forte."

"Norte forte...like the north forty?"

"Si. Si." Luz had to remind herself to cease this blabber. Her father had requested many times to remain humble about the farm, especially around Americans. She felt a sudden fright grip her chest. Her father had warned her about something called the CIA, and that they always came as wolves, but dressed like sheep. Her feet became clammy, and she would not reveal anything about the family-owned jewelry store around the corner. "Enough about all this, Señor Rand." She lifted the sheet and turned him over on his stomach. Straddling him, the heat of her undercarriage warmed his rear end as she worked firm hands from his spine to neck. She was pleased to feel his muscles yield to her touch. If he was a spy, he was cooler than Bond.

She turned him over and things only got better for a ten-minute reality lapse before they continued with their chat. They connected, as if old mates. His eyes cleared and captured her. She kissed him again. And the process repeated.

It was well after noon when Luz awoke to grill carne asada. Rand chewed happily with this unexpected royal treatment. As he pulled his clothes back on, Luz watched him from the bed as he answered the question in her eyes. "I will call you the next time I come to Mexico City."

She wrote out her number and led him politely to the door. Stunningly naked, she reached up on tiptoe to kiss him one last time. Unable to watch the departure, she slid into the still-warm bed and wrapped her arms around herself while she listened to the slam of the taxi door and the engine roar. Half of her was afraid that she would never see her first one-night stand again. The other half reminded her that every premonition she'd ever had, every last one, had come to be reality. And this particular premonition was by far her most vivid, this pilot from New Orleans, tall, funny and gone.

4. Pablo Who?

She ran in panic, without shoes, from a wild pig of some sort that grunted, snorted on her heels. Finally she fell into a pile of leaves deep in the woods. As the horned swine charged, she screamed. Her legs kicked and bounced off the spring of a cheap mattress. In a cold sweat, her heart raced as eyes opened. Again she could not move her arms. The smell of adrenaline propelled anxiety as her hair dripped additional sweat onto her soaked nightgown. Blue eyes darted left to see a blank white wall and further left to see the moon... no it was a clock. She looked down to see the predicament with her arms. Confused at the big buckle at her chest and the tight nylon straps, she questioned if her arms were amputated and why. She was on fire and the rampage in her heart brought horrific news: This was not heaven. Judy Chapman screamed at the top of her lungs. And nothing came from her mouth.

Her mind flashed with scenes, a runaway Rolodex. She remembered dozens of pills. How long ago was that...? Years maybe. She looked again at the clock that read twelve o'clock. It disclosed nothing. It could be noon. It could be midnight. It certainly said nothing of the month or day. Bright florescent lights under clinical plastic blared into her soul. She looked away and was drawn to a black book that lay peacefully on the metal table next to the bed. Her pulse began to slow. She saw a closed door open.

"Mom?" Rand tiptoed over to the bed. "How ya feelin'?" He scanned her chalky face and flinched at tight nylons straps that bound her arms across her chest. "Oh my God."

"Where am I, Rand...?"

"Mandeville." He unbuckled the straitjacket quickly. "Let's get this damn thing off." He hurled the restraint into the far corner and took her cold hand, the strong hand he knew so well.

"The nut house...?" She looked around the room. "So... this iss Mannn... devil." Her mouth was a desert and her breath reeked of death. "How dih... I geh... heh?"

Rand was uncertain how much he should tell her. His head throbbed with stress and last night's bird strikes. "How ya feelin'?"

"Groggy...so groggy." She slurred as her eyes lost focus and closed.

He moved to the bathroom to find a water glass. He filled it from the sink and went back to her bedside but she had slipped back into hell. He held her hand for an hour, gently weeping while she slept. Please, God, look over her. He stroked her lanky damp hair. "Hang in there, mom," he whispered in her ear before he left.

Numbly, Rand began his clip-clop across the Causeway back to New Orleans as the sun faded into the horizon. Reaching the end of the concrete span, curiosity wheeled the SS through Fat City, the restaurant and nightclub district of Metairie. Rand slewed thirty years back in time as he entered Guzzo's, the old man's favorite haunt. Haze of stale smoke hung over a dozen rumpled-suit regulars, mostly salesmen. He found a stool at the center of the new universe.

"Whatallitbe cap?" The bartender was there before his feet hit the bronze support under the huge bar. A tender in a drinker's bar knows not to be tardy. He spun a cocktail napkin down and kept his eyes on Rand as he dropped back like a quarterback, reaching for the bottle rack. This guy was All-Pro.

"Howsa 'bout a Wild Turkey, splash of Seven."

"Lime?"

"You know it."

The glass crashed hard into the ice drawer and came out packed; bird was poured generously to the rim. All-Pro grabbed the soda gun out of its holster and shot for a thousandth of a second. In one blink, he snatched a lime out of thin air and set down a concoction that twinkled in the dim light.

Rand's night vision kicked in. He could gradually see more people in the far corner: a man with a woman, certainly not his wife, and a few alone, having affairs with gin-and-tonics. He did not see his father.

"You're Earl's boy aren't you?" The raspy voice came from Rand's right.

"Yessir."

"I'm Wally Romero. I met you at a Saints game las' year." He held out his hand.

"Oh yeah, I remember. How ya doin'?" Rand shook the clammy hand and surveyed the creased face.

"Fine. Hey, sorry to hear about your mama."

"Yeah, thanks." Rand didn't quite know what to say. "Hey, have you seen my dad?"

"Not yet. He was in here yesterday." Wally took a sip and a long pull from a Marlboro. "Haven't seen him today yet. Hey, you still on the radio? I heard a diffrent guy doin' da traffic dis mornin'."

"Nah, I got a new job, flyin' a corporate airplane. Just started last week." The door opened and another business suit landed on a stool, a pelican on a harbor piling. Rand sipped the bird and the burn hit his throat. All-Pro wasn't fooling around.

Wally pointed at his glass and drained it just as the replacement arrived. No money was exchanged. "It's a shame 'bout ya mamma. I met her a few times." Wally had only heard that she was critical, maybe she had died, he wasn't sure. By the time Wally got the word, it had usually been through a few adjustments.

"Yeah, I just saw her at the hospital. I think she's gonna be fine." Rand took a more aggressive sip and the burn was nearly gone. So was the tension in his back. He took another sip as a quarter hit the bottom of the jukebox and Sinatra started in on That's Life. "I was hoping to catch him here to talk about her."

"Well, he's probly over at Carol's." Oops.

"Carol's?"

Wally's loose tongue kept him in constant turmoil. "Did I say Carol's...? Oh dat's right, he don't go in dare much anymore." He looked at Rand to see if he bought the sloppy retraction.

"Yeah, I know about her. Can't figure it though." The line was cast, the bait was tasty, the fish waterlogged.

"Well, ya know your ol' man is a good-lookin' guy. Wish I had his looks." Wally sensed turmoil and took a sudden interest to the pelican one fathom and two stools right. "Hey Russ! Ya goin' to da game on Sunday?"

"Fuck no. I hate dem goddam Saints."

Rand turned to his left. Three martini drinkers discussed a welfare system fix. They were going to spring into action to save it... first thing tomorrow... And the goddamn press. The jukebox paused and the panel of experts became louder as they waxed on about world problems between sips.

Rand took a deep relaxing breath. Within this black hole in a Fat City strip mall, all problems had simple solutions. Midway through his second euphoric bird, it hit him: So this... this... is where he had been. So many nights he had waited in the driveway hoping to see the familiar front grill come down the hill on Tchefuncte as all the other fathers passed by, in time for dinner. As dusk turned to dark, he would begin looking for familiar square headlights before finally giving up, eyes tired from the strain. This... is why his mother held that twisted look on her face at dinner, the head of the table, vacant. This... is why he came home with that smoky smell and crawled around the house on hands and knees. This is where he was... all those lost days and nights. All... those years.

Through low cirrus of Camel and Marlboro, Rand saw his reflection in the mirror behind the bar. Ohh... shit. The image of glass to lips produced a stinging epiphany. Like father, like... He flinched as revelation beeped faintly through his brain and seemed to echo throughout Guzzo's. Every head turned toward him with pointed glares as if his skin had been painted black. Confused, Rand wondered if everyone had heard him think. Beeps continued for several seconds before it dawned on him that the new-fangled device hooked to his belt had activated. Penetration from the outside world was a clear and present danger to the sanctuary of Guzzo's.

With an awkward fumble, Rand finally muted the damn thing. He threw down a five and moved from the time-warp to a rusted payphone on the mall's brick wall. He dropped a quarter and spun eight numbers with the rotary dial to reach the home of the great Captain. Hotchkiss picked up on the first ring.

"Hey partner, we got some flyin' tomorrow. Let's say an oh-six-thirty show for an oh-seven-forty-five wheels in the well. Washington National, overnight in D.C. and down to Pinehurst, North Carolina for a couple days. Back late Thursday night. There's nothing on the weekend. Ya get my beep?"

"Sure did. I was in church," Rand deadpanned. "I'll be there by six." He hung up and fished a dime from his jeans. His index finger went straight to the three on the dial, hesitated before a quick spin. An outside force dialed the last six numbers. She answered. He froze for a second. "Do you know who this is?"

"Hmmm. Could it be the guy who hasn't called me in five and a half days?"

"Four and a half." Rand smiled with relief. "Hey, so what are you up to this weekend?"

"This weekend?" Reni wanted to squeal. "Nothin' I can't escape."

"Ya wanna sha-wing over to Destin?" He held his breath.

"Who's dat on da phone, baby?" Mrs. DuVette stopped dead in her tracks on the way to the dinner table with a steaming bowl of pasta.

"It's Rand, mama."

Dat Gawd-awful Lakefront Airport. "Oh."

Reni shooed her mother away with her hand, then put her lips close to the receiver. "Yes!"

Brophy Wales possessed an esoteric education that would make scholars weep. His father had taught him that life was a sweet cherry and that the only thing... the only thing... that could rot the fruit, was fear.

In the early Sixties, an opportunity was presented. The great airlines suddenly needed more pilots than they could find. Airline careers were available for the alert as twenty-year-old Brophy Wales rushed out to Ryan Field in Baton Rouge to secure his private and commercial pilot certificates. Within two months, he submitted his application to TWA in New York and was immediately hired. He rode sidesaddle on the 727 for two years before a bid to the co-pilot seat for three. And when the first 747 was taken out of the box, Brophy Wales sat in the right seat of the jumbo globetrotter before the first wrinkle had invaded his face.

Seven years later, the four Gs—general public perception of an airline career of girls, grub, glamour and glory—began to fade with reality of acute circadian dysfunction. The routine time zone blur of seven-day trips from New York to Paris to Los Angeles to Honolulu to New York had begun to retard his physiological mainspring. He began to find himself wide-awake in the middle of the night, every night, losing his memory due to prolonged exposure of high-altitude radiation. His circadian rhythm began to decay his fit body and his sharp mind with a dozen nights a month in strange beds and time zones. He became lethargic, impotent and miserable.

During an annual vacation, Wales began an exploration for a vocational adjustment. He considered starting a charter operation or a flight school. His first stop was Lakefront Airport. On the second day of his mission, he shuffled through the hangar just west of the terminal building, checking the planes with For Sale signs on them. He noticed a tall rugged man peering into the cabin of a Beech Bonanza. "Nice machine," Wales observed.

"Si...uh yes...it is."

"Is it yours?"

"No. I wish it were."

Wales immediately saw the window of opportunity slide open. "Are you local?"

"No. I'm from down south."

Wales laughed, "South of what? We're about as south as you can get."

"You know Merida...in the Yucatan?" The man stepped down from the wing to hover a half-foot over Wales. He held out the large callused hand of a rancher. "I am Luis DeSoto."

"Brophy Wales."

"It is nice to meet you."

"Likewise." Wales looked him over. "You're not Mexican."

"That is correct. My fam-i-ly comes from Colombia." DeSoto needed to shake the bushes. "Do you work out here?"

"Hell no. I don't work. I'm an airline pilot."

The leathery face creased with a laugh as Wales dreaded the next question. "Really. What is your route?"

"New York to Paris mostly." He couldn't stomach another explanation and recall of his actual route. "Are you looking to buy a plane?"

"Yes."

"Would you like me to help you find one?"

"Yes."

"Let's go grab some lunch."

Over red beans and rice at the Lakefront's terminal restaurant, Luis DeSoto realized that his mission had just taken a giant step forward as Wales unloaded his recent frustration. "Airline pilots are a strange lot," he began.

"How so?"

"To be a first officer, you have to bend your personality to each new captain. For instance, the last trip I flew, the captain preached the gospel for six days. He had the Bible out and read scriptures to me and the flight engineer while we cruised over the Atlantic." Wales entertained his companion while DeSoto devoured a cup of seafood gumbo, stocked full of lake crab. "The captain on the previous trip read phone numbers and shared his experiences at Paris brothels. I never know what day it is or who I should be."

"So you do not see a long career working for TWA?"

"Not my first choice. But it's hard to quit."

"Okay." DeSoto put down his spoon and looked into eyes of intelligence. "I have a proposition for you."

Wales answered with raised eyebrows: Spit it out...

"I am part of an enterprise that needs an airplane to carry items from point A to point B."

"Items?"

"Yes. Farm items, broccoli mostly."

"Broccoli?"

"Broccoli is a big...moneymaker." There is a harvest on my ranch—point A—that is ready for shipment to customers at point B: Santa Maria, Calyfornia."

"How much...broccoli?"

"Enough to fill a tractor-trailer...like we used to. But it is too risky to drive across the border with the entire harvest."

"So you need an airplane?"

"Yes sir." DeSoto cut his eyes to confirm that they were not being overheard. "And some of my neighbors could use this airplane also."

By the time pecan pie was served, Wales had decided a career change was imminent. By mid-afternoon, he had become an instant aircraft broker and tracked down an old DC-3 that was parked over at Corpus Christi. DeSoto paid cash for a Lear charter to Corpus and for the retired, fully-fueled Douglas. The next morning, Wales took two hours of instruction from the former owner atop his first tail-dragger before DeSoto played co-pilot for the inaugural leg to Tampico. They laughed like kids when they realized halfway through the leg that Wales didn't know jackshit about the plane he was flying and that DeSoto wasn't even a pilot; stuff like that becomes hilarious with a touch of hypoxia. Wales' first landing resembled a beach ball bouncing down the runway. They refueled again in Villahermosa before the last leg to Merida. By the third landing and after seven hours of hand-flying, Wales had the classic airliner mastered.

His initial broccoli run paid more in one trip than he earned in a year at TWA. But two years into his career adjustment, just south of Tegucigalpa, Honduras, the right engine on the DC-3 ceased at liftoff on a flight back toward the massive, unguarded Texas border. Over-grossed with product, none of which was broccoli, he was forced to return to the Tegucigalpa airport, where curious authorities checked the smoldering engine. He was subsequently tossed into a feces-infested cell with two petty thieves and Camille Mouton, a coonass who had been stung and busted for buying fifty keys of ganja from the Presidente's cousin.

Eight years later, Mouton and Wales could reminisce wryly about arranging a hundred greenbacks just to get the damn cell cleaned out. When that worked, they paid $500 to get a private cell. Two hundred more bought a catered meal from downtown Tegucigalpa. And $2,000 eventually bought a new addition to their cell, along with the only window unit air-conditioner within miles. Wales' hot account from home would fly in for conjugal visits, bearing crawfish and po-boys from New Orleans. One night, the prison staff threw her a surprise birthday bash where champagne flowed from an electric fountain. Twenty thousand thrown in the correct direction terminated their correction, and the hottest party spot in Honduras was history.

Not surprisingly, Wales' absence from T-Way did not go unnoticed. But not long after he was fired, his income rocketed with DeSoto's introduction to the Cartel and the primo new product with less bulk and more yield. He traded the old Douglas to the Louisiana Mosquito Control fleet for two Piper Senecas.

After his first two runs using the old drops-into-the-swamp method, he established a base for his aircraft modifications at a small airport in the rolling hills of western Arkansas near Mena. He acquired a hangar and an array of material to customize small planes. He hired two full-time mechanics to modify the Senecas with fuel bladders, eventually replacing the obvious fifty-five gallon drums to free up valuable cargo space. Trap doors were designed to drop contraband into a large soybean field outside of New Roads where a Hughes 500 helicopter retrieved and the empty Seneca continued innocently to Mena. Once Wales landed, he'd roll up to the hangar door, which was raised for the fifteen seconds it took to coast into obscurity. He kept an apartment above the hangar stocked with food and drink for a week-long hideout. Most of the plan was overkill, but it made him feel invincible. Invincibility produced a damning, shit-eating grin.

Wales bought a home with a half-million in cash close to Jimmy Swaggert and the slippery governor. The locals began to talk. Whispers found a path to the East Baton Rouge sheriff, who ordered a permanent stakeout on the Wales home. Soon there was no doubt that Brophy Wales needed a long Angola visit. One night, as the sheriff walked out of his favorite steakhouse, he noticed Wales munching happily with his new wife. They made eye contact. The shit-eating grin grabbed the sheriff's goat. As he passed their table, he whispered, "We're gonna get your ass one day."

"Get this Fife," Wales shot back. "You are way too slow." He laughed as the sheriff stormed out.

So on the fine Louisiana day when a call came into the East Baton Rouge sheriff's office from a Florida D.A. asking if anybody knew a Brophy Wales, the sheriff got right on the line. His adrenaline flowed to a smile as he listened to a fluke tape recording: The Feds had wiretapped a second tier dealer out of West Palm Beach, who mentioned that Wales was the moneyman behind a 50,000-Quaaludes run from the Bahamas. Just after the dealer's oil-dripping Piper Aztec landed in Palatka, Florida with the goods, a warrant was issued for Wales' arrest. So that's what that bastard's been doin'... runnin' Quaaludes. Wales was charged with narcotics trafficking that carried a fifty-year visit to the big house.

Out on a $2 million bond, Wales raced with ideas to run to the hills of Thailand or South America, but soon wondered if these same authorities would listen to his fish story, as unbelievable as it might sound. He made a call to the DEA office in Miami and jumped the seven a.m. Eastern 727 out of Moisant to meet with the boys.

They met him on the departure level at Miami International in a black-walled Ford Galaxy. Two agents chauffeured Wales across Rickenbacker Causeway and through the pastel buildings of South Beach. "If you guys help me out..." He watched the back of their heads as he delivered his knockout line. "I can get you Vilez, Ortiz and even Pablo himself." Now you boys know who you're dealin' with. He sat back and waited for them to stop the car to kiss his big fat ass.

The driver casually made eye-contact through his rear-view, painfully ignorant of the world's main cocaine source. "Pablo who...?"

5. Papa Dee

Florescent red and orange leaves lit up the Shenandoah Valley below as the Merlin cruised north at 17,000 feet. Descending at 280 knots over Dulles Airport, they were handed off to approach control on an assigned heading of zero-one-zero. Hotchkiss pointed out National upon the west bank of the Potomac as they passed the airport on a high downwind leg. Rand also spotted for the first time, within a chaotic street layout, the Capitol dome, the Washington Monument, RFK Stadium and the Lincoln Memorial.

"Okay partner, I'll fly this one. The next time we come here, it will be your turn." Ken found the upper Potomac, camouflaged in fall, and waited for the clearance for the River Visual Approach to National.

Shadowing the river on the final course, Hotchkiss whistled Yellow Submarine while Rand viewed landmarks and the silver Eastern 727 that sashayed four miles ahead. The Potomac widened before the infamous Watergate Hotel passed on the left. The Pentagon appeared strangely vulnerable a mere 1,000 feet below Rand's right thigh as he dropped the landing gear. He caught a quick glimpse of the White House as they zipped by at 600 feet. The great captain hugged the left bank of the river until a hard right bank over the Key Bridge to the centerline of Runway One-Eight. They crossed a small park where people gathered to watch planes shoot over their heads at low altitudes. Rand could see a dozen airliners lined up for takeoff. Hotchkiss pulled back smoothly on the yoke with his left hand and slid the power levers to idle with his right as the wheels kissed asphalt.

Awed by his sudden ascent into the big leagues of aviation, Rand cleared his throat and picked up the mike. "Merlin Eight Bravo Charlie clearing Runway One-Eight for Butler Aviation." The airport buzzed with dozens of DC-9s and 727s. "Nice landing, Ken."

"Thanks. That one worked out pretty good." Hotchkiss let out a sigh and taxied smoothly to the lineman's hand signals on the north end of the field for engine shutdown. Rand made haste to open the airstair for the popular president of Benson Dredging.

Ken had spoken highly of Jim Benson, the founder's son, who had grown the firm beyond his father's wildest expectations. But today, instead of stopping to chat with the flight crew, he just gave a brief smile to the new co-pilot and nodded "thanks."

Benson was preoccupied with problems. Five multi-million dollar Corps of Engineers contracts signed during the last administration had just been cancelled by the new power. In a move that would surely appear brilliant in the short term, the thespian in the White House had cut spending to the Corps to free billions from the federal budget for tax cuts. The nation's channels and waterways would someday clog without the maintenance, but Benson would be bankrupt long before.

While Mr. Benson set out to lobby for his survival, his two pilots crossed the Key Bridge in ignorant bliss. From the back of a rickety cab, wide-eyed Rand took in the sights. En route to the Georgetown Marriott, Ken pointed behind the Lincoln Memorial to 1600 Pennsylvania Avenue, "That's where true power lies, partner."

After they checked into adjoining rooms, Hotchkiss called for a debrief. Ken handed Rand the usual post-flight glass of J&B and suggested a place for dinner.

"Hey partner, ya ever tried sushi? There's a great spot down the street."

"Sushi? What is it?"

"Raw fish and pickled rice, wrapped in seaweed." Hotchkiss spat Copenhagen into the hotel's small water glass.

"Damn. Sounds fabulous."

Just across town, inside the basement of a historic house with gigantic columns, a young Marine lieutenant colonel labored with feverish energy. As a special operative freshly endowed with power, "John Cathey" had traded in his Marine fatigues for a cheap polyester suit. He was poring over a report straight from the Vice President of the United States. The landslide victory over the impotent previous administration had given the new White House carte blanche for a change of course. It seemed to Cathey that he was now working directly for the VP, the former head of the CIA. He suddenly had at his disposal, access to the world's best armed forces, unlimited cash and the most sophisticated intelligence network on the planet. He had permission to play and win any game. John Cathey was becoming... invincible.

All through his Marine Corps ascent, he had participated in special operations, special this and special that. Bar talk for years had revolved around a running mystery: Who the hell really calls the shots? With this latest step up a more exclusive ladder, the picture had begun to clear.

His new post had evolved quickly and quietly. The civilians who tapped him were obviously extremely well connected. The interview had begun with a G-II pickup at Butler and proceeded to a landing at Rickenbacker Air Force Base outside of Columbus, Ohio. A non-verbal driver in a black Cadillac delivered him to the home of an $8 million soft donor, who referred to his distinguished houseguest as the Maestro. Drinks were poured and dinner was served. The colonel soon learned that an elite group needed his services and that Acta non verba would become his new Semper Fi. He learned that he would operate under an assumed name under assumed rules.

The steely blue eyes of the Maestro assured Cathey that he would enjoy absolute coverage, and that an esoteric wink was permanent as a thousand documents. After the second round of double malt, they had wryly discussed the effect "disinformation" has on a nation with an attention span of a Collie while the colonel checked pictures of staunch conservative senators and congressmen smiling with the silk-suited Maestro. Cathey recognized Ohio's Adjutant General between the host and the governor, cocktails and Cubans in hand.

"The key to a good disinformation campaign is to sell it to a..." the Maestro held his hands up to indicate quotation marks, "...reliable source. As word spreads through an established reliable source, it becomes common knowledge, which provides a warm blanket of Papa Delta, good old reliable Papa Dee."

"Papa Dee?" Cathey asked innocently.

"Plausible de-niability." Steady eyes looked straight into Cathey's. "Acta non verba," he added coolly, as if he had only whispered the phrase for the last thirty years.

Cathey listened with disbelief as the man described his new workspace. Someone's seriously yanking my chain. This lying bastard was telling him that his new office would be in the basement of a white house... the White House. Bull... shit.

His feet-wet mission was to rid the world of a crooked Third World government located in the mountains of Central America, specifically

Nicaragua. The problem was that the inept Congress didn't quite see the grim situation in the same light as the administration. This forced activation of a covert plan.

The mission would begin with a disinformation campaign to label the new Nicaraguan leaders as a dreaded Communist regime, scarier than liberal, which worked so well in the last political campaign. The Maestro reaffirmed that he would not tolerate Kennedy-type bleeding hearts.

While the Maestro spoke, Cathey mentally replayed the Zapruder film shot in Dallas. Clarity arrived in waves. Again and again he had watched Kennedy's head being blown off by a bullet that obviously struck from the front. Papa Dee had said that one man from the rear had delivered three perfect shots from an impossible angle. No…shit.

Rand woke at five a.m. Though it had only been a couple hours since he hit his own bed for the first time in three days, he could tell that the sleep process was over. He rose to the kitchen cupboard for a cup and saw the usual swarm of roaches perform a silent Houdini act into the cabinet. He loaded two scoops of freeze-dried, one sugar, a touch of Coffee Mate and boiling water to a roadie cup before he descended to the SS.

The Causeway clip-clop induced a trance that lasted the full twenty minutes to the Northshore. He wound east on US 190 past downtown Big Branch to a slow left into the secluded, pine-guarded institution, home to a strange mix of chemically induced relaxation and centuries of anxiety. Distant screams echoed behind closed doors as he entered his mother's ward. In a room between two snoring patients, Judy Chapman lay wide-awake, staring at the ceiling, her arms restrained with straps bolted to the bedside. He immediately turned to the nurse. "Is this necessary?"

"'Fraid so."

He took his mother's cold hand. "Mornin', mom."

She smiled for the first time in weeks. "Oh… Rand." She lifted her arm to touch his face and the slack in the strap expired. She began to sob.

He stroked her hand and tried to catch her eye. "Hey, I went to Washington, D.C. this week. Just got back last night."

"That's wonderful." She stared at the far wall. "How did I become such a failure, Rand?"

"A failure? You are not a failure. You're just having a bad spell. It's raining and one day the skies will clear and the sun will shine." Rand wanted to believe his own words. "I spoke to your doctor yesterday and…"

"You spoke to Dr. Johnson?" she asked incredulously, as if Johnson were the school principal.

"Yeah, on the phone from North Carolina."

"Did he say I was crazy?" She faced the ceiling again.

"No. He said you were sick and that he was going to make you better. Better than before."

"He did?" She turned to look straight at him. She remembered the fear she saw in those very eyes after he stepped barefoot on a bee at age six. She saw the same fear now. Some things never change. Again she reached for his face. And again she was restrained.

Rand bent down so she could touch his cheek. A tear streaked down it onto her neck. "Remember what you used to tell me, Mom, that we're just building character? We will work through this."

"What about your father?"

"What about him?" Rand was puzzled. "Has he been here?"

"No." She sighed. "He wants a divorce."

"How do you know that?"

"He told me."

"You're kidding. He told you he wants a divorce?"

"Yes. It was right before his birthday. We were on our way to the airport to pick up Bill and Jule with our first... only grandchild. He'd been drinking and said that he wasn't happy with his life; that he wanted his freedom. And I was devastated. It ruined the moment. It ruined the night. It ruined my life."

Rand's face flushed and he thought about the Guzzo's crowd. How can that be so damned important? "Why didn't you tell us?"

"I've known it for years." Her unfocused eyes pointed at the bright overhead lights. "You know...I hate ceiling lights."

"I know." Rand held tightly to her warming hand. He swallowed. "Mom, I'm not going to lie to you. We have a lot of hard work to do." He looked into her eyes.

She looked back. "How can I ever go back to that house again? I'm a worthless, washed-up old lady with a husband that doesn't love me. I gave him three children and raised you all...with all my might. And now... I've been discarded... like... oh, I don't know what."

Rand let her go on, releasing three decades of therapeutic pressure. He held tightly to her hand and could feel her relief. It was the first time he had ever heard her complain.

"Mom. This will pass." A Bible was next to her pillow. "Where did you get this?"

"Mrs. Burns from the church came by."

He picked it up. "Mom...?" She had slipped into instant slumber. He placed the Bible against her heart and tried to pray as best he could through a surreal cloud. Judy was fast asleep when he walked away from her and her fellow cellmates.

The SS moved eastbound through traffic on the I-10. Rand pushed the ol' girl up to eighty-five, switched on the AC and plugged the radar detector into the cigarette lighter. Reni edged closer to him from the middle of the seat. Bernstein had released her for a fictional eleven a.m. doctor appointment on this cloudless October day, the thermometer stuck on eighty degrees. Destin lay four hours ahead, tucked on the Gulf side of the Florida panhandle with white-powder beaches and clear blue water; still an unspoiled treasure that few tourists had found.

Reni took his hand. "How's ya mama, Rand?"

"Not so good." He wheeled around a gravel truck as he entered the seven-mile bridge on the east side of the Pontchartrain. A J-boat, canvas sails full of a gentle breeze, tacked between the bridge and the railroad bridge that paralleled the I-10. "I feel bad for her."

"I'm sure."

"These shrinks are scary... detached from emotion... talk about her like she's a lab rat. 'Could be bi-polar... could be schizophrenic... could be addicted to drugs.' Jeeesh. The place gives me the creeps."

"Can they make her better?" Reni leaned her head onto his shoulder.

"Say they can. Gonna take some time though."

"I'm sure."

"Felt guilty leaving there this morning. It's tough to see her in that... situation." Rand stared ahead.

"Has your dad been there?"

"No." Rand tightened up. "Don't think that's gonna happen."

"Look, Rand...we don't have to go. Why don't you go back over and see her?" She slid away and looked back at him.

"I asked the doctor about it. He said these next few weeks are critical, that many things could upset her. He thought it better to stay away, let her de-tox and allow some dark moments alone. You know, darkest before the dawn and all." He smiled at her. "Thanks." He pulled her back over and felt her warm leg on his. Rand wrapped Ray-Bans around his ears. "So, how did you break the news to your mother?"

"Well, I had to embellish a tad." Reni smiled mischievously. "I told her we were meeting some of your family over there...aunts and uncles...cousins."

"Young lady! I'm shocked." Rand raised his eyebrows. "Is that any way for a good Catholic girl to behave?"

"Only if I'm to avoid the nunnery." She rummaged through her handbag. "Look what Dawn gave me before I left work."

"Young lady! I'm gonna have to spank you!" Rand eyed the tightly twisted cigarette.

"Yeah, she said you can't go to the beach without one."

"Well that's nice. Uh… could you hold that down a little?" Rand spotted a state trooper in the right lane and coasted down to sixty.

"Oh my God." Reni didn't know what the penalty was for such a cigarette, but it didn't matter, her mother would kill her first. She held it beneath the seat in her sweating hand as the state car passed.

Suddenly, Rand reached across her, looked straight at the unsuspecting trooper, raised his middle finger, and laughed evilly. The trooper flinched.

"Have you…lost your mind?!" Reni looked at him with her mouth wide open. *He just ruined my life.* "What are…you doing?" As the cars reached the shoreline, Reni watched in silent horror as flashing red lights reflected in her side-view mirror. *He's a moron. I'm in the car with a moron.*

The trooper proceeded cautiously to the driver's side, his right hand close to the 357 Magnum holstered to his waist. He saw the window slide down and two hands come out… empty, wisely showing no harm.

"Hurry up, butt-wipe. I ain't got all day!" Rand yelled, flinging both arms out of the window so the guy wouldn't shoot him.

Reni shoved the joint under the seat and watched the trooper peer at Rand. A slow smile lit up the officer's face as he broke into a huge, toothy laugh.

"I should have known!" Trooper Charlie roared and held out his hand for Rand to shake, greatly relieved that he wasn't gonna have to shoot somebody. "You crazy sonofabitch!"

"Sorry man… but I had to yank your chain." Rand laughed as he looked toward a stunned Reni. "Charlie, this is Reni DuVette."

"Ma'am, I'm gonna have to advise you to come with me. This man is crazy." Charlie checked her long legs, a full halter top.

"You know him?" *Thank God.* Her tan had faded to white.

Trooper Charlie took off his hat to jump in the back seat. "How you been, boy?"

Reni sat quietly, occasionally glancing back to flashing lights, as the boys laughed like kids recalling their repertoire of buzzes and the good ol' throwing toilet paper rolls from the airplane days.

Once back on the road, Reni could finally speak, "I thought you lost your marbles."

"I'm sorry... can't help myself... there is... something wrong with me." Rand grinned and punched the back of his head lightly. "Hey girl, let's fire that bad boy up."

"I've never smoked before." Reni looked straight ahead. "My innocence is melting... mel-ting."

Ten minutes later the trees were greener, the sky was bluer and the SS floated above asphalt. Rand pushed Let it Be into the tape deck. A blanket of tranquility began to settle until Reni punched his right arm, hard.

"Hey!"

"I can't believe you did that back there."

"Wha..?"

"Flippin' off a state trooper, that's wha... Did you see the look on his face? He was pissed." She giggled. It was all such a silly, funny joke. "How can a certain finger... raised into the air... cause such rage?" She lifted her middle finger. It was too damn funny. She laughed hard.

"Havin' a good time?" Rand looked over at her. She just laughed harder as she shot the bird toward Rand and out her window. A tear slid down her left cheek.

As the SS glided over pavement, clear blue water and pure white sand magically appeared. She was dreaming, but totally conscious. A thousand masterpieces were painted before her eyes. The trees, taken for granted all of her life, were now unfathomable miracles of color and moisture. The road itself, winding smoothly along the coast, was evidence of man's ingenuity. Who made this happen? Who...? God. How...? Who cares? She pictured the engine stroking effortlessly under the polished hood. Does anybody really understand how that works? She looked to her left and saw this beautiful guy, wearing a t-shirt that read Louisiana Yard Dog above a fierce cartoon alligator.

Rand turned left at the beach and sent the electric windows down. "Ahhhh. Feel that, girl." Warm Gulf air circulated the car as palms swayed easily in the breeze. The planet was magically small.

Rand wheeled in beneath the welcome sign of The Las Palmas Hotel. The place was deserted. He scored a beachfront room for forty beans a night because the weekend forecast had called for a drenching rain until the approaching cold front stalled over northern Alabama. "Weathermen should stick to tellin' us what happened yesterday", Rand grinned as he slid the key into the knob. Reni hesitated a moment, anticipating a life event behind this door.

Rand dropped his bag and lifted her over the threshold into a dark and musty room. He landed her softly and found a light switch. The bulb barely burned. The damp odor was creepy. Fighting a growing wave of panic, Rand moved quickly to the dark window. He fumbled for the cord and gave it a tug.

A heavy curtain moved behind sheer white cotton. Sunlight made a spectacular entrance. Rand pulled the second cord and the cotton danced aside to an unobstructed view of open water and white sand. They both gasped. He slid the glass door open and a sweet sea breeze instantly blew the dank Florida smell away. Four-foot waves crashed the beach in a masterful serenade. A balcony held two lounge chairs, a huge wicker chair and a glass table. Palms clapped at God's performance. Beautiful.

"Let's go swimming, Rand!"

"God yes." Rand unzipped his bag, found his trunks and stepped out of his shorts. Reni watched his back muscles move with easy coordination. As he pulled up the suit, he turned slightly and she saw all of him.

"Hey!"

"Oh... sorry."

Rand smiled as she dug for her two-piece. She turned to face the beach and untied her halter, loosing bosom before she hooked the new bikini top. She drew a deep breath and dropped her shorts, exposed for the first time to the opposite sex. What the hell. She pulled on her bottoms and turned around, semi-proud of herself. But he was gone.

Rand came out of the bathroom to see an elegant French cut bikini and the smile of sweet surrender. "Look...at you, woman." He pulled her toward him. "What did I do to deserve this?" She giggled as Rand parted her lips and fell to the bed.

"I've wanted to kiss you all day," she whispered, running her hands through his hair.

"I was sending subliminal messages." Rand unhooked her top with one hand and took a long gaze beneath a shower of hair. Valve closure below locked in high pressure.

Reni held his neck and her breath. He rolled her beneath him and he departed south. "Where ya goin'?" Rand tugged her bottoms past her knees, past her feet and dropped them to the floor. His suit shared the same destination as he surveyed perfection back to sweet lips. Nude bodies met and pressed euphoria as Rand moved his leg between her thighs. Oh my God... this is it. The dream began. She squeezed with virgin muscles. "Oh..." Reni felt his pulse within her, on her chest and his hands.

"You okay?"

She nodded and covered his mouth with hers. A power wave pushed surf to thunder and gusted wind into the drapes. "Yesssss."

The sun hung just above the horizon of the deserted beach when they finally made it to the powder sand that squeaked pristinely with each new step. Rand slid his arm around her waist and motioned toward the setting sun. "Hard to believe that baby is ninety million miles away."

"It doesn't seem right."

"Okay, somewhere around there. Say ninety-two million."

"Not that." She smiled. "This day...this is the best day of my life, Rand." Waves lapped at their ankles. "And it's everything I've been taught not to do."

"By who?"

"The church. My mother." Her head cleared with each draw of sweet oxygen. "If she could have seen me today." She shook her head.

"Feelin' guilty?"

"I don't know. No, not for myself." She looked at him. "You're not Catholic."

"Huh? Oh no. Press-by-terian"

"But you're a believer?" A dune a dozen paces off the water silently offered a seat to watch the changing sky show. Rand lay back in the sand as darkness began to fall.

"Oh, I believe. Look at the sun, heating and cooling the earth. Things that enormous don't just... happen."

"But not in Christ?" Her hair blew due north.

"Whoa...deep already. I don't know."

"You don't know?"

"I hear people say they have turned their life over to Jesus Christ and they seem so content and satisfied. But those same people talk about war and revenge and the death penalty."

"You're against the death penalty?"

"Isn't that one of the commandments?"

"Thou shall not kill. Yes." She took a deep breath. "But what about the victim?"

"The one that has gone to heaven? Revenge doesn't do them much good. When did Jesus preach vengeance?"

"So you do believe in Christ?"

"I don't know what I believe." Warm wind wafted over white surf.

"Do you believe God invented pot?"

"Of course." The sky darkened in waves.

"Then how can it be illegal?"

"You tell me. You take a couple of puffs and everything's beautiful. You do it everyday, it's vegetable city. Just like booze or anything else." Rand swallowed. "I wish my dad had abused pot instead of booze. He probably wouldn't hate himself."

"Your dad?" Reni's eyes opened. It was darker but the horizon glowed. "Drinker, huh?"

"Oh yes." He looked away to the left. Far away. "Lives in a gin glass."

"You don't get along with your father?"

"Tried. Can't do it. He never made time for me."

"Why?"

"Wish I knew." Reni saw that his eyes were unfocused.

"There should be a rule that your father has to adore you."

"Yeah." He looked over at her. "Take a note." He gave a slight smile. Darkness arrived in waves above.

"Rand?" She stroked the back of his head. "There's somthin' I been...dyin' to do"

"And what would that be?"

"This!" She got to her feet, slid her bottoms down, popped off her top and sprinted naked to the crashing surf.

"Well, I'll be damned." He stripped and followed.

"Oh my God Rand! This feels sooooo good!" She held her arms up toward the stars as she back-jumped into the waves. An enormous harvest moon rose above the dunes, bathing them in magical light. "Yeeessssss!"

6. Clip-Clop

With a long pull of Pall Mall, Leonard Monde watched Hattiesburg, Mississippi dissolve through his rearview. He had left behind his bulky TV and incinerated his Delroy Chemical wardrobe of four ties, three jackets, six pairs of slacks and five button-down cotton shirts in a gasoline-ignited bonfire at the trailer park's burning area. He would miss that burning area. Four flannel lumberjack shirts, two pairs of Wranglers, a drawer's worth of socks and underwear, shaving kit, steel-toed work boots, a decade of Penthouse and two cartons of Pall Mall were all that remained of his worldly possessions. The twilight ahead faded into night as he motored westward on Mississippi 166.

The glove box held $2,200 in cash for five years and six days severance, car title, registration, and a .44 Magnum. Beneath the driver's seat was the little .38 that served as his security blanket and ten inches of razor-sharp, jagged-edged Gault knife. As blackness engulfed his Wildcat, the complex organ that seemed to control life had again found erection. He looked to the darkened sky for the light that was not there.

An hour later, a junction appeared in the headlights. He'd begun the turn up the north ramp of I-55 until rotten memories of Tennessee swerved the Wildcat back to the underpass. He gunned the accelerator southward toward the sign that read New Orleans.

Jimmy Swaggert had convinced Monde that the past is done. Let bygones be bygones. The preacher had spoken directly to him for the last week of unemployment through the final days of the blinking RCA Victor. Swaggert had sweated defiant conviction, holding the opened Bible with trembling hand. Jeee-zuss understood the unbearable pain of his life. Jeee-zuss knew all. Jeee-zuss would shine an everlasting light against the darkness of Satan. Today! And all he had to do was send a hundred dollars to Jimmy Swaggert. The televangelist boldly promised that the investment would double by... day's end.

It was the Jeee-zuss-knew-all part that made Monde's hands sweat. Nobody knew all. Nobody knew that he really hadn't earned a bachelor's degree from Tennessee-Martin or that he'd changed his name; that his father had ripped him from bed repeatedly in the middle of the night; that his father had killed his mother in the black market snuff film he'd stumbled upon one morning while the old man was locked up for a month. Nobody knew that he'd raged inside as the flick-flick-flick of that projector mortally wounded his soul. Nobody except daddy knew that he'd sloshed the doublewide with gasoline and torched the whole damn thing before his great escape at age sixteen. Nobody knew that Sarah Jenkins or Gabrielle Simmons or Mary Beth whoever had all died during his black moments. Nobody would ever know that he was the true victim; that it was his daddy that should be strapped into Ol' Smokey at Angola for releasing this terrorized soul to rage upon society, not him. The jury would soon read with fear and outrage, the atrocities rising with a bad moon.

Shallow taxpayers would soon pat themselves for the capital punishment of the child abuse and rape victim. They would soon feel a sense of vindication, of justice, of sweet revenge with the news, painfully ignorant that this child had never felt a kind hand upon him; never knew love or a thread of compassion; never had a chance. Nobody knew that he lived in constant fear that either his father, Charlie Jenkins or the sheriff would barge down the door. Nobody knew that he was scared as hell. Except Jeee-zus?

Early this morning, Monde had doubled Swaggert's hand and stuffed $200 into an envelope. He'd walked to the general mail drop at the Mobile Mansion to lay his offering upon seven others addressed to Baton Rouge, Louisiana.

Monde pushed the Cat up to eighty. New leaf... turn over a new leaf.... He looked to the sky, but there was no light. The pilgrim exited I-55 to the I-12 eastbound at Hammond and followed signs to the Causeway. Make friends... get a job.... He pushed in a Haggard cassette, fired up a Pall Mall and began to relax as Merle sang of becoming a better man, a kinder, gentler man.

Five miles north of the Causeway, a Tulane med student anxiously held out his thumb, wishing he'd taken his mother up on her offer to drive him the thirty miles into the city. The oil pump on his 240Z had failed last week and Paul Riley held ransom for tomorrow's release from the engine shop in his wallet. A lift across the Pontchartrain to meet his fiancée at Lakeside Shopping Mall would end his transportation dependency. A Greyhound passed and Paul wished he'd thought about the bus an hour ago. Behind the hound was a Buick Wildcat which slowed to a stop fifty yards south on the gravel shoulder. He picked up his small duffel and sprinted the distance easily.

Paul pulled the big door closed behind him, breathing slightly harder than normal. "Thanks man, where ya headed?"

"New Orleans."

"Great. I'm trying to get back to Tulane." Paul eyed Pall Mall butts that overflowed the ashtray to join a dozen more on the floor. The stale nicotine smell nearly triggered his gag reflex. "My fiancée is picking me up just past the bridge at Lakeside." The temperature seemed high.

"Hell, I'll take you all the way," said the friendly voice, face half-shrouded in darkness.

"Perfect." The car slid back to blacktop; tail lights disappeared into night. "Where ya coming from, sir?"

"Memphis."

"You working in New Orleans this week?" Riley had noticed the Mississippi license plate.

"Actually, my friend, I'm lookin' for work. Memphis is stocked full of assholes." Shut the fuck... up.

Paul cut his eyes toward the large man behind the wheel. What the...? His neck and back muscles clenched with sudden tension. Monde slowed for a toll booth and began to dig into his pockets, cussing, until his passenger produced a dollar. Paul resisted a notion to yell to the impassive black attendant as Monde forked over the bill.

The Wildcat sped over shallow brackish waters as conversation ceased and the impact of front tires against each thirty foot section of the world's longest concrete bridge produced a clip; leaving the rears to answer with the traditional clop. Some Northshore commuters swear that the bridge warps time and they can't remember anything out there and some claim that the methodical clip-clop keeps them steady across, no matter how tired or drunk.

The planet had rotated all sunlight past the western horizon, painting the sky and water identically black. The northbound bridge was a string of lights heading for home, while southbound traffic was virtually non-existent. The Cat's headlights pierced the dark void. Paul closed his eyes to the Causeway's hypnotic spell.

Monde began a trance with tumultuous memories of the Jenkins ranch in central Mississippi. Following the trailer torch, he had run scared to the I-55, hitched south in the cab of an 18-wheeler, drifted to a cattle ranch that was in dire need of young, strong backs. In the beginning, it was a comfortable match and the rancher's wife had welcomed him by cleaning out the old guest trailer and stocked it with books from the local library's clearance sale.

The Hemmingway stuff was good reading, but it was the mathematical instruction manuals that drew his interest. Cold numbers became his friend. He had finally discovered something to trust. He would work long days in the field bailing hay, feeding the cattle, running the tractor and work numbers with MIT precision by candlelight each night. There was even an attempt at a traditional education but the wasted days at Folsom High only brought ridicule and shame while he inwardly scoffed at the math teacher's ignorance. He dropped the attempt, skipped the enrollment at a university and proceeded straight to forging transcripts and ID cards.

The rancher's wife had also befriended him in confusing, sporadic nights of Chardonnay binges. The final night on the ranch ended with an awkward midnight visit. After three bottles, Sarah Jenkins had stumbled incoherently out to Leonard's trailer to perform a pathetic strip tease. Her breath reeked of alcohol as she progressed to a nude lap dance. As she teetered on unconsciousness, Leonard helped himself to the goods while she began mumbling how sorry she felt for him being such a b-big l-loser. The words caused a rage that brought his massive hands to her throat. He had always wanted to kill someone during sex, but his father had always forced him down. He squeezed hard enough to cut off her breathing and Sarah attempted to wiggle from a tight penetration. He jammed and she squealed. This registered as rape and she knew it. She began to scream toward Charlie, asleep for three hours, in a drunken stupor: "Rape...! Ra.."

Monde got his left hand to her neck and braced it flat against her throat. His right hand grabbed her hair and with one swift pull, snapped her neck. Silence restored, he finished her, rag doll style before a retreat down the road and through the woods.

Charlie Jenkins was not a stupid man. He awoke at three in the morning with socks still clinging to his feet and his wife absent. He searched the house, shaking his head with each empty bottle before finally sliding out to the trailer with tingling curiosity. The mess he found was no rape. At least not the beginning... The rancher knew exactly what to do, as always. He went straight to the small shed next to the house and moved a heavy shovel aside so he could get to his trusty twelve-gauge. He brought it into the house and set it next to the bed. There were a few questions he needed to ask of Sarah so he went to the trailer and carried her to their bed where she belonged. He lay down beside her and kissed her cheek before pushing the business end into his mouth. His last human touch was the trigger through his socks. The sunrise an hour later was the first that Charlie and Sarah Jenkins had missed.

The posse that surely must be following needed to be duped. The degree from Tennessee-Martin and Mississippi driver's license he designed were masterpieces. His new last name was a scramble, derived by the force that drove his soul. His license increased his age three years.

Monde squeezed the wheel. This damn clip-clop dropped memories like an old 45. The next cut was his attempt to permanently shift $180,000 from the multi-million dollar account that he'd managed for Delroy into a ghost account on Grand Cayman. His plan had just one more move that would have netted enough tax-free funds to put infinite miles between he and the posse.

Five years earlier, Monde was convincing during the interview with Delroy's president, Ezra Sorenson, and landed the open position with identification that proclaimed his age at 24. The accountant proved extreme competence, showing early and leaving late with balanced books. He had pulled it off, but a genuine education would have warned him of the Securities and Exchange Commission and watchdogs against bank fraud.

Monde now pictured the plant supervisor, ear to phone, talking to Hattiesburg Trust about suspicious activity in the company account. The clip-clop tweaked his aggravation and he squeezed the steering wheel tightly with both hands as the eruption began at his scrotum and exploded from his throat. "You dumbass!"

Paul sat up quickly. All he could see were centerline stripes. "What happened?"

"Fuckin' nothin' man. Don't worry about it."

Paul's heart galloped. Oh Mona, wait till I tell you about this guy. Clip clop, clip-clop. He cut his eyes sharply toward the driver.

Monde tranced back to Hattiesburg. "Ezra wants to see you Leonard," Sorenson's secretary whined over the phone. "Right away, too." Monde recalled the panic that came with the call. Though just a secretary, panty-less Cindy Lou Thigpen was actually the most powerful creature within the barbed wire fences that surrounded Delroy Chemical. He relived sitting in the waiting area while she typed a letter, using most of the White-Out in the state of Mississippi. As she reached for a phone call behind her in the wheeled office chair, her legs spread to give Leonard an unobstructed view of the most powerful corporate tool known to man. She taunted him with a steady pose. That cunt.

The worst-kept secret in plant history was her closed-door dictation in the president's office with phone lines on hold, bleached blonde flowing onto Sorenson's desk, holding her sweet target up like a catcher asking for a high hard fastball. The president climbs up for a mount, reaches for the stiff handle… Monde reached below the seat and squeezed tight. All energy channeled into his right hand.

A violent chest punch raised Paul out of his seat. His heart thumped outrageously. He reached over to grab at the wheel, but his hand moved so… damn…slow. Clip-clop…clip…clop. What's broken? He followed Monde's eyes to a black handle, stuck in the middle of his chest. For a second it was comical as a Saturday morning cartoon.

Slowly, Monde extracted the knife. Dark fluid spurted to the dashboard with an audible splash. Paul felt life drain from his severed heart. The Mile 13 marker passed in slow motion. His neck was numb. He looked toward the heavens until his eyes slowly crossed. His groin began an infinite free-fall. I can't move my arms, was his last thought. Clip…clop… clip…clop.

The heavy foot smashed the Wildcat beyond the 100-mph mark as Monde fingered the electric windows down, popping his ears with the radical pressure change. Violent crosswinds splattered both faces with fresh blood.

The Mile Five marker streaked by in a blur of white before Monde screeched into the crossover at Mile Four. With great urgency, he flung his door open, circled behind the car to pull his leaky passenger by the underarms. He extracted the ransom wallet before a clean body-jerk over the concrete rail to a splash forty feet below. Monde screeched into reverse, and forward toward the lights of Metairie. He thumbed through the wallet and counted out exactly $400. Swaggert had delivered. Again, he looked up for the light. This time, it was there, defeating the horizon to his left: an enormous moon rising.

At the Mile 1 marker, he lit up a Pall Mall, inhaled deeply with an odd mix of fear and bravado. "Welcome to the Big Easy."

7. YAHOOS

The Vice-President of the United States had passed the Top Secret file down to the basement after his briefing with the National Security Advisor. Cathey now read that he might have a new weapon at his disposal in the administration's War Against Communism. A guy had just surfaced in Miami, via the DEA, who had been very busy since his termination as an airline pilot, according to the NSA.

As Cathey read over the file it became abundantly clear that Mr. Brophy Wales needed to squeal like a pig if he were to avoid spending the next four decades in a government vacation facility. Information and skills that Wales possessed could only expedite Cathey's ascent: Unsurpassed knowledge of Colombia and Central America. Bilingual. Photographic memory. Connections with the Cartel, Noriega and the underworld. A red question mark was dabbed next to the last item and then, in black ink, a note about an unconfirmed $20 billion cocaine market per annum. Wow...who is this guy? Cathey made the call to Andrews for his favorite new perk. The right engine turned as he boarded an Air Force C-21 for the hop to western Arkansas.

Brophy Wales huffed up wooden steps to the hideout inside his private hangar. He opened the door and found a stranger in his chair, the chair in which Wales had often sat with invincibility in these secluded Arkansas woods. The intruder sat comfortably in his sanctuary, projecting an arrogant smile that could only belong to a gun-toting, government-backed agent of God only knows which covert agency. The look of confidence made Wales want to salute the obvious Special Force member. *Finally, someone I can relate to.* Wales wanted to jump to attention, but instead held out his hand.

"Take a seat, Mr. Wales." The man didn't reciprocate and Wales' hand floundered in thin air. Wales found an old wooden-wheeled desk chair and squeaked it over to sit across from his visitor. Cathey examined the overweight smuggler and calculated how much time it would take him to get him into shape. He concluded that it would be a major waste of time. "Mr. Wales, thanks for coming. I am under the impression that you have got yourself in some deep doo-doo with the states of Florida and Louisiana." He watched Wales swallow and his face turn pasty. "I am also aware that the United States Government would be willing to jump into the fray...resulting in many years in government facilities for your activities, which I am just now beginning to understand." The man did not move behind the desk and his eyes did not blink. "As devoted Americans, our mission is to purge this country of the cancer of drugs that has encompassed our society and to severely punish those who supply us with this filth. From what I understand, you can lead us to the source that is illegally transporting to the U.S." The righteous man lifted an eyebrow.

"That is correct."

"Well, I am telling you straight that this is of utmost importance to me. And frankly, Mr. Wales, if you work with me on a trial basis, we could see about getting your sentence reduced."

"Who exactly is we, Mister...?"

"Cathey. John Cathey. Let's just say that I am from very, very close to the very top of our government."

"The CIA...? DEA...?"

"Yes." Cathey looked him straight in the eye. A boyish smile revealed a gap between the front teeth.

"I should get my attorney."

"Let's get something straight Mr. Wales. We...err... I don't leave paper trails. This will put you in a precarious position, I know. But believe me, it's your only chance to stay out of the big house. Your problem is that you have a big mouth, and this has already caused me some grave concern. The East Baton Rouge sheriff would like to hang your ass from the highest tree as it is."

"I'm aware of that," Wales conceded with a dose of humility.

"Now, we have some very important issues before us. Very important." Cathey looked sharply across the table. "I've heard a lot about the Cartel down in Colombia. Let's start with these yahoos."

"Yahoos...? I'm not sure you know what we're dealing with. These guys are bigger than any life form down there. They are ruthless and constantly suspicious. I wouldn't be surprised if they knew you were here talking to me." Wales watched Cathey's smile fly away. "They have traced me to some remote areas in the world, and they continually quiz me to reconfirm what I have told them in passing. I guarantee this, Mr. Cathey: On more than one occasion, if I would have answered no to a yes question, my fat ass would not be sitting here in front of you now." Wales did not smile. "Their intelligence works from the hot end of a Mac 10. It's amazing the 411 you get when the guy at the hot end figures his last words will be a lie." Wales grinned.

Cathey realized instantly that his leverage would only go so far. "What I need is a quick, hard hit. Can we do a proving run this week?"

"Whoa boy. Proving run? This ain't a new car."

"We need immediate action. The wheel of justice is a steamroller coming at you and once you get smashed, there ain't a whole lot I can do. I need 200 kilos by next week. You make that happen and we will talk about the next move."

Cathey held up both palms, moved them together in front of his face and slid them from left to right to imitate a prison door closing with a harsh "clang." He dropped his hands. "Nobody said it was gonna be easy."

Wales realized his days of freedom were now officially over. "Two hundred kilos. It can be done. Where do you want it...here?"

"No, in the usual place."

"What usual place?" There is no fucking way that he knows about...

"The ranch in New Roads." Cathey's brown eyes said it all.

This mother fu... A jet engine whined outside as a Learjet, renamed and painted in Air Force colors, taxied up to the door of Rich Mountain Aviation. Cathey popped up out of his seat. "You got your first order. Don't let me down." He descended deftly down the narrow stairs and moved through the shade of the hangar to enter the clamshell door of the Lear, which opened just long enough for him to get his body through. The left engine restarted as the C-21 taxied out and rocketed into gray alto cirrus.

Through his picture window at Lakefront Airport, Jeffrey Bernstein saw Ollie hold arms skyward as screaming Garretts moved close enough to rattle the glass. Finally, the sleek Merlin came into view. As usual, the pointed nose of the turboprop made an impressive sight on his ramp.

Bernstein's mood soured quickly when Rand Chapman followed Jim Benson and Ken Hotchkiss down the airstair. He watched Reni appear to greet him, hair and sundress fluttering lightly in the breeze as they walked arm in arm to the hangar. Bernstein's gut clenched. He had long given up on Reni. Everyday he wondered how much she remembered about the night he'd talked her into dinner at Galatoire's and poured two bottles of Dom down her throat during a disastrous attempt to score while Rand was in Mexico. Now that she was off the open market and no longer pulled in enough extra business to justify inflated wages, Bernstein waited patiently for a chance to terminate his Achilles heel. She...has got to go.

"What the matter, hon?" Rand's eyes circled her face.

"Nothing."

"You sure?"

"Yeah." Reni kissed him on the lips. "I missed you."

"Yeah, it's been almost eight hours." Rand recalled the start of this day in his new apartment in the Quarter.

Hotchkiss walked over to Reni and kissed her gently on the cheek. "Hi sweetheart."

"Hi Kiss. How's life?"

"J-F-B. Just beautiful, my dear. I've got the best plane and the best crew on the field. How could it get any better?"

"I don't know." Reni looked away. The Merlin's left wing passed an inch over the tail of a Piper Seneca as Ollie maneuvered her expertly into the crowded hangar. Hotchkiss watched Reni closely. Something's wrong. "Who died?"

"What?" She quickly snapped back into happy-girl mode. "Nobody died. I just had a long day."

"How ya like the new place?" Hotchkiss' eyes made the circle.

"It's perfect. We'll have to have you and the Mrs. over for dinner. The courtyard has a swimming pool."

"Sounds great." Hotchkiss moved toward the lobby. "Hey, I gotta go beat the traffic. Wheels in the well at oh-seven hundred, partner."

"I'll be here at six." Rand glanced at Reni.

"Six? Where to?"

"Just over to Houston. Be back tomorrow afternoon." Rand calculated logistics. "Hey, wanna ride with me?"

"What about my car?"

"I'll drive you back in the morning."

"Yeah, sure."

The SS came alive with ignition and an Animals version of House of the Rising Sun, the volume way up. "Whoa." Rand turned the V down. "Musta been rockin' this mornin'." He smiled out of the corner of his mouth.

Reni looked over to her Mustang, picturing it in the lot all night, a clear message that the Catholic girl had swerved from the road of righteousness. Her mother constantly pressed her about the nights she had vanished while her father quietly hoped that Rand would make an honest girl of her one day soon. Turmoil stirred in their home. Today, it stirred in her gut.

Jeffrey Bernstein came around the corner and her gut got queasier. He made quick eye contact and looked toward his Mercedes, as if he didn't see her. Things were not good with her boss. What... did I do?

"Hey, Jeff." Rand waved at Bernstein and didn't notice that it wasn't returned. "There's your boyfriend," he teased Reni.

"He's been strange lately."

"How so?"

"Hardly talks to me." Reni stared down at her hands. The gold bracelet Rand gave her for Christmas sparkled in the late afternoon sun. Her eyes moved toward his neck. She wanted to grab him with both hands and tell him everything she had learned and everything she had felt today.

Rand glanced at Shelley Arms as it slid past, roaches surely snacking on the remains he left in the pantry. "Glad to be outta that hole." He pointed with thumb as they moved up Downman Road. "Popeye's!" Rand saw the sign for the local fried chicken place. "Whaddaya think, girl?" Al Copeland's spicy, greasy chicken had caught on fast in New Orleans. Reni and Rand would escape at lunch to Popeye's for takeout, make their way to Shelley Arms, get naked, and eat greasy yard bird. The relationship grew when they discovered the sinful onion rings.

"Not tonight darlin'." Reni watched the fast-food joint go by. As usual, there were no whites in the long line.

"No Popeye's? You sick, woman?" Rand raised an eyebrow.

"No darlin'. We've got all that gumbo left."

"Even better." Reni's sister-in-law had cooked up some gumbo for a party, and offered it as they left on Saturday. It christened the refrigerator when he moved in on Sunday.

Rand's first move after a salary jump on the Merlin was to trade the dump on Downman for a two-bedroom French Quarter apartment. A former student had mentioned the prime vacancy and he acted quickly to secure the old slave quarters at 300 beans a month. Scarce parking was the only drawback.

As they entered though the wrought iron gate tonight, Reni wondered if the extra bedroom signified anything for the future. They passed the main house entrance through a large ivied courtyard with a rock swimming pool and climbed wrought iron stairs to the second-floor conversion. Inside the elegant apartment, the walls were sponged light maroon. A painting of St. Louis Cathedral that Rand had bought in Pirate's Alley after a lengthy stop at

Pat O'Brien's, hung in the living room; the price remained a painful mystery. He refused to buy a TV. Reading lamps were plentiful and Reni had already moved some of her books into the living room.

Rand dropped his day bag onto the couch. He blew dust from a wine glass, selected a California Merlot from the built-in wine rack, uncorked the bottle, filled a glass for Reni, moved to the icebox, filled a glass with ice, poured a long bird and waved a Seven-Up across the top. He handed over the wine glass. "Better let that breathe a little." He took Reni's hand. "So you had a long day." The first sip warmed his throat.

"I went to the doctor today." Her hands trembled slightly.

"Ohh?" Oh....

She looked straight and seriously into his eyes, ready for an honest reaction. "Rand, I'm pregnant."

The trap door dropped as his face flushed. He looked from eye to eye. "How can that be?"

"I don't know. I missed a few dosages, but only a few."

"Well, mama, I guess we're gonna have a baby." He could hardly believe what just came through his lips.

She began to cry. "This isn't how it's supposed to be...Rand." A tear slid from her pale blue eye. And another.

He pulled her close. Her hair smothered his face and he felt her chest heat and heave. He moved his hand down to her ribs and rubbed gently. "Hey...it's okay."

"Mama's gonna kill me."

"She'll get over it." Rand swallowed. "As soon as she holds her little grandbaby in her arms."

Five o'clock came fast and Rand woke to a slight headache. They had both drank more than usual to shift into strange gears, alcohol the clutch. Reni had her shorts and running shoes on as coffee percolated on the gas stove. "Superdome and back mister." She tossed his shorts over his head.

Reni ran strong and Rand dragged. Some days, the legs need a rest. Sweat came slowly and he finally began to feel better, as poison streamed from his body. He watched Reni run, steady as always, her breathing barely audible. As they turned the corner at St. Charles and Poydras, the Superdome peeked through the buildings, a giant alien craft that had landed in the Central Business District. They circled the dome and made their way back through the Quarter, past dilapidated Lafitte's. Rand dug the key from his shorts as they reached the gate and huffed through the courtyard, fears postponed by runner's high.

Soon the SS chugged against rush hour traffic out to Lakefront on the crisp February morning. "Darlin'? Do you think we're doing the right thing?" Reni had repeatedly asked herself that question during a sleepless night.

"Oh hell yes. The I-10 is the way to go. If we went down…"

"That's not what I'm talkin' about." She slapped his leg.

"Do we have a choice?" A G-II smoked out of Lakefront ahead as they approached the high rise and Rand watched the cream of corporate jets climb.

"I don't want to ruin our options. Your options." She was anxious. "Maybe we should think about this. Maybe wait until things are more secure."

"That ain't gonna happen anytime soon."

"Maybe if we were already married."

"Okay, let's get married. Tomorrow."

"No." She began to cry. "Everybody will know."

"So fucking what?"

"My mother…will never forgive me." She looked out to the distant swamp. "I think we should wait until the time is right. We're so young."

"It's totally up to you… I'll do whatever you want."

As he wheeled into the lot at Aero, he pictured a little baby in the back of the SS. He imagined the car sitting there empty after a fatal crash. Just like Rick. Right before Christmas, Rick Simmons and Charlie Rowls had crashed a Jet Commander into the pine forest near the small town of Many, Louisiana while taking the boss to a cocktail party. Both the pilots died and the boss was still comatose a month later. The pilots' cars had sat eerily vacant for almost three weeks before someone finally removed them. Rick had a wife and two little boys. Rand pictured the SS with an empty baby seat strapped in the back, waiting patiently for him to return.

Reni kissed him with taut lips. "We'll talk about it."

"Yeah." Rand hit the hangar door just as Ollie was hooking the tug to the Merlin's nosewheel.

"Ooh weeee. Look wha da cat drug in." Ollie was cranked. "Comin' in ta fly da man's plane. All gussied up." He pulled the Merlin out into the ready area and rolled a red carpet to the airstair.

Rand moved through the cold cabin to retrieve the coffee container and the ice drawer. He filled the drawer with cubes from the icemaker and walked into the lobby to brew a fresh pot of java. He heard Hotchkiss on the phone in the office checking on the weather and filing a flight plan with the Feds. On his way back, Rand grabbed a Times-Picayune and placed the paper on the aft seat. The front-page picture was of the sixth prostitute who'd been brutally murdered in the past two months. While Ollie hooked up the external power unit, Rand did a final walk around and spun the propellers blade up as the passengers rolled up.

"For Jesus' sake…George." Mrs. DuVette thumbed through the Picayune. "If da worl don't have enough trouble." She checked the picture of the lost angel of the Quarter. "Our little girl is out dare amongst murderers and heathens. My sweet Jesus." She sighed and thought about her daughter's perpetual absence. Dat Gawd-awful Lakefront Airport.

8. Monkey Strike

Scuffed white pumps beneath a tight orange skirt swung into the Wildcat's passenger side. The lost child of the lower Quarter slurred through restraints of weed and blow: "Evenin', honey...." Her weathered face reflected distant neglect and heartbreak that had trampled a sweet angel into a callused street hooker. Her recent family tree sprouted a father into a Cleveland junkie and her mom hit the road when she was three. One snowy Ohio morning, she had found $200 on his dresser and immediately called a cab to the United ticket counter at Hopkins to purchase a one-way ticket to New Orleans.

Rumor was that her mother's family was from the far-away place and she went a-lookin'. The seventeen-year-old spent the first elegant night sharing a bottle of Boones Farm with a homeless woman who sent her to the right people for a small finder's fee. Two months later, her pimp cruised the Quarter in a shiny new Caddy. Except for a couple of rough sessions from the endless line of conventioneers, Japanese businessmen and oilfield workers, she had not been treated too badly. For a hooker, she had been lucky. At the ripe age of twenty, her bosom lay sadly to chest, worn from an average of eight intercourses a day, three or four anally. She enjoyed any drug that her dick offered, preferred heroin to cocaine; cocaine to marijuana; marijuana to cheap wine; cheap wine to straight whiskey. She smoked any cigarette that wasn't trampled upon the grimy street. She had never been to a dentist who could have filled the fourteen cavities, fixed the broken bicuspid and washed layers of bacteria from her mouth.

Monde exited the back Quarter on Dauphine with the quiet approach. His last date was a disaster after he'd read the fate of Swaggert, ruined by a big-mouthed hooker. But let's let bygones be bygones. Tonight was for celebrating the new job he'd landed. He pulled out a Pall Mall.

"You mind?" Loretta reached for the pack.

"Not at all."

"What's your name, handsome?"

"Leonard." He looked over as she fired up.

"Where ya from?"

"Jackson."

"Jackson, Mississippi?"

"That's the one."

"My girlfriend is from Jackson. She says it's a good place to settle down and have babies. You got any babies Leonard?"

"Hell no."

"Whoa boy. I hear some hurtin' over there." She noticed that his fingers were squeezing the wheel tight as the Cat rollercoastered the Industrial Canal high-rise on I-10. "Hey...where we goin'?"

"Shut your... dicksucker. Don't you ever stop ta..." Monde checked his speedometer at eighty. "Goddammit to fucking hell!"

"What? What is it?" Loretta sat up.

"Fucking cop." Monde eyed the motorcycle on his ass, the blue lights flashing from the clean white and blue Harley-Davidson. The big cop pointed to the right shoulder. Monde eased over just past the Downman Road exit. "Fuck!" he screamed.

Loretta was sure that she was deathly afraid. She couldn't choose who scared her more. "Ahh...shit," she mumbled under her breath.

"License and registration please." Patrolman Bethke stood a full step behind the driver, his holster unbuttoned and his hand an inch off the handle of his 357 Magnum. His right hand held a huge metal flashlight that doubled as a headbanger.

Bethke followed the driver's hand with his beam as it moved over the orange skirt to pop the glove box. The ten-year NOPD veteran sensed a five-alarm. He pulled his Magnum and moved back a step. "Step out of the car, sir!"

Monde's gut sank. This is it. He pulled the door-release and stepped out, hands purposely away from his body.

"Hands up against the car...on the roof!"

"No problem, sir." Monde's hands went straight to the roof and he spread his legs for the upcoming search. His mind raced to his blade and a .38 under the driver's seat. Shit. "What's the matter, officer?"

Bethke patted down the slightly taller and much heavier driver. "Well, for starters, I clocked you at eighty-one coming down the overpass, twenty-six over the limit...for those counting. Who's the lady?"

"Just a friend."

"What's her name?" Bethke finished the pat down and stepped backward.

"Well...haven't got that far yet, just met her in a bar."

"You been drinking?"

"Na-sir"

"Okay, get back in the car. I'll be back in a minute." He walked back to the bike and reached for his radio.

Monde plunked down on the seat and immediately pulled the .38 under the seat to under his right thigh. He fixed on the rear-view mirror. "Goddamn."

"Are you...uh we...in trouble?" Loretta looked back at the cop.

"Turn around, goddammit! What are you...fucking stupid? What's your f-fuckin' name anyway?" Monde reached for his blade. He stopped.

"Lo-retta." Creep.

"Nice to meet ya." Loretta...Loretta.

Bethke found nothing on his radio call to headquarters except that Leonard K. Monde had been licensed in Louisiana for just over a month. He approached the driver's window. "How long ya been in town, Mr. Monde?"

"Ahhh...just moved here a month ago. And just found a job today." Monde fingered the trigger on the purloined .38. "Don't really know anybody in town. Thought I'd go out to celebrate a little." Now... ain't that sweet.

Bethke leaned on the driver's open window. His brown eyes searched and his instinct screamed. "Ma'am? Are you okay?"

Well fuck no...I'm not O Fucking K. I got a psycho drivin' my ass to who the fuck knows where...a fucking cop asking me questions...I got a rap sheet twenty three and a half fucking pages long...I had four strange men up my ass today...haven't had a solid dump in six fuckin' months...no place to live...a pimp that beats the piss out a me every other day...my tits are fucking gone...I've had seven abortions...this sickly fuckin' cough for a month...Am I okay...? Fuck no! "Yessir." She looked straight at the dashboard while her hands sweated. She would never find her mother because the answer just killed her.

"Where ya gonna be workin sir?" What is... that smell?

"Hey, I got a job downtown. La Petra, I'm an accountant." Monde silently raged inside. How fucking stupid...asshole. Tell him your life story. He squeezed the handle.

"I guess I don't have to tell you to slow down. Drive carefully, sir. Goodnight ma'am."

Monde eased his grip, rolled up the glass, put the warm .38 back under his seat, gave a brief smile to his babe and rammed the Cat into drive.

Bethke moved back to his bike against oncoming traffic. Blood. It smelled like blood. He turned around as tail lights faded into traffic, the silhouette of the big guy in the left seat and his small slouching friend in the right. Did I just screw up?

Wales could not sleep for the first time since the perpetual jet lag of his commercial pilot days, fifteen years earlier. He laid in his king canopy bed and played the old second-guessing game as his head clicked into overdrive with dozens of hypothetical scenarios. He did not beat himself up when he realized that he could have been a senior captain at TWA by now, bidding the best schedules at a hundred grand a year.

Wales knew that the airline career is the most overrated job on the planet. His new-hire classmates at T-Way were all stressed out, burned out and divorced. Pilots came home exhausted and grumpy from forty hours of flight time in six days, only to face piles of bills and chores in a sea of negligence. The burden caused countless domestic implosions and the pilot usually had to remove himself or be removed from his family.

But it was the lack of control that created the most grief. Investment bankers schemed with airline management to create bankruptcies and leveraged buyouts, all designed to purge the senior guys out on the street. Pilots' careers were under siege while airlines filed for Chapter 11 to abrogate labor contracts, or sell off assets to start-up carriers that repainted planes as People Express or Northeastern. The furloughed pilots would crawl over to live in Newark at a fraction of their former salaries and a carrot of stock that would make the village idiot run for the hills. Wales smiled with the knowledge that he still maintained some control over his destiny.

Brophy Wales never bought into the Joe six-pack mentality. He couldn't get the visual of coming home, mowing the lawn, going to the grocery and hardware store...taking up golf, watching sports on the TV, drinking a few beers and going to the LSU game loaded on Saturday night to yell for the Ti-guz. He did not bomb his photographic memory with booze or the fancy drugs that he imported for the fast-laners. His satisfaction was that he made their black-tie shindigs and Washington balls, their bashes at Studio 54 and on Sunset Boulevard, their weddings, funerals, and all-night parties. His clients included car dealers, real estate agents, executives, congressmen, governors, governors' brothers, and even the VP's sons. Click.

He pictured Jean Lafitte. His fascination had begun with a kooky Gregory Peck black-and-white film about the Frenchman. Soon afterwards, he was drawn to the Cabildo in the Quarter and stayed for hours, reading all about the pirate turned patriot. There, in silent darkness, he had felt a strong connection to Lafitte as he swept through history in the old museum next to the great cathedral. And in silent darkness, the connection clicked.

He was in nearly the exact situation that Lafitte had faced. The challenge was to convince the high powers in Washington that he really wasn't a bad guy, and that he could offer immense knowledge acquired along the way in the underground. What drives these people? His body lay still while his brain hyper-spaced for three hours. Click.

Power. Cathey represented a direct line to the White House. He owned the keys to the drug of power, the euphoria of crushing anyone. Any-one. Click. Wales quickly devised a plan that would blow Mr. Cathey away, retreating with the outlaws to a long, secluded, ultra-wealthy life in the Colombian mountains. But America was his home, and he had the chance to become a patriot who would destroy an invincible force aimed at the very root of American society. Just like...Lafitte.

Wales had a thousand questions. How filthy dirty does all the power make those people? Click. Where am I going to find an experienced pilot to fly my support airplane? The barrage of clicks drove his feet to the carpet and a stroll to the kitchen. He dressed, fixed a BLT, picked up four digital beepers from their re-chargers, and departed from the garage in his black Mercedes.

At oh-three-fifteen, in moonless predawn, he wheeled east toward Lakefront Airport, skirting north around the Pontchartrain, away from a predictable route. In the dumpy industrialized town of Hammond he slalomed easily around infinite potholes on empty streets, past black, shotgun neighborhoods, across three railroad tracks to a lone payphone at a corner grocery held up by cracking paint and rotting wood planks. He rammed the big car into park, stepped up to the building's lone improvement, a touch-tone payphone. He took the position.

With feet spread, he wedged the receiver between his right ear and shoulder, and dug into square waist-level front pockets of his Mexican wedding shirt for the 200 quarters racked at the bottom. Wales took two handfuls in curled fingers to the coin insert. He got a dial tone and thumbed the first quarter into the slot and smoothly moved the next one in line up to the ready position. Before the first quarter hit the coin box, four more quarters were en route down the slot with his patented two-handed coin roll. Thirty quarters and ten seconds later, he dialed from memory, zero followed by a five and a seven, the Colombian country code, in front of the secure number of the outlaw Jorge

Ortiz. The phone rang two short rings that could be confused for a busy signal. Wales figured that, as the least patient of the three Cartel leaders, Ortiz was the weakest point in their wall of invincibility.

Ortiz jumped angrily out of bed. Unlike Wales, he regularly used his own product. His night had started with two lines and shots of Stolichnaya at seven o'clock. The staff had arranged to deliver a seventeen-year-old local girl whom Ortiz had spotted walking through town. Her father was passed a cool $10,000 when he drove his cab to the hidden castle at four in the afternoon, hours before the ill-tempered Ortiz awoke from his daily slumber under a ceiling fan. Initially happy to see her, he could not perform; the cocaine had taken its toll. For the past two hours he had watched the back of the girl's head move up and down on his limpness. Just when he felt life finally returning to Jorge junior, the damn phone rang.

"Goddammit." Ortiz never let this phone go unanswered. He fumed toward the dark, empty study to feel for the light switch that illuminated his hand-carved mahogany desk. An outlawed gorilla's hand sat next to the crystal globe on the right side of the desk, the fingers arranged to the flip-off position. "Bueno."

"Bueno. El Gordo aqui."

"Si. Buenos noches." Ortiz spit in disgust.

Wales could hear his own voice bounce off the abandoned building across the dark street; the streetlight was shot out years ago. He wouldn't be surprised if there were fifty homeless camped inside. He watched for movement as he spoke in Spanish to one of the world's most dangerous men. "We must meet. Things are getting too warm up here my friend."

"How so?" Ortiz cooled slightly at the satisfaction of what could be a major business problem.

"The new presidente is a big politician. It could be that we withdraw for awhile." Wales pushed his words clearly through the payphone.

"Stop now? That is impossible." Ortiz was backlogged with product bound for Rio, which also had political problems. He sat on 1,000 kilos. "Have you told Pablo?" Ortiz sank into a $40,000 leather chair.

"Not yet. I had a bad signal on his phone," Wales lied. "Your phone is clean." The deception began. Electronics was one thing the Colombian boys didn't grasp. "You may want to tell Pablo. I suspect it is from somewhere outside of Colombia." That ought to narrow it down some. Wales smiled wryly.

"Where do you think?" Those goddamn Brazilians.

"I have an idea." Wales was ready to get off the line. "Two girls with big titties."

Ortiz pulled a laminated sheet from the top drawer. He fingered down twenty-two code lines to the two girls prefix and over to the next column labeled big titties. He read the solution. Wales would be at his place sometime in the next afternoon. "Okay. I hope you're having a good time." Ortiz read the coded confirmation and the line died.

Wales rolled back into the leather-seated Mercedes and headed over to US 90 toward Ponchatoula, Madisonville and Mandeville. At the Causeway tollbooth, he slid a Washington to the lethargic attendant and pushed the German engine up to 140 mph, slowing to fifty-five only to elude the potential pitfall of cops at the crossovers with radar every four miles. Clip-clop...clip-clop.

Half an hour later, Wales wheeled into an aluminum T hangar on the east side of Lakefront Airport owned by Fat Aviation, one of his skeleton corporations. He towed the fully fueled Lodestar out with his mini-tug and re-parked the Mercedes in the hangar. Quiet darkness was shattered as he fired up the radials and taxied out to Three-Six Left. With the tower closed until five, he cleared himself for takeoff to the north before a hard bank over the Pontchartrain to the south.

Ever conscious of the possible tail, he flew toward logical airports to a fix over the Petroleum Helicopter pad in Leesville and slowed to Bell 212 speed. Once past the last rig, he wavetopped into tranquil, mid-Gulf air. He climbed to 800 feet and methodically switched on the autopilot to heading and altitude hold. Damn, it's good to have a steady autopilot. Click.

He contemplated a new smuggling route across the pitch black Amazon into Brazil and Argentina. Click. A new life in Sao Paulo or La Paz or Santiago. Click. He pictured gapped-toothed Mr. Cathey frustrated that he had disappeared. Click. He smiled recalling what he'd learned about Jean Lafitte from the literature at Cabildo. Two hundred years earlier, as the governor and controllers waited impatiently on the bank of the Mississippi for their riches to arrive, Lafitte would lurk within the tall grassy marsh of Barataria as journey-weakened ships and crew slipped helplessly into his grasp. And when the time was right...the booty was gone, and Governor Claiborne would order: Kill that bastard!

But when the excrement hit the fan, and the Red Coats planned an attack to capture New Orleans from up the Mississippi, the powers wisely employed Jean Lafitte to gather intelligence for the upcoming battle. And he saved their arses. Wales remembered that Lafitte had stolen from just those dumb enough to come upriver half-asleep with guns unready. Life is hard...and harder when you're stupid. And when his country needed him the most, Lafitte obliged. Legend had it that Lafitte was ultimately double-crossed and assassinated by the government. Click. There was something vexatious about Cathey. Click. Things needed to go right. Click. He considered his own mysterious disappearing act. Australia...Click. Thailand...Click. Africa...Click. South America.

An hour north of the Yucatan, as the sun rose, Wales caught a major sinker. The Lodestar's reliable two-axis autopilot held steady heading and altitude as the pilot unbuckled. In the tranquility of the open Gulf, awake twenty-five hours with an achy back, Wales moved back to the modified lone passenger seat and pushed stiff legs straight. He put his head back for just a second... and fell dead asleep.

As the plane plunged south, Wales was in a spaceship with the steering wheel of a 1966 Impala. Uranus in his windscreen, a hostile missile's sparkled wake streaked from behind as the piece-of-shit steering wheel dislodged from the kooky instrument panel. His airspeed read 10,000 knots just as his craft impacted the planet. Wales' heart thumped with eyes closed to realign his cosmic clock. He heard the groan of the Cyclone to his left and opened his eyes.

He peered out of the window and wondered who was flying so damn low over the water until he realized that he was the pilot. He rushed forward to eye the fuel gauges. The tanks were nearly empty, and the navigation instruments waved with no reception. He looked ahead to the horizon and saw only open sea. The altimeter read a steady 900 feet. He jumped into the left seat and set the VOR on Merida, waited impatiently until the orange digital reading from the DME finally came up at 25.3 miles. He centered the needle that confirmed he was one lucky man. As bleary eyes cleared with fresh energy, Wales disconnected the autopilot and descended to wavetops as white beach appeared ahead of thick green trees. He took his usual heading at the usual smokestack and held his course for twenty-two minutes before he spotted the ranch of his confidante. Wales circled to the dirt runway at about eighty degrees on the compass.

He touched down lightly on the dirt-packed runway, recalling that the hairiest segments of each trip were the two takeoffs from here, especially the last one, fully loaded with cargo and fuel. The Lodestar needed around ninety knots of airspeed on the wings to fly the airplane fully loaded. Cool temperatures help an airplane fly while heat has the exact opposite effect. Wales' normal operation was to fly at night, for many reasons, but most importantly so that his airplane could indeed fly. He bet his life on every takeoff that the engines would run, and run well. One night, Camille had asked Wales what he would do if he lost an engine just after takeoff.

"Turn off the landing light," he had replied, straight-faced in the orange hue of instrument lights.

"Turn off the landing light? What the hell good would that do?"

"None. But why watch what's going to happen? It's gonna be ugly." Brophy grinned. "Just turn out the damn light."

Wales now taxied up to the 10,000-gallon fuel tank, skillfully hidden under an oak tree on the north side of the strip. He rolled a ladder to the right wing, lifted the nozzle to see blue Avgas sparkle in the sunlight as the Mexican sun scorched his back.

Four miles to the south, a gentle breeze circulated through the hacienda. The rancher's twenty-year-old daughter, visiting from Mexico City, read peacefully in a wicker chair below a high ceiling fan. The south wind carried the sound of the Lodestar away and she didn't hear the engines as El Gordo pushed the throttles to the forward stops.

Wales held the brakes with his feet until the engines ran at full power. He released the brakes and the plane lurched forward. Peripheral vision told him the plane was too heavy. Halfway down the runway he glanced quickly at the airspeed indicator. It read only forty knots and he considered an abort but the stubborn side of his brain had already made the decision to go, the same side that controlled his right arm and sweaty hand that held both throttles at full power. The plane rolled at fifty knots. With just 500 feet to go, a small fig tree beyond the end of the runway entered his vision. He pulled on the yoke, but the main wheels remained on the ground and bumped through rough grass beyond the runway. With 300 gallons of highly flammable Avgas in the wings, thoughts of a massive explosion surfaced.

Wales felt the metal throttle arms begin to bend as he pushed to the stops and pulled the yoke to belly. The wheels left the ground and the dust blew in the Lodestar's wake as the fig tree filled the windscreen. As the nose popped the tree, he grinned with irony, congratulating himself for not panicking as the Big One hit. Debbie and his kids came forward in his mind. The fig tree moved down the center of the undercarriage as his problems magnified with a windscreen filled by a fifty-foot oak. Wales wished it was night, so he could turn out the lights. The eerie stall warning horn squeaked. He amused himself with the thought that a bird strike on the window is nothing uncommon, but a squirrel strike would be a new one. The Lodestar hit ten feet below the treetop as Wales anticipated the big boom. Shade darkened the cockpit as engines churned through leaves for the longest three seconds in world history. And suddenly, the tree was gone. He looked ahead to open sky while engines groaned maximum power. He glanced quickly at the airspeed and couldn't believe his eyes...ninety-five knots. Ahead was only blue sky as his arms and lower back burned with a rush of unneeded adrenaline. Wales smiled big, completely unscathed. He felt two strong hands at his shoulders. He looked to heaven. It's not your time, my brother.

Four hours after takeoff, he defeated the Colombian coast west of Barranquilla and found Ortiz's private landing strip near an aluminum hanger under a gray sky. As he flew the final approach to the grass runway, rain streaked his windscreen. Touching down, water splashed from the wheels up to the bottom of the wing as mud grabbed the landing gear. He used double power to taxi the plane over to the party of four waiting near the hangar. He spotted a white plantation hat atop a stallion. It was Ortiz.

With his ancestors' dark mix of native blood and Spanish conquistadors, Jorge Carlos Ortiz cast a statuesque shadow upon his muscular Irish thoroughbred. He galloped through mud as the Lockheed's engines shut down.

Wales opened the door. "Buenos dias!" He watched the pony show through narrowed eyes.

"El Gordo! The great American piloto!" Ortiz pulled hard on the reins.

Wales found stiff legs. He remembered that the weakest link to the Cartel was also the most dangerous. "Bueno Señor, como esta?"

"Bueno. Bueno." He rode a cocaine-fueled celebration of invincibility.

Wales noticed an oak twig stuck in the plane's elevator under the tail. He decided not to share his near-deather with the Colombian. He also noticed the ever-present bodyguards just outside the thicket, with Russian AK-47s slung over shoulders. Another guard thirty yards to the left was down on one knee with a deer rifle. "Beautiful fucking day. How long has it been raining here?"

"All morning. Did you have a good flight?"

"No problemas." Except for a fifty-minute slumber and a near squirrel strike. "I am glad I can talk with you Señor Ortiz. We have interesting problems arising in the Estados Unidos."

"Ohhh?" Ortiz dismounted.

"The new politicians have announced serious action against the flow of illegal products into the country. It is mostly a big show. There is a plan to fly radars in stationary blimps attached to cables up to 6,000 feet along the U.S. border to detect airplanes flying in." Wales looked straight into the conquistador's eyes. "We have a very short time to make a big hit before these blimps are operational."

"Is that so, Gordo?" Ortiz focused on his three men across the runway.

Wales watched the eyes of Jorge Ortiz. "I have a few ideas to discuss with you first." Wales leaned against the leading edge of the taildragger's elevator as mist floated on lush greenery. "I would like to make a very huge run in the next ten days. The time is right."

"Ohh?" Ortiz considered the failed Rio delivery. Good.

"Then..." Wales looked around. "Can those men behind me hear what we are saying?"

"Of course not." Ortiz answered immediately. How in the fuck... did he know? It was aggravating at times to work with El Gordo.

"Good. I am working on a new method to transport the goods. A way that will work with a hundred blimps along the coastline." Wales smiled. "With this big run, I can secure equipment I need to make it happen."

"Is that so?"

Wales answered with great seriousness. "I have a plan to purchase a very big airplane, and to make one huge run that would normally take ten trips. I have tested the night vision drops and have gathered a dedicated team that will execute a flawless plan with the least possible risk. One problem remains, for which I will need your help."

Ortiz looked over Wales curiously. This man had never asked for assistance. "And what would that be?"

"I need a new re-fueling strip somewhere in Mexico or Central America."

"That's it?"

"Si. But it must be at least 5,000 feet long and it must be paved," Wales continued in Spanish. "And runway lights would be nice." Wales knew that with such a field, there must be some government agencies involved; the bonus fish for his new pals in Washington.

"Runway lights. I am sure we can work that out, Gordo." Ortiz thought of all his connections in Central America. "When?"

"In the next two or three months. And in the meantime, I will make three fast runs in the next week if you can supply it."

"Gordo, this is a surprise."

"Yes it is. There was an article in Aviation Week about all the money allocated for the blimps. They will be operational in a matter of six months."

"Yes, and then what?"

"Then I will have my new plan in place."

"Which is?"

"I will buy a new plane; a Learjet that can fly as high and as fast as the airliners. That will enable me to piggyback into the U.S. at night, with all lights off, completely undetected."

"Piggy...what?"

"It is a term for flying close formation. The radars pick up metal and transponders, which an airliner has. If I am flying close formation with no transponder, there will be virtually no way to detect my airplane."

"Will not the passengers see you?"

"No. I will be flying at night just behind and above the tail."

"Can you fly this Learjet?"

"Of course."

Ortiz held up his right hand and a young girl came out of the thicket ahead of ten peons. Ortiz barked an order: "Okay, load the plane!" He looked at Wales. "Gordo, it is time for you to fly. I will load your airplane to the top and I will see you fly off into the sunset."

Cocaine. The fucker is loaded on cocaine. "Tomorrow, mi amigo. I must rest overnight." Wales eyed the muddy runway. It would be suicide to attempt a takeoff now.

"Rest? You are joking. We do not rest around here." Ortiz pulled the girl up behind his back before he brought the horse to a muddy gallop down the strip.

Wales watched grimly as mud splashed. He felt a cold sweat as a tractor filled with product emerged from the holding hangar. The peons loaded the Lodestar to capacity within ten minutes. Wales signaled Ortiz over to him. "Señor Ortiz!"

The Colombian galloped the horse to the plane. He breathed hard as the teenager held her arms around his waist, her dark shoulder-length hair frayed. "Si, Señor?"

"I have a problem that needs your attention."

"Si?"

"The landing strip is much too wet for a takeoff. I need to wait until the strip dries so the wheels will not sink into the mud." Wales tried to explain a weight and balance aviation problem to a cocaine-laced pseudo-dictator on a white stallion.

"You will take off, Gordo. I have heard you are the greatest piloto on the Earth." He pulled an Uzi from the saddle. "I will help you be motivated if you would like." He held the machine gun skyward and released ten quick rounds. "I will see you again in two days."

Wales reluctantly stepped into the plane. He taxied out to the far end while surveying the strip for dry spots. He pushed up the power and held the brakes. The dry portion was on the right side of the grass runway. He released the brakes and was pleasantly surprised at the acceleration until the plane moved into an area of standing water. She struggled to eighty-five knots and took to the air like the last shot out of a Roman candle. Wales had the throttles at the firewall again while he eyed thick forest approaching the nose of the plane. He was sure, for the second time today, that he was toast. He comically pictured a monkey strike.

This time, the nose of the plane hit a major branch of a tree, about fifty feet in the air. The windscreen cracked instantly and Wales was slammed against his shoulder harness. Cargo flew forward to smash his head against the instrument panel, opening a gash over his left eye. His vision went dark except for stars. His face went numb. The plane made a hard right wing-over as propellers churned wafts of pine. He heard the right wing snap and knew his beloved Lodestar was history. The whoosh of a blaze would certainly close his coffin. The cockpit separated from the left wing and Wales and the booty were a wingless lawn dart pointed at the earth below. A branch at thirty feet kicked the tail right, nose left, as the cockpit hit with great force on the co-pilot side with a thud. The tail was sheared from the fuselage, and the pilot was out cold for twenty peaceful seconds.

It's still not your time... but I will promise you this... one day soon, you will die... and all that you meet will die. I will be there, my brother, for you and all that you save.

"Howit I do that?"

If you pray with them once, I will take it from there. The Truth is me and I assign you to spread Truth in your final days on Earth.

He awoke in hell. Wales looked down to his blood-covered shirt and pants from a gash over his eye. He could not see his feet because of the mangled mess beneath him. Fuel ignited a rage of violent pops that surrounded Wales, pinned to his seat. Through heavy black smoke, he saw two peons run from the plane with bales of cocaine. Those bastards. The obvious order from Ortiz was to save the load, not the pilot.

Fire disintegrated the fuel tanks and the wings that had fallen fifty feet behind the cockpit, but the damp forest was in no mood to be burned. After the last bale had been recovered, the Colombians pulled Wales from the cockpit. As they dragged him out, he saw his legs were still attached and his feet moved with each try. What a life I'm having here....

They took him into the ranch, where he slept for sixteen hours after a local doctor had stitched and bandaged his forehead. He awoke in a groggy mist with a splitting headache and sore limbs. His life was no longer reality as he clicked through the fire, the eerie sound of propellers surging and churning through branches and pine sap. Click. The smell of burning fuel and rubber tires. Click. A federal covert agent in his chair in his hangar. Click. The fig tree and the oak tree. Click. Ortiz shooting an Uzi over his head. Click. The standing water on a sloppy wet runway. Click. The TWA job. Boring a straight line over the north Atlantic, landing at seven in the morning at Orly, dog-tired in the back of some hotel shuttle while Parisians walked through town in sophisticated dizzy energy. Click. The big loss of yesterday: The Howard Lodestar. It can't be real. His eyes sprang open and he was more awake than ever. And on the way, I was born again. He looked to his right. A Bible lay on the table.

Hello, my brother. I am with you.

A deep voice addressed him in Spanish. "Buenos Dias, mi amigo." Jorge Ortiz entered the bedroom and stood next to Wales. "You are a very fortunate man."

Wales' vision went black and a sharp pain entered his right ear. "How so?"

"I have found you a new airplane. It will be here in less than one hour. I hope you have better luck than yesterday."

"What type of airplane?"

"It is a Cessna 421."

"I will have to find a place to refuel it." Wales felt every mile from Baton Rouge. "I will have to get back home and bring down a plane with long-range fuel tanks. I can not stop every 500 miles for fuel. Wouldn't look good at the hearing."

"Do not worry, Gordo. I have arranged for you to land in Managua for fuel and then you can go the usual way."

"Managua?" You must be joking. "How can I land there?"

Ortiz handed him a napkin with four numbers on it. "Put these in the transponder and act like you are landing at Kennedy Airport."

Wales looked over the numbers: 6666. "Managua." So that's it. "Okay." Wales glanced at the eyes of the madman. Payback's gonna be a bitch for you.

"I spoke with Pablo. He is going to meet you in Managua."

A gentle knock at the door preceded the peon who brought Wales' mended and washed clothing in a neat fold. He painfully dressed before a jeep took them down the dry dirt road to the airstrip, two miles north. Wales was pleased that it had not rained since yesterday and the runway seemed dry. He looked to his left and saw the hole he had bored into the forest, the charred trees and the burial ground for his beloved Lodestar. He allowed himself a moment to recall the good times in the ol' girl. Flying low across the water, the engines purring and the world sliding by under the steady wing. He closed his eyes a moment. Goodbye old friend. And the moment was gone.

The sound of the twin-engine Cessna brought his attention to the right as the 421 cleared the trees, touching down hard enough to cause a bounce and another as the pilot struggled to bring the plane under control. He stopped just 200 feet from the thicket. Wales stood next to the white hat as the pilot delivered a new plane to the world's most successful drug smuggler.

Wales' critical right eye moved over the plane, performing an intense preflight inspection, as his left remained swollen beneath black stitches. This plane was a typical Cessna, nothing fancy, clean and reliable once the fuel-injected Continental engines started.

The young Colombian pilot disembarked as Wales limped slightly up to the white airplane; a green stripe ran down the fuselage and up the tail. He climbed up on the wing and felt a quick shot of pain through his neck and into his temple. He was pleased that the plane was well-maintained and that the engines were not leaking oil. There were navigation charts for Central America and landing instructions on a clear plastic clipboard. The peons loaded the bales recovered from the crash site and he climbed behind the yoke. He found the airspeed indicator first, re-gauging in his mind where the needles should be when he flew this baby over the trees he was unable to clear on his last attempt. The Continentals started and he taxied to the end of the dried strip. He looked back at the strange wing and engines to make a mental adjustment. He pushed up the throttles for the first time and he cleared the trees by a hundred feet. He glanced quickly down for his last sight of the ill-fated Lodestar as it zoomed beneath the left engine.

He banked toward the western Caribbean on a northwesterly heading while his head ached and vision blasted blurred images. He cringed with sharp pain as stars blinked though moments of darkness. He picked up the clipboard and read the attached note.

Land at this strip 7 miles south of Managua Airport. Follow the road south of the city and land to the north. Put 6666 in your transponder to alert allies.

An arrow pointed to the strange field and he was hit with another sinker. Ortiz's plan. Flying into Nicaragua with a load of cocaine. What could possibly go wrong?

He crossed the coast and strafed the treetops. He rose with the hills and hugged the valley before the brown flat capital city. The sun was near the horizon, nearly blinding him with illuminated haze. He recognized the open space of the main airport outside of the city and saw his east-west road. His pulled and turned the yoke, sending the Cessna straight over the road at 400 feet as Managua churned beneath the propeller. He checked his airspeed at 200 knots and hoped his allies in the radar room were winking some serious approval. The road wound as depicted on his new chart and he hawked the smaller north-south strip. Wales took a deep breath and pulled the throttles to idle for flap extension on a right downwind leg.

A huge backfire came from the left engine and the plane yawed severely left. Wales had seen an orange flash shoot upward out of the corner of his watering eye when the plane jolted into a 30-degree left bank. His heart pumped adrenaline as he glanced out to the... that was no fucking backfire. The front of the engine was gone and the remaining cowl section spewed fuel-injected fire.

But first things first: A metal warehouse next to the jammed highway filled his windscreen as he descended through a hundred feet in a 40-degree bank. Quickly, he pushed a hard right rudder and pulled the Titan to level flight. He needed constant right rudder to keep the airplane straight. Working leg, working engine. He found the cutoff lever for the left engine and the fire extinguished. The plane was headed north and would not turn. A bullet hole outboard of the severed cowling confirmed that someone had just shot off his engine and that maybe not everyone was on the same 6666 page.

He held a ton of back pressure and realized that this airplane was going down. The only mystery was the location. He looked for a place to land, a highway or an open field, anything smooth for about 1,000 feet. His brain clicked through options and he calmly decided on a small flat strip of terra firma adjacent to a railroad track. The Titan barely held sixty feet above a neighborhood of tin-roofed shacks as he realized he was flying away from the intended airfield. I wonder if... He peered intently ahead through haze, pain and black flashes and... hell if he wasn't lined up perfectly for runway One Zero Left at Managua Fucking International. The adrenaline junkie smiled with a colossal fix.

9. You Will Pay

Reni was already wide-awake as Monday's dawn broke gently through the window over the courtyard. The decision had been made. The appointment was at nine. She called Bernstein at home with a fictional bout with the flu, decided to skip the daily run and felt instant guilt. More guilt.

Rand awoke to an empty bedroom. He found her in a deep stare out by the pool. "Mornin' darlin'." He reached past his heavy heart for a handful of thick hair. He stroked her head and lightly massaged her cheeks. He felt moisture. "It's after eight."

"Yeah." She moved up the stairs. Rand followed. They dressed without words.

He wheeled the SS into the parking lot of the plain white clinic. The sign said something about family planning. Rand circled to open her door but she was already headed for the entrance. The receptionist pushed a clipboard over the counter. Reni took a seat and began to check appropriate boxes. The place was ice cold.

A sixteen-year-old girl sat opposite with her straight-faced mother. They looked poor. Rand and Reni wondered if their own age considerations were flawed. A nurse came out, looked at Reni and nodded. The couple moved through the door and into the procedure room, the patient behind a partition as per the consultation on Friday. Reni reemerged in a light blue hospital gown.

The doctor entered and Rand checked his cheap scuffed shoes, blood-stained white coat and stethoscope. His fingernails were dirty and his face was ice. Eye contact was as likely as a day trip to the nearest star. He strapped Reni's feet to the stirrups, nodded for the nurse to administer anesthesia. He asked

Rand to leave the room. Thank God. He walked numbly to the vinyl black couch in the adjoining waiting area and ignored the strong energy that called to him.

Reni felt a plug pulled from her electrical system momentarily, followed by bright lights and total darkness. She entered a nightmare: A big man stood over her. She panicked and began to choke.

The nurse switched the vacuum on and a beating heart was discarded into the steel fetal tank. The terminator turned off the machine and headed back to his office for a swig of straight vodka.

In a cold sweat, Reni awoke. Her heart raced. The nurse wiped blood from her inner thighs as the door opened. Rand's face paled when he saw all the blood. Reni saw, clearly, the departure of life from his eyes. Things could never be the same.

Twenty minutes later, Rand led the groggy former mother out to the SS. In the parking lot she fell to her knees and vomited onto the asphalt. Rand bent down to comfort her but he could only watch her convulse and gag in the bright sunlight. She found her legs and made the remaining thirty feet to the car. They did not, could not, speak, paralyzed by the horror of the morning.

Reni clutched Rand's arm going up the apartment's stairs to crawl into bed. When he left for his afternoon flight, she cried. Rand stared straight ahead as he drove in to Lakefront for what Hotchkiss had called a weeklong adventure to Old Mexico. No music flowed from the radio. The first night would be Mexico City and the next would be a town that he'd never heard of, south of Veracruz. The Merlin was airborne at four-thirty and Reni was left alone in darkness as tears flowed like the mighty Mississippi, a half-mile away. She slept through a bizarre set of nightmares and woke at dawn.

A glorious trumpet echoed from blocks away. Reni recognized Rampart Street Blues, her favorite Dixieland number. She wondered groggily why someone would be playing so loud and so early and fell back into restless slumber, chased by nightmares until she checked the clock: 10:42 AM. Panic was added to her emotional fray as she grabbed the phone. Dawn answered.

"Dawn... it's me. Is Jeff around?"

"Yeah. Where the hell are you? He's mad as a hornet."

"I'm at Rand's."

"Jeff called your mom. She said she didn't think you were sick."

"Uh-oh."

"And now you're missing Mardi Gras. It's a madhouse out here. The ramp is jammed with airplanes."

"I'm sorry, Dawn, but I'm really not feeling well."

"Yeah, well, me either," Dawn snapped. "I'll page Jeff."

Louis Armstrong played while she waited on hold. "This is Jeff Bernstein." He sounded out of breath.

"Jeffrey...It's Reni." She felt a sinker.

"Yeah?"

"I'm sorry for not calling earlier." Deep pain slashed from her pelvis. "I'm not feeling very..."

"Look, I don't have a bunch of time right now, Reni."

"I think I can make it tomorrow."

"Great, it'll all be over by then. Whenever the hell you do decide to come back, I want to see a note from your doctor." He slammed down the phone, yet there was a slight smile. Sweet justification had been delivered on a silver platter.

Reni slipped back to sleep as Fat Tuesday continued beyond drawn curtains. A strange mix of murder trials and parade trumpets punctuated her rest until Ash Wednesday began at midnight. She lay wide-awake in the quiet darkness before dawn within a black hole of guilt, afraid to pray, unworthy of asking anything from anybody. She sobbed as the sun rose and shuffled to the shower.

"Mr. Bernstein...I'm sorry about yesterday."

"Fine, Reni. Do you have a note from a physician?" Bernstein looked coldly into her face. Something had changed in this girl. Her eyes were red around the edges and her nose was irritated.

"No." She stood. Pain surfaced in her stomach. She grimaced. "Jeff, I've had some very personal problems."

"Okay, stop right there." Bernstein held both hands up. "Reni, we run a professional operation here, with tons of competition. I can ill afford to stop my business every time someone has a personal problem." He swallowed. "You crossed a big line yesterday by not showing on Mardi Gras, of all days, and furthermore by not calling in."

"Yeah, but Jeff, I couldn't sleep and..."

"Reni. Listen to me. Between you and me, I like you a lot and have been happy with you for the most part. But I must draw the line. It's not fair to the rest of the workforce to let you get away with this." And I've been patiently waiting for you to screw up.

"No... You're not going to fire me." She felt sorrow push up toward her eyes and a sink in her chest. She fully expected to cry, but she was out of tears. She sat stunned. His eyes were ice. He's killing me.

"We will give you two weeks severance and you can even file for unemployment. You can take as much time as you need to get your personal life back in order." Bernstein slid the check over to her, pleased it was going so well. "I'm sorry."

Reni looked over the check and the pink release slip. She got to her feet somehow, on numb legs. "Okay." She heard chatter followed by silence as she ascended to the lobby on autopilot. She tried to hold her head high as she felt each eye upon her. With a dainty nod toward her suddenly former co-workers, she continued out the glass door. Reni had left the building.

She stared unfocused at the galloping Mustang on her steering wheel. It was over. She turned the ignition. In a stunned silence, the Mustang seemed to know that the shell-shocked girl needed to go straight to the lakefront. Empty parking spaces called her to the spot in front of the Mardi Gras fountain. She rolled the window down and killed the engine. A breeze brushed her face, rustling her hair slightly. She waited for the great sadness to arrive. And waited. Finally, she cried. But the miraculous streaks down her face were tears of joy.

Reni pressed her hands together and looked past her darkness to energy above. "Forgive me Father. Forgive me Father. Forgive me Father." Her door opened. She was not alone as she crossed Lakeshore Drive to the seawall. The Pontchartrain's steady waves lapped concrete stairs that disappeared into brackish water. She sat on the top step and looked over the horizon. Warm air massaged her face. She gazed at the water and was blessed with a deep relieving breath. Consider the water. Nothing can change it. It will always be there. And so will you.

She took another deep, easy breath and felt stress evaporate from her back. He captured her. And He spoke clearly: I have your child. I will hold him and love him for you. And you will see him. And you will love him. Reni held her palms toward heaven as she wept.

"Thank you, Lord."

They looked like hell. Hotchkiss and his tall sidekick sweated profusely as they slogged down the main street of Coatzacoalcos. They eyed the grim catch of the day laid out on the sidewalk. "Yum," Rand allowed. Ninety degrees Fahrenheit heated up the village and flies swarmed the fish, no doubt caught in the grimy polluted river that sloshed through town. The day before, Rand had managed a three-mile run along the riverbank, amazed that fish could survive in the filth. He saw five dead bloated dogs along the bank, stinking to high heaven. Villagers picked through the fish as a creased old man watched over shoppers to gladly accept the few pesos for his effort.

"Goddamn. The people that badmouth the EPA should see this." Hotchkiss was at the end of his rope. For three days, the pilots had been playing the waiting game while Benson and his engineers were in the field, scouting the area for possible dredging jobs. So far, they'd come up empty.

Families sheltered themselves from the blazing sun in makeshift dirt-floor homes and tin-roofed shacks. Neighbors and their naked children were exposed for all to see. There were no movie theaters, golf courses, or amusement parks. Today's entertainment was two gringos walking around town. Occasionally a filthy child would run up and hold out a hand to beg for money. The gringos felt guilt and politely refused.

"The talk I had with Benson on Tuesday was a tad disturbing."

"What talk?"

"When you were putting the plane to bed, he pulled me aside."

"Oh."

"The new administration's budget cuts have had a huge impact on dredging companies. All our contracts with the Corps of Engineers are in jeopardy. He said flat-out that this could effect virtually everyone in the corporation."

"Shit. We're in the corporation."

"Talk about a warning shot over the bow." Hotchkiss was not happy. This was not part of his career plan either. "I've never heard him talk bad about anyone before. He was steaming over the political games with his livelihood. At some point, dredging will resume, but he said we might not be in business when everything backs up and the work needs to be done."

"Shit." Rand's mind spun with instant job insecurity. When things begin to roll backward... "What time frame are we talkin' here?"

"We all know the perils of a corporate pilot's career. The first thing to go is the airplane. And I doubt they would keep us on the payroll to show them how to get to Moisant." Hotchkiss laughed. "Maybe me only." Back to the game face. "There is a small chance they would keep us on as a tool to search for new jobs or for new bids. To be perfectly honest though, partner, they are well aware that this could be a single pilot operation."

That statement took wind out of Rand's sails. Blood rushed his cheeks. "Wait till I tell em' how cheap I can work. Hell, I could turn in the company car for you."

"I think I'd rather be laid off than fly here every week."

"No shit." Rand held the door for Hotchkiss as they entered the lobby of the best hotel in town, replete with luxurious electricity.

"Thanks, partner." Ken hesitated a moment. "You know I will continue to be in your corner, partner." Hotchkiss tapped on the counter to rouse the fat man from his siesta beneath a large fan.

"Si Señor?"

"Any messages?"

"No señor."

Rand nearly laughed at the crush of disappointment that dripped from the face of his boss.

"He's got to call today, Kiss. They wouldn't leave us here forever... would they?" The two climbed the tile stairway that led to their rooms on the second floor.

"I don't know, partner." Hotchkiss managed a smile. "Gotta blow mud. I'll check with you later if I don't hear anything sooner."

"Okay, boss." A small fan blew on the highest setting in Rand's tiny room. Dust was thick on the dilapidated wooden table and chair in the corner. A rock-hard bed waited for him to lie down in his underwear. His feet hung over the end.

Mandeville seemed air-conditioned sanity as thoughts of his mother began another downward spiral. He tried to visit at least twice a week, so she must wonder where he might be by now. A simple phone call from Coatzacoalcos was impossible. His father had vanished into a blur of gin with his new girl. He had tried to talk with him on a few occasions but it was always mixed with gin, tonic and confrontation. The message was clear: You aren't shit, and you never will be. Face down in a gutter. Rand lay on the bed and stared at the ceiling, an anchor tied to each ankle.

Reni made a brave choice not to let yesterday's events bring her down as she dabbed rose lipstick in the bathroom. The Times-Picayune lay open on the kitchen table, but she had barely glanced at the front-page story of another murdered prostitute. She'd gone straight for the classified ads and circled several prospects in the Help Wanted section. Jeffrey Bernstein would not get the best of her. No way Jose.

Leaving Lakefront had rekindled Reni's desire to work in the CBD. Top of her list was an office in One Shell Square, the tallest building in all of New Orleans. The man on the phone sounded very nice and set an appointment for an interview. With Picayune in hand, Reni pulled the glass door open to a comfortable waiting area with leather seats. The middle-aged receptionist greeted her with a warm smile, a welcome change from her envious Aero colleagues. Reni noted the two-carat diamond ring on the woman's left hand and felt free from competitive, insecure glares.

A tall man dressed in a dark blue suit approached her and held out a big hand as she rose to greet him. "You must be Reni." He instantly liked her.

"Yes, sir. Reni Duvette. Nice to meet you, sir." She smiled up at the big man.

Dark green eyes were careful not to look further than her soft face. "Come on in. I'm Leonard Monde."

Rand sweated through his second novel of the trip as the fan groaned through the fourth day of dirt. The Gulf Viking was beginning to seem like a fine job when a soft knock on the door snapped him into the present. "Who is it?"

"It's your savior."

Rand jumped up and swung the door open. "Tell me anything good."

"Jim Benson called. We're outta here in an hour, partner."

"Hot shit."

The Merlin pounded down the rocky runway at noon and when the wheels finally lifted off the pavement, the pilots began to breathe again. "Gear up, partner."

"Gladly." Pollution stunk up the Merlin, in equal hurry to get out of town. The dusty downtown area slid by and the last sight of the greasy river. Black smoke billowed from the coal power plant. Good riddance.

The haze layer stopped at 12,000 feet as they climbed into light. High cirrus hung above to welcome them back home. Rand pulled out the chart and punched in the coordinates for the north route over calm Gulf water. An hour into the flight, Benson made his way forward. "What's the ETA?" He seemed to have grayed a bit in the long week.

Hotchkiss took the question. "We're three hours out of Lakefront, touchdown at oh six-thirty." He pulled back from the GNS. "So how was the trip?"

"Money-losing proposition." Benson looked over at Rand who didn't turn around, but listened intently. "I'm not sure about sending all our equipment down there. Call it a bad gut."

"Tell me about it." Hotchkiss laughed.

"Yeah, it's a filthy place. I'd hate to send forty people down there knowing what I know. The handwriting is on the wall." He pulled the catering tray from the couch seat. "Ya'll want some sandwiches?" He handed up the ham and cheeses and returned to the leather seat just behind the wing, satisfied with the fair warning. He would miss his Merlin. The plane was as comfortable as his living room and had saved him countless hours at the terminal in Atlanta, waiting for yet another delayed commercial flight. Benson watched the right propeller cut through the Gulf air as they crossed the shoreline just south of Grand Isle. The powerful hum of the engine was bittersweet.

Lakefront Airport received her journeyed tenant. The passengers were gone by the time Rand got off the plane. Ollie set the chocks around the nose tire and disappeared into the hangar without a word. Hotchkiss circled around the tail and set the propellers in the down position. "Who died, partner?"

"Hell if I know." They entered the lobby and the only sign of life was Dawn behind the counter, working with her head down.

"Hey girl!"

She casually looked up. "Hey, Rand. Good trip?"

"It was interesting." Silence. "Where's Reni?"

"I think she's off today"

"On Friday? She's never off on Friday."

"I don't know. I don't set the schedules." She looked up past Rand. "Hey Ken, here's some messages for you."

"Thanks, doll." Hotchkiss moved toward the counter.

Rand watched Dawn closely as she looked down again. Her eyes came up slightly to see if he had left the room and when she spotted him, instantly looked down again. Rand quickly put the Merlin to bed.

The apartment door was unlocked. The bathroom light was on and Reni's jewelry box was open on the dresser above an opened drawer. He moved toward the closet as the bedroom telephone rang. "Hello?"

"Hey. You're home."

"Yes, I am." Rand looked toward the closet. "Where y'at darlin'?"

"I'm... uh... downtown."

"Where downtown? Why weren't you at Lakefront?" Rand was bombed with strange vibrations.

"Hey, it's Friday. Come meet me at the Rainforest." Reni was upbeat.

"Rainforest? What the hell is going on?"

"I've got some good news, Rand. Don't spoil it."

"Well hell. I'll go to anywhere for some good news. When?"

"ASAP."

"Hey, I haven't had a hot shower in a week. Let me scrub Mexico off my ass and I'll be there in forty minutes."

"Perfect. See ya then. Love ya."

Rand hung up the phone and stripped. He cherished the warm water that blew from the showerhead and savored the luxurious lather from a green bar of American soap. The grime on his skin washed away. He stepped out a new man as he walked naked to the freezer and piled ice cubes into a plastic go cup. The numb buzz of a weeklong trip could only be cured with a few bird strikes. The wrench in his back subsided with each sip as he dressed. Drink in hand, he strolled through the courtyard and out onto St. Philip to hail a cab on Dauphine. "To the Rainforest...uh the Hilton."

Rand found the express elevator to the Rainforest, and tossed the cup of ice in the trash behind the club's waterfall display. Simulated thunder began behind the dance floor. He found Reni alone in a padded booth against the panoramic window above the mighty Mississippi.

"Hey darlin'." She stood as Rand approached with a quizzical smile and kissed her softly on the lips. Reni wanted to go on longer, but he pulled away. "What in the world...?"

Reni's curls crashed over padded shoulders of a new navy power-suit; her lips were touched with gloss and she wore just a hint of blue eyeliner. A new perfume yelled directly to a week's supply of hormone excretion. "How was the trip?" She gripped his hand tightly.

"Bullshit. I went to hell and back." Rand watched the dance boat, SS President, leave the dock below. "Now, why weren't you at work today, young lady?"

"I was at work." Reni sat up. "I got a new job." A white smile burst through full lips as she circled Rand's face for a reaction.

He sat back incredibly, "A new job? Where?"

"I'm working in the CBD! You're looking at the new manager for Accounts Receivable at La Petra Corporation at One Shell Square!"

Rand froze. "Reni, what the hell are you... drunk or somethin'?" Rand pulled away from her as the waitress cruised up and looked down at the two.

"Oh, he finally showed up." She winked at Reni. "What'll you have, sir?"

"A double bird. And soon." The waitress set down a fresh bottle of Dom Perignon for Reni. She poured it into the slender crystal glass and the bubbles within created a miniature celebratory fireworks display.

"Girl...what the hell?"

"Well, that asshole Bernstein fired me on Wednesday and..."

"Fired you? For what?"

"I called in sick on Tuesday. You know, Mardi Gras."

"Ooops."

"Yeah. I wasn't feeling so good after Monday." Reni worked through the week and got to the interview at La Petra. "So this big guy comes out to interview me and he seemed kinda creepy at first, kinda like a thug almost. But he takes me back to the offices and explains the whole operation to me and gives me an application to fill out at this empty desk looking out over the Superdome. After I finished, Mr. Monde read it over and ushered me into the president's office and Mr. Simpson offered me the job."

"Monde?"

"Leonard Monde. He's my new boss. He seemed weird at first but he's real nice."

"And Simpson is the president of La Petra?"

"You got it." Reni smiled big. "And the empty desk I filled the application out on... is mine." She drained her glass and refilled it. "The only creepy part is the girl I'm replacing disappeared two weeks ago."

"Disappeared?"

"She's the one that's been in the papers. Her parents have a reward out to find her. Last anybody saw her was at her... uhh my... desk."

"Wow." Rand took the double bird that flew in from behind the Rainforest bar. He checked an adrenaline lapse with a mammoth sip. "Wow."

Rand woke at dawn to the sound of chirping swallows in the courtyard. He was alone. Cocktail hour had burned late, and Reni's early excitement had soon turned into a bitter recount of the events at the clinic. After she drank herself into total numbness, Rand had poured her into a cab and sent her home. As he stared at the textured ceiling above, his ears rang with Garretts and bird screams.

He pondered the demise of the Merlin job. He figured a flight instructor position could be found, but that seemed unimaginable after getting a whiff of turbine fuel and comfortable living conditions. He wondered...

The phone rang loudly and Rand jumped. It must be Reni. Who else would call at five in the morning?

"Hello?"

"Rand, you're home again! Where have you been?"

"Mom?" Rand adjusted the phone to his ear. "What's going on?"

"I just wanted you to know that I feel soooo great. It's time for me to get on with my life and forget about all the bad things that have happened and get a job and maybe move to a new place and start my life all over again and fix a healthy breakfast every morning and change my hair and turn in the car for a new one and..." Rand's mouth dropped opened as he listened to the manic machine gun. "And when I finish the remodeling I will take my Realtor's license and open my own office and hire fifty-two agents to work for me because I'm really not a bad person and I have three great children and we will still be a great family even without your father and I living in the same house."

"Mom?" Rand waited for silence.

"Yes?"

"How ya feeling?"

"Honey, I feel great! I think I know what was wrong with me and I need to get going with my life and plant flowers in the garden and be nice to the elderly because you know we have elderly in this place and they don't have many friends and I can be a great friend to all the older people that don't get to see their families or the husbands and their wives have passed on..." A mammoth inhale. "I could make sure that if their sons and daughters need a house in the area I could send one of my agents over to get them a nice house so they could just stay in the guest house without having to stay here at this place. Rand?"

"Yes?" He held the phone away from a near yell.

"I have to go, I need to call the Realtor board to see if they still have my name and if I can start interviewing people right here at the hospital. I'll talk to you later darling and you know I love you so much and I couldn't have done it without you."

"Mom...Mom. I don't think anyone's there at five in the morni..." Dial tone.

He rose, showered, grabbed a quick cup of java and began the familiar journey across the clip-clop under gray overcast that matched the choppy Pontchartrain. The bridge trance lasted until he reached the Northshore.

As he crossed the lawn at Mandeville, the metal door to the cafeteria opened and a line of patients emerged from the building. They all looked fairly sane except for the man with no shirt and a cotton ski hat and the woman who walked with her pants and underwear in her hand. But it was the tenth patient that made Rand stop dead in his tracks. Clad in a red sweater, black pants and clean white tennis shoes, his mother shuffled in small steps, her pale face staring straight ahead. Rand stepped off the sidewalk onto the lawn as the line passed, but he was invisible to her. He followed her into her room. "Hi mom."

"Oh." Blank stare. "Hi Rand."

"How ya feelin'?"

"Tired." She took a seat in a wooden chair and stared at the floor.

"Why?"

"Because I've done such a terrible thing and let everybody down. How embarrassed you all must be."

"Mom, that's ridiculous. No one is embarrassed. We just want you to get better. That is all that matters. We all love you." He looked at her for a response and got one. She was asleep. He turned down the sheets and placed her in the bed. She began to snore as he held her hand and knelt beside her. *Dear Lord, here I am again.*

Light streamed into his dark bedroom. Leonard Monde froze in fear. The cops...? He couldn't see the face of the male silhouette. He reached for his knife under the pillow. The knife was gone. As the intruder moved over the bed, Leonard went for his .38 in the drawer. It was also gone. Strong hands grabbed his jeans at the waist and yanked him clean out of bed, pinning him to the floor. Light from the hallway lit up a familiar face. "So ya burned the fuckin' trailer down, ya little motherfucker," his father screamed. He stripped his son naked and began a series of slow punches to the side of his head.

Drenched in rage, he awoke in darkness. All was quiet, except for a thumping pulse of adrenaline snaking through his brain. Monde reached under the pillow and the blade was there. He opened the drawer to feel the .38. He looked at the backlit alarm clock. It read 1:32 AM. He grabbed a Pall Mall from the pack on the night table. He felt a surge of wild energy as he began to visualize those lips. Money. It takes money to score a woman like that.

As two o'clock rolled around, the accountant began to devise a master plan. There was $5 million earmarked for Loffland Drilling out of Tulsa that he could easily reroute. Maybe this Thursday. He pictured a call to his peer at Loffland to promise a wire by the following Wednesday at the latest. But this wire would cross offshore to Grand Cayman. They might start looking on Thursday or Friday. I can...we can...get way down the road in three days. From then on, the beautiful plan only got better. He crushed the cigarette into the ashtray.

His hand slid beneath the blue jeans he wore as a barrier against expected attacks. The fifth massage in twenty hours began as he closed his eyes to picture wavy blonde hair and clear blue eyes looking down from above.

Reni's thoughts were jumbled as she made her way down Poydras on Monday. She recalled Rand's pale expression at the clinic. It was just last Monday but it seemed a year ago. Her heart sank with guilt momentarily, yet she found comfort by turning a palm skyward. Courage and faith pushed her around the corner at St. Charles toward Hibernia Bank while a dozen suits eyed her covertly and another half-dozen did so overtly.

The leather briefcase in her left hand held a million-dollar cashier's check from La Petra made out to LM Properties. The deposit was made without complication, allowing her time to join the lunch crowd at Mother's on Tchoupitoulas.

Monday is a no-brainer at the popular CBD eatery. As she slid her fork under the red beans-and-rice special, a party of four young businessmen smiled in her direction. Reni was suddenly aware that there might be other possibilities within the $500 Dior suits that worked the CBD. She felt a strange distance from Lakefront Airport, Jeffrey Bernstein, Ollie, the Merlin... and Rand Chapman.

Rand had changed. His voice was monotone when he called on Saturday to inform her of plans to spend the weekend on the Northshore with his mother. He mentioned that there was another exploration trip on the schedule for Monday that could last the entire week.

As the week progressed, there were no calls. Perhaps there were no phones where he was, yet she cried herself to sleep each night with thoughts of other possibilities. Wednesday brought a deposit of $2 million. Friday afternoon, another $2 million was deposited into the account of LM Properties. Reni picked up the phone on her return from Hibernia and dialed out to Lakefront.

Her heart sank as Dawn informed her that the Merlin had landed two hours ago and that the gang was meeting at Ichabod's on Lakeshore for happy hour. Tears streamed her face as she drove home in rush hour with the radio tuned to WWL. A new voice flew above with traffic news.

Reni was out the door for a five-miler before a quick shower. She wore her white sundress lightly over a runner's high as she pushed the door open to Ichabod's. She moved through the bar area to the large wooden deck that overlooked the harbor. T.G. was regaling the group with tales of a fishing boat buzz. Their laughter was punctuated by clangs of halyards against masts within a late afternoon breeze. Sunset was a blue and pink masterpiece over the Causeway to the west.

"Hey girl!" Rand jumped to attention and waved her over. He kissed her gently on the mouth and she thought perhaps everything was all right.

"How was the trip?"

"A long one. Five days on Martha's Vineyard."

"Where's that?" Reni felt uncomfortable in the old crowd. Beth had brought her new fiancé, Ashton. Bridget's laugh bullhorned at every story along with the giggles of Reni's replacement, a nineteen-year-old brunette with sapphire eyes.

"Off the coast of Massachusetts, just north of Cape Cod. Cool little island with lots of bluebloods." Rand turned toward his colleagues. "Hon, say hello to Dawn Davis. Bernstein's new target." Everybody laughed.

"Hi guys. It's been awhile." Reni moved closer to her territory. "What's going on up in Cape Cod?"

"There was a sailboat harbor that needed to be deepened in spots, but it doesn't look like its gonna happen. Not enough work to justify the project." He looked at T.G. and made damn sure not to even glance in the general direction of the new Dawn. "I may be looking for a job soon. A real one."

Rand quickly brought Reni into the loop, and she chattered on about her new job and the glowing bustle of downtown New Orleans. After a few rounds, she called Rand over for a sidebar on the far end of the patio. "I need to talk to you." She held his hand and he returned the squeeze, but it wasn't the squeeze. "What's going on, Rand?"

"Going on...?"

"Who's that little brunette?" A lake breeze blew a strand of hair across her face and into her mouth. She finger-combed it away. "You're not looking at her like you used to not look at me."

Rand pulled up two deck chairs and motioned for her to sit. "I don't know, ask Bernstein. I doubt she's old enough to be in here. Hey, look...there's Ted's boat."

"Aren't there phones on Martha's Vineyard?"

"I don't know." He chirped from bird. "Things aren't going so well. I'm probably going to be on the street very soon looking for a job. And I've got work to do with my mom." He sat back and placed his feet on the bottom wooden rail over the harbor.

"Well, I won't spoil your night. I may just go find some people from work." She got to her feet. "I'm outta here."

He continued to stare into the water with his plastic cup hinged on his lower lip as her shoes clicked away.

T.G. and Bridget came over after a quiet moment. "Not going so well anymore with you two?"

"No it's not." Rand stopped the waitress. "Could you bring me another please?" He held up the empty cup as Bridget cackled loudly. Another bird, another story, another cackle shoved harsh reality into the lake.

A new flying student joined the group. Mona Seaver had soloed for the first time this afternoon. As per tradition, her shirttail was cut to midback, exposing her bra strap. She had the shorn tail to prove it, and she held the memento up with huge grin. They all cheered and clapped. T.G. stepped forward. "Mona, this is an old instructor, Rand Chapman, now a big time corporate jock."

"Nicetameetcha."

Another bird, another story, another joke. The new Dawn and Bridget had a party to attend. T.G. had a date to pick up. Beth and Ashton had needs and departed in his RX-7. Mona ordered another Johnny Walker Black Label.

"Scotch?"

"Yeah. An acquired taste." The disco began pulsing music inside as light turned quickly to night. Except for the occasional waitress, they were alone under a gazillion stars.

"You said you're from Covington?"

"Mandeville."

"You're kidding. I was a Skipper."

"I thought you looked familiar." She popped his thigh. "What's your last name?"

"Chapman."

"Billy Chapman's brother. God, I know you."

"Bill. At college he became Bill."

"You dated Becky."

"It's all comin' back."

"My dad wanted to kill you."

"Yes, he did." Rand smiled. "What's Becky up to these days?"

"She's at LSU. Living off campus, and into Jesus."

"Becky…Seaver?"

"Yep. She's been born again."

"Once was never enough for her." Laughter. "You went to Tulane, right? And dental school?"

"That's right." A sip of Black Label. "Last I heard you were at USL."

"I lasted a semester. You still dating Paul?"

Silence.

"Mona?"

Tears slid on both cheeks. She looked past the harbor to the horizon, ironically lit with lights from the Mile 4 Causeway crossover. "You don't know?"

"What?"

"He's gone."

"Gone?" Rand sat up. "Paul Riley is dead?"

"Presumed… dead."

"Why doesn't Bill know about this?"

"He disappeared. There is no finality. No news."

"Disappeared? How?"

"He'd gone home. And his car was in the shop." She laid her head on Rand's shoulder. Johnny Black and sweet innocence took a hand that on last sighting belonged to a former life that she wished would magically return.

"I waited for three hours at Lakeside. I called his parents and they said he had left before sunset. I called his apartment all night…the next day. Our date was set. I began to wonder…if he'd bailed on me. A week passed. A month. No one had seen him. No one has seen him since."

Reni cruised Lakeshore with sorrow as she visualized a split from Rand. She tried to imagine a date with one of the CBD suits. She began to drift with comfort until a wave of insecurity lapped her back to nights at Destin, fried chicken lunch dates, runs through Audubon Park, dinners at Commanders, long drives in the country. She wheeled the Mustang back to Ichabod's to salvage the times of her life. She pulled the large wooden entrance door open and moved past the maitre d' into the lounge. In the hour that she'd wandered aimlessly, the club's large varnished bar had come alive and the dance floor was crowded. A gallant charge from an LSU sophomore landed her a margarita. She scanned the lounge while keeping the sophomore hopeful with the minimum interest required for companionship. She saw a few people wander out from the disco area to the peace of the patio. Energy brought her to feet as she pushed into the night. The Lakefront gang had departed. A couple here, there, one sitting against the wall. The guy looked sort of like... "Hello, Mr. Chapman."

Bird-induced confusion swarmed him. Mona brought her head from his shoulder, tears still streaming down her face. "Reni," Rand began, "this is..." Reni stormed away. "I'll be right back." Rand chased her down and grabbed her elbow. "Hon, she is an old..."

"Old enough to be your...good God, Rand. It didn't take you long."

"She's a friend of my bro..." Mona approached. Low- cut black Levis set off long, athletic legs. Her stomach was exposed where her instructor had hacked her shirt. Brown hair pushed away from an alluring face. Rand stopped her. "Mona."

She touched Reni's arm. "Hey, I'm sorry, Rand and I were just..."

"Please go." Reni snapped.

Mona headed for the front door. Rand was in a tight spot. "Mona, please wait outside. I'll be right there. Please wait." She nodded affirmation. He pulled Reni back as she tried to escape his grasp with tears of fury.

"Reni! Listen!"

"No! You listen." Barry White began. Reni yelled above the cheering crowd. "Let me tell you something." Veins streaked her thin neck area. "You aren't the only guy in town. You bastard!" He reached for her arm.

"Hon, listen..."

"Is this what you want?"

"Reni." He looked around. "I don't know. I hope not."

"You don't know? After all we've done. You don't know?" She welled up. "Well, I can tell you this. It is over Rand. I'll make up your mind for you. It is over." The patio door opened behind him. "And I'll tell you one thing. You will pay for this. You will pay. I will get even."

Rand stepped back. Her hair blew forward as her dress furled in the breeze. The backlight haloed a brilliant outline.

"I gotta go," he whispered.

10. Alien in the Mirror

Rand began an afternoon transformation. With eyes closed, he pictured a huge rock spinning though vast emptiness. On it were millions, billions, trillions, gazillions of gallons of salt water. A humongous ball of fire kept the rock warm from an impossible distance. Rumbling volcanoes shook its surface, scaring thousands of bizarre species. Animals with great intellect designed explosives to destroy other animals' habitats. There was enormous bloodshed. As cranial hyperactivity jolted him, Rand realized that he was actually on this rock. He felt his bones and visualized blood pumping through a body that he did not understand. The phone rang. Rand commanded his arm to pick it up.

"Wheels in the well at oh six-hundred, partner." Hotchkiss paused. "This could be last call."

"Oh well, I was getting tired of the old bird anyway. What'd we get? A seven-two-seven?"

"Yeah, right." Hotchkiss laughed. "It's not for sure but a potential owner wants fresh motors. We make one stop to drop off the boss in Houston then we'll take her out to Midland for the overhaul. They still haven't said anything about us."

"Maybe we can fire up some resumes while we're there."

"I'll be closing Ms. Darlene's account, partner." Hotchkiss coughed for the third time in a minute. "But feel free to use me as a reference."

Morning came fast and the Merlin dropped the last passengers at Houston Hobby before a mid-morning punch through gray clouds into an ocean of blue over illuminated white undercast. Rand pushed on defensive Ray-Bans against the intense Texas sun. They climbed to 16,000 feet on a northwest heading.

"Well partner." Hotchkiss waited as a long silence passed.

"You ain't gonna cry... are you, boss?" Rand smiled from the left seat.

"It's been a good run, partner." He looked over to his protégé. "I'm gonna miss this gig." Kiss had debated with himself as to who should fly the last leg before deciding to give it to Rand. The gesture did not go unnoticed.

"It's gonna be hard to beat this one." Rand looked to the man that had transformed him from a good stick to a wise pilot. "But that don't mean we ain't gonna try, right boss?"

Hotchkiss smiled the final smile. "Right, partner."

Sun baked the oil-rich Permian Basin as the Merlin descended toward its tumbleweed and sand with the towns of Midland and Odessa in the windscreen. The plane touched down smoothly and taxied to the large engine overhaul hangar. Within minutes, mechanics had unbolted the seats and removed the engines from the wings. By sunset, the turbine blades would be out of the Garretts for infrared inspection.

The loaner was a 1976 Corvette and the boys headed for the Odessa Holiday Inn. Hotchkiss worked his account while Rand fought the War Against Boredom with a venture into local bars that were swamped with cowboys and roughnecks. There were plenty of women and he figured that the odds were good... but the goods were odd. So he returned to his room for an early sleep.

The beautiful plan was working well. With five million dollars safely in his personal account, the chief accountant at La Petra cleanly transferred $3 million into an obscure account on Grand Cayman. On Friday, he had checked the bail, and that, too, was perfect. Eastern had a seven p.m. to Miami that connected with the midnight Varig to Rio. Way gone. He had scored two phony passports with Reni's mandatory employee picture.

At nine-thirty sharp Monday morning, Leonard Monde called the Hibernia branch manager to alert him about a large cash withdrawal, a little walkin' round dinero of two hundred grand. He confided that a huge land deal hinged on the cash before a second call to Loffland Brothers' accountant in Tulsa to confirm that the wire transfer would be there by midweek. All systems go.

Monde was confident when he emerged from his office. He wore a starched white shirt and his tie hung just slightly askew over his belly roll. "Good morning, Reni."

"Mornin'. You have a nice weekend?" The two top buttons of her white cotton blouse were loose and he inhaled full cleavage. He caught a vision of the new couple cavorting in luxury beneath piles of cash.

"Yes, thank you Reni." He swallowed. "Reni?"

"Yes, Mr. Monde?"

"Could I ask a great favor of you?" His hands sweated heavily.

"Sure."

"This afternoon, I have an appointment out at UNO. But, uh...my car is in the shop. Could you...uh...do you think you could give me a ride out there after work?"

"Sure thing, Mr. Monde. What time?" She scanned a large ledger for a lost receivable.

"You can? About five would be perfect."

"Sure, whenever you'd like."

"Thanks, Reni." His mouth was dry. "The reason I need a ride out to UNO is that they have asked me to speak to an accounting class."

"Really?" She tried to look suitably impressed.

"But the class doesn't start until seven, so I wondered if I could buy you dinner to kill time."

"Uh, dinner?" She looked over the Superdome directly ahead and thought quickly. "I'd love to, Mr. Monde, but I was going for a long run tonight. I don't mind giving you a lift out there, though." No need to lie.

"Great, Reni. And if you change your mind... dinner is on me." Monde paused. "Reni?"

She looked up past the scraggly mustache toward dark green eyes, unfocused and intense. "Yes Mr. Monde?" A tingle started at the back of her neck.

"Could I have the keys to your car, Reni? I have some materials I need to take with me tonight that I'd like to load in." He stared out over the city.

"Uh...my car? Uh, sure." She dug the key chain out. "This one opens the trunk. I'm parked in the lot next door at Carondelet."

"I know," he whispered.

Shortly after noon, Monde descended three sets of marble stairs from the lobby of One Shell to Poydras. A two-block trance left him moist as he pushed the glass door open to the spectacular Hibernia lobby. Monde didn't stop to admire the forty-foot-high painted ceiling with gold trim, pristine marble floor or the dozen marble pillars that held the entire building. He marched directly to the branch manager's huge oak desk, behind a three-foot polished oak barrier.

"Oh, Mr. Monde." William Parris stood. "Nice to see you again, sir."

"Mr. Parris." Monde put the briefcase on the big desk. "I hate deals like this, but its part of buying property around here. Cash negotiates well."

"I have the forms for your signature." Parris pushed across Notification of Cash over Ten Thousand forms for the IRS and a withdrawal-of-funds slip. "I'll be back in a few minutes."

Monde's hands shook and he flashed a quick glance at the security guard that had been called for the major cash transaction. By the time he completed the forms, Parris was back to look over the papers. "Follow me, gentlemen."

The men took the brass-caged elevator down to the vault, where another .44-toting Hibernia guard stood at the entrance. The Pinkerton man hung with his peer as Monde and Parris proceeded to a table that was stacked with hundred-dollar bills. Parris counted out 2,000 pictures of Benjamin Franklin into Monde's brown leather briefcase.

Ten minutes later, Monde loaded the briefcase into the trunk of the Mustang. He drove Reni's car to Eastern's ticket office on St. Charles, where he counted out eight Franklins for two one-way, first-class tickets to Miami on the early evening Whisperjet. *The plan...is working.* Monde was back at One Shell by three to check his watch every two minutes. At precisely 4:55, he straightened his tie in the mirror in the executive restroom and tucked his shirt back into his pants. He managed composure as he opened the door. Reni stood in the hallway.

"Hey, Mr. Monde. Are you ready?"

"All set. I can't tell you how much I appreciate this, Reni."

Reni found conversation with her boss difficult. "You have some long legs," she managed as she adjusted the seat forward to reach the pedals. Monde had retrieved the briefcase from the trunk of the car and laid it on the backseat. After turning left onto Canal to the I-10, she pushed the speed limit in uneasy silence.

He finally spoke. "Reni..." He looked at her with a slight smile. "I have some excellent news for you."

"You do?" She glanced at him and back to the road, and took a longer look at the peculiar smile. "What?" She noticed Rand's old apartment as they headed down Downman Road toward Lakefront Airport.

"Pull into the parking lot at Lakefront, Reni. I have something you have got to see." His eyes glowed as the sun set.

"The parking lot...?"

"Yeah, Reni. You're not going to believe this."

She passed the hangar at Aero and tried to pick out familiar airplanes. She noticed the Merlin was gone. Just past the old terminal building, she pulled into the empty lot next to the shocking statue of three naked women and one naked man bathing in a fountain. "Here?"

"Perfect, Reni." He reached into the backseat and grabbed the briefcase. With trembling hands, he opened it and sat back to get a perfect view of her reaction. "Well?" He smiled big.

Rand spent a restless night and woke at eight. He read the Midland paper and found nothing of interest as usual. At nine, Hotchkiss knocked on his door and they made their way out to the maintenance hangar in the Vette. They found the Merlin on jacks as mechanics tested the landing gear system. Rand observed retraction with a third cup of coffee. Hydraulic pumps whined as the gear doors slammed shut under 3,000 pounds of pressure. Hotchkiss entered the small office in the hangar to make a call back to One Shell. He emerged with ashen face.

"Partner." Ken swallowed hard. "I got some bad news."

Rand looked down at the great captain. His hair seemed grayer. Uh-oh. He had anticipated the layoff, but this was still going to hurt.

"Last night..." he paused to look straight at Rand. "Your Reni..."

Reni...? He stepped back with surprise. Ken's eyes followed him and pierced like never before.

"...was kidnapped..."

Sure she was.

"...and murdered."

Rand looked at Hotchkiss with incredible disbelief. The straightforward statement seemed legitimate. His legs nearly buckled. "Where did you hear... that?"

"I just spoke with the office. Everyone's been looking for you. It's all over the papers." He saw Rand go very pale, his lips parted. "God, I'm so sorry, partner."

A king cobra had delivered a fatal bite to Rand's brain. He searched for a place to fall as the past month's events shredded him. Gonna pay for this... Rand. The hangar was full of strangers. More strangers in the business office surrounded the only phone in sight. He asked for and received car keys from Hotchkiss and drove in numb shock over to the terminal building on the far side of the field. He parked in desert heat, hurried in to find a payphone and dialed her home number.

The DuVette's small house was crowded with family and friends when the telephone rang for the hundredth time. Mrs. DuVette sat in her favorite chair holding a picture of Reni in pigtails at age six. Tears rolled down her cheeks as she recalled the hour it took to braid Reni's hair that morning. An hour. What she would do for just one more hour with her little girl. Outside, George DuVette rocked back and forth on the swing-set where he had spent hundreds of hours pushing his sweet little girl through the air. Her laughter still echoed from the redwood fence he'd built. His hand clenched the gold necklace she'd worn to work just yesterday; it was the only item he could positively identify among gruesome remains.

Dazed by unanswered questions, Reni's brother Brian finally picked up the phone. Adrenaline smoked his brain. "Hello?"

"Brian?" Rand stood in the carpeted concourse. The voice on the end of the line seemed normal. Maybe it's all a mistake. "It's Rand." He stood in silence, the phone pressed to his ear in a death grip. "Please tell me it's not true."

Brian felt his throat swell again. He choked back an eruption to whisper: "Yes...it's true."

"Oh my God." He banged his head on the top of the payphone as the second wave of disbelief stormed him. The abortion. "Brian, what happened? Who did this?"

"They caught the guy. It was... where are you Rand?"

"Midland, Texas."

"So you haven't read the papers?"

"Papers? No." In the papers. Everyone knows...?

"Yeah. His name was Leonard Monde, he worked with her downtown. Did you know him?" Brian needed more answers.

"Monde?" Rand ran through his active mind. "Monde? I don't think I ever met him." He flashed to the last time he saw Reni, alone on the dance floor. She was so beautiful...and so upset. That strange look. He pictured the silhouette and the dress. I'll get you Rand. His gut sank, and strength departed his knees.

"Yeah. Sounds like a real sicko. He drove her around for hours last night. Cut her throat, shot her and set her on fire... the Mustang too."

"Whaaaat...?" He heard Brian gasp for air. "Good God! How's your mother and George taking it?"

"Not good," he barely choked out. "The bastard poured gasoline over her and set her on fire. They're doing an autopsy on her right now."

"God." Rand felt each mile between the hellhole and the Pontchartrain. "I'll fly back as soon as I can."

"I gotta tell you, Rand, you probably aren't the most popular person around here right now."

"I guess not. What... timing." The sinker found the bottom of the deepest ocean. "I'll call you later. Tell George and your mother how sick I am. Please."

He hung up and stared at the phone. A vision of her beauty engulfed in a roaring gasoline blaze blasted him. How can this be? Another clear vision of hair popping and skin melting slammed him. He numbly moved out to the car until his legs failed and he dropped to the asphalt. Dry air blew against his hair and he nearly puked. He flashed to Reni in this very position outside the clinic. His eyes focused on the horizon, over the tumbleweed and under a blue sky. "Where have you gone?" He visualized her rise into the universe with eyes on him.

He drove silently back to the Holiday Inn to fall on the bed. Murdered? It made no sense. Rand stared at the ceiling for three hours until a light knock snapped him into delirious hope. Disappointment hit when he saw Hotchkiss standing in the doorway with Darlene behind him. He handed Rand a full glass of Scotch. "Thought you might need this." Kiss didn't know quite what else to say.

"It's unbelievable...I hope I wake up soon. It's got to be a nightmare." Rand saw a vague image of his boss, but his eyes remained unfocused. "I need to get back to New Orleans. I don't know why."

"I already checked on flights out of here, partner. Nothing until seven tomorrow morning. Let me know if I can do anything in the meantime." Hotchkiss decided not to share the other two major pieces of bad news of the catastrophic day. "Keep the car tonight. We have Darlene's." Rand caught a look from her that made him feel like a leper.

"Thanks, Kiss." He closed the door and lay back on the bed. A slide show played endlessly inside his head: runs through the French Quarter, parties, games at the Dome, trips to the beach, lunch dates, the time she climbed a big oak tree on Lakeshore and waved playfully from the giant branch. Her smile. He watched the images in silence.

A cheap clock radio on the night table automatically broke into his thoughts at midnight. "And here's the latest number one from Willie Nelson...." The Texan began his nasal twang:

Maybe I should have loved you
All those lonely, lonely nights
Maybe I should have held you
But you were always on my mind
You were always on my mind

Tell me
Tell me your sweet love hasn't died

He stood and walked to his suitcase. He found the hidden twisted unit, stuck it in his pocket, and pointed the Vette into the dark desert. The lights of Odessa disappeared through the rear-view as he drove with no destination in mind, floating on the deserted highway under a blanket of stars. Rand picked an abandoned road at random, followed it to an abandoned wellhead and crept to a stop. He killed the engine, rolled down the window and pushed in the cigarette lighter. He stared ahead until the lighter popped. Smoke poured upward with a deep pull. Peering into infinite darkness, he was stoned as a pony.

A powerful magnet drew his eyes to the millions of twinkling lights above. He stepped out of the car and climbed onto the hood. The heat of the engine warmed his back as his mind journeyed far into the universe. A shooting star streaked from left to right. And another. And another. Soon there was a full-blown shower, with hundreds, thousands of streaking lights. He couldn't move. His heartbeat thumped audibly in his ears.

And there she was. Sitting...no, swinging from a star, just the way she had from the branch on that live oak. She smiled the same smile and spoke in the same playful tone.

"Hi darlin'!"

He heard her voice so clearly. And next to her....Was it a... baby? What else could make her smile so big?

11. Fuzz

A tall man lurched out of Lafitte's hideout. Though young and muscular, he stumbled with dysfunctional legs toward the river on cracked cobblestones. His head began to swirl at a rate the legs could not process and he splashed into the grungy gutter under the rear bumper of a parked Chevy. Face down. After enjoying a moment of peace, he pulled himself to his knees and crawled to the opposite gutter to repeat the performance. Face down in a gutter. The bastard was right.

Using the strength of ten men, Rand found his knees, shaking from the seven birds and ten Jagermeister shots. He crawled to the gate of his courtyard and climbed to his feet, steadying himself with a stiff right arm to pull his keys from his pocket, turning it inside out like an ear. He dropped the keys after missing the keyhole by six inches. "Oughta put fuzz around the goddamn thing." He giggled aloud and finally found the target. The gate crashed shut behind him and he stumbled down the brick tunnel to the courtyard. "Fuzzzzz around the goddamned thing ...fuzzzzzz...around the goddamned thing... fuzzzzzz...." With dawn breaking the darkness above, Rand scraped his arm on the redbrick courtyard wall. He felt no pain as his skin broke at the surface. "Scraped my goddamn arm," he muttered. "My goddamn arm is broken. Put some fuzzzzzz around it...." Three blue swimming pools danced in his vision. "Should soak... my goddamn arm... in the goddamn pool... then put some goddamn fuzzzzzz around it...fuzzzzzzz...." He leaned forward to lower his bleeding arm into a blur of blue. The brain did not register the black barbecue grill directly ahead and he clanged it with his knee and tripped into a face-first splashdown. He opened his eyes wide to a thousand sparkling bubbles and black charcoal ascending to the surface. "Goddamn bubbles...goddamn swimming pool." He inhaled half a lung of water as he spoke, surfacing in the shallow end and coughing loud enough to wake the landlord in the main house, still holding on to the keys.

"Meant...ta do that...meant ta..put some fuzzzzzz around it." He pulled himself up without the ladder and managed to hoist one leg out, and the other, before a pratfall back into the pool with another great splash. "Meant ta...do that." He finally found the ladder and took a full minute to reach the patio. As he meandered up the stairs, the landlord peered from the second-story window of the main house, watching water drip steadily from the fully dressed tenant.

Rand turned the knob and tumbled into the kitchen. "Looosie, I'ymmm...home." he slurred. "You got some 'splainin'...ta do." He started to fall in the hall, but slid down the wall into the bedroom, over the pile of clothes and into the unmade bed. Rand pulled the sheet and blanket over his soaked body and was instantly comatose.

On the floor in the brightening room lay the copy of the Times-Picayune he bought on the day he returned from Texas, two weeks ago. There was a black-and-white photo of a big burly man, shirt unbuttoned, tail no longer tucked, a V-neck undershirt half-covering a protruding belly. His black, greasy hair was disheveled. His long face was centered with a bulbous nose and his mouth hung slightly open below a wispy mustache. A veteran NOPD detective held the prisoner's arms handcuffed behind him, clearly sickened by the sight of the man. The story read:

WOMAN SLAIN, BODY SET AFIRE

The burning body of a young New Orleans woman was discovered in a grove of willow trees alongside Paris Road about 10 p.m. Monday, police said. Police arrested a suspect in the woods nearby.

Homicide detectives believe the woman was either beaten or stabbed to death. They said the upper portion of the body was burned and there was a gash on the neck and a large cut on her thigh.

The victim was identified as Renelle Jacqueline DuVette, 21, 44 Swallow St., New Orleans.

Police say they have booked Leonard Monde, 30, 666 Pontiff Avenue, Algiers, with first-degree murder and simple kidnapping.

Monde was DuVette's supervisor at La Petra Gas Company at One Shell Square, where she was a secretary, police said.

The body was discovered by a motorist who saw a fire and reported a burning "mannequin" about 200 yards south of Interstate 10 and about 30 feet off of Paris Road in a sparsely wooded area.

When the fire trucks arrived on the scene, they discovered the burning body.

Police were called to the scene, and K-9 officers flushed Monde out of the woods, police said. He was taken into custody.

DuVette's automobile, a late-model white Mustang, was found about 100 yards south of the Interstate near a levee.

Gasoline was poured on the woman's body and on her car, police said.

DuVette apparently was a kidnap victim. At 6:30 p.m., a bulletin was issued by the New Orleans Police Department asking officers to be on the lookout for DuVette.

According to police, DuVette and an unidentified man were seen arguing in a parking lot at the Lakefront Airport. A security guard saw her jump out of her car, and scream to the man inside, "Put that thing away."

He forced her back into the car and drove away, police said.

Police say they are uncertain about the motive for the kidnapping and murder but there was a large amount of cash found at the scene. Police said DuVette and Monde left work together in Duvette's car Monday afternoon.

The news had yellowed and Rand's severance check from Benson Dredging, along with the official pink layoff notice, lay between the front page and the Sports section. The Merlin remained in Midland, waiting for a new buyer; the first prospect elected to go with a Cessna Citation. Hotchkiss had called two days after Rand flew home with more bad news: The pilots had been reduced to an "as needed" status until the plane was sold. "But you may have to cover those trips for me, partner. I just got back from the oncologist."

Rand was already in the bag at four in the afternoon. "On...c-cologist...?"

"Yeah, partner. This old man has lung cancer."

Reni's autopsy results did not enhance anyone's recovery process. It determined that there was both anal and vaginal penetration, and that the official cause of death was head trauma. There was also a bullet found in her Mustang, an entry wound in the right thigh and an exit wound just below the right kidney. Her throat had been cut deeply from ear to ear and Monde's belt was fastened around her neck, leaving tormented minds to imagine the horrific last hours. The lungs revealed no fume contamination, indicating that she was already dead when he torched her lifeless body.

Rand's watch hung loosely around his slack wrist as he slumbered in soaked sheets. He had not eaten for ten days. The closed-casket funeral had been at the great St. Louis Cathedral in Jackson Square. Every seat was taken. There was no invitation to join the family in the first three rows, so Rand had slipped into the last pew. He felt angry glances from Reni's relatives as they sat together, holding hands, crying on countless available shoulders. It was abundantly clear that he was one of two culprits who made their sweet angel's last weeks on this planet a living hell. He was a leper. You'll pay for this.

Tears streamed steadily down Rand's cheeks. He hadn't thought to bring along tissue, so his nose ran like a river, and he could only wipe the mess with the sleeve of his dark blue suit. Through blurred eyes, he saw Christ upon the cross and the grandiose spires that rose behind the altar to the heavens, the elaborate stained glass of each window, murals on the ceiling that seemed higher than 1,000 feet. He sensed each human in the cathedral searching for answers to this incomprehensible act of brutality. Each of those searches seemed to course through Randolph Chapman.

Rand conducted his own third degree, going back to the decision to abort. That would have changed everything. Reni was afraid of the reaction that was now, an obvious act of God, the creation of a human life. It was guilt that made her afraid. Guilt and fear. Rand pictured Reni and his son walking through Audubon Park hand in hand.

Rand's was the final car in the long snake behind the black hearse to Oak Lawn Cemetery. The front seat had never seemed emptier as he drove in stunned silence. Rand put his hand on the spot where Reni had sat so many times. As the last to arrive, he got the worst parking space of all the mourners. You will pay. Rand walked alone to the burial site, where about a hundred people had gathered.

He could barely stand to watch Reni's family approach the flower-strewn coffin one by one. Finally, after everyone had passed, he moved forward on numb legs. He placed his right hand upon the varnished cypress casket and felt a wave of penetrating heat on the palm of his hand. "I love you Reni." He choked back tears, and wondered if she could hear him. "I love you, darlin'." His Ray-Bans hid swollen red eyes as he wiped his nose again with his moist sleeve. He turned away, feeling two hundred eyes upon him. Empty sorrow and a spiraling loneliness nearly tackled him to the manicured lawn. He stepped slowly through the silent crowd... and kept walking.

Mrs. DuVette watched Rand move away. *Lawd... have mercy on 'is soul.*

In a blurred dream, Rand found the SS and turned the key. When he neared the entrance, his hand was magnetized to the volume knob. Willie waited.

> Tell me that your sweet love hasn't died
> Give me one more chance to keep you satisfied

He drove the old girl back toward town and exited on Carrollton Avenue. A streetcar clanged on the track in the neutral ground. At the Riverbend, he passed the Camellia Grill and pictured the last time he and Reni were in there, laughing with the quick-witted black servers. He pushed down St. Charles and the Audubon Park came up on the right. Rand and Reni had spent countless hours there, running the paths up to the river and back to the Avenue. Some days, they would take the riverboat from the Quarter to Audubon and run back. Other days, she would act as his caddy on the park's golf course, smoking twisted cigarettes as they made the rounds, laughing in deep tranquility.

The SS continued beneath the bowers of St. Charles, Victorian ladies and plantation houses tucked behind giant oaks. Another streetcar clanged by on the tracks, the single headlight burning dimly. He stopped for a red light at Napoleon. Just a few blocks to the right was Tipitina's. Reni loved Tip's. They spent countless nights there, dancing to zydeco and all the great New Orleans bands: the Radiators, the Neville Brothers, Harry Connick Junior, the Cold, Dr. John. He pictured Reni twirling on the dance floor, hair and skirt flying. To the left lay Baptist Hospital, where they both were born. Across the street to the right was Copeland's outside patio. He pictured her there in the afternoon sun, sipping Merlot, just four weeks ago. To the left a few blocks sat Pascal's Manale, her favorite restaurant in the world. He recalled the night they stumbled drunkenly into the kitchen to ask for the famous barbecue shrimp recipe. The gregarious chef gladly obliged. Their history was so young in his mind, yet suddenly, so old.

A horn blew from behind and Rand drove on in a daze of memories. A cruel mind played back the murder scene vividly. He knew the last hours were hell, Reni screaming with disbelief after she was shot, early in the encounter. Rand pictured her with her skirt and panties ripped off, fighting for her life, and losing. How she had taken a double raping, while he punched her in the side of the head to unconsciousness and finally, to death. How scared she must have been, knowing that she was going to die.

Rand crossed Canal and found a spot on St. Philip, and with each glance, an old memory and new grief. He made his way to the apartment, popped the cork from the bird, wishing after half the bottle for the strength to stumble down to the swift river to jump in. He ripped the ringing phone off the wall and dove into a black hole.

Days later, he woke at nine-thirty. Today was the day. He was bombarded with the hopelessness of his mother's situation, his frustration with his father, the loss of his dream job. Reni was dead. Kiss was dying. Faith was non-existent.

His head throbbed as he barraged himself with questions. Why should he continue to live in this hellhole only to die painfully, sixty or seventy years down the road? He found no reason to play this stupid game, and he was sure of his decision. It was time to go.

In the bathroom mirror, his beard was two weeks past the sharp end of a razor. He was surprised by the red veins around his nose as he splashed water on his head and peered closely at an alien with his own piercing blue eyes. Rand stepped toward the dresser and kicked the severance check from the Picayune into the open.

"There you are, you bastard." He threw on Levis, brushed his wet hair back, stuffed the check into his back pocket, splashed down a straight shot of bird and headed out. Just past Lafitte's, he spotted the SS where he'd parked her after the funeral. No doubt she'd been waiting patiently to ambush him with that damn Willie Nelson song.

A voice called out to him, asking the time. He pressed on, knowing that it too, would pass. The voice yelled louder. "Señor! I asked what time is it?" She saw him pick up the pace. "Señor Chapman!"

Rand stopped. He slowly turned. Who…in the fuck? As she moved up Bourbon, her shape began to look vaguely familiar. She flashed a big smile and he made one connection. Her olive skin and shoulder-length, jet-black hair made another. The dark rose suit over heels that lifted classic beauty produced a semi-positive ID. His vision must be playing tricks. It couldn't be… "Luz?" He pulled off his Ray-Bans. "Luz, is that you?"

"The one and only!" She rammed his body with arms open and kissed him hard on the mouth. You, mi amigo, are a hard man to find."

MENA, ARKANSAS

12. Mach This

Rand pulled back to see her face and was stunned by dark penetrating eyes under thick, manicured eyebrows. Her skin in the bright light was as perfect as it had been in the heat of the night. Her Latin lips were full and her hair hung to ample breasts that funneled to a slim waist and strong legs. He felt her press against his chest. "What the hell...are you...doing...here?" He squinted, not sure that he wasn't tripping.

"I came to see you." Luz smiled. "It took a couple of days to find you...to remember the name of the bar you told me about."

"What bar?"

"Lafitte's Blacksmith. I just remembered this morning." She pointed back at the dilapidated building and the brown French doors that were boarded until cocktail hour. "You told me it was your favorite bar the first time we met."

"I did?" He struggled to find her pupils within sapphire irises.

"I have been out to the Lakefront Airport looking for you but nobody seemed to know where you live. I got your phone number from the girl at Aero Services, but there has been no answer for two days." Luz kept her arms around Rand. "She said no one has heard from you in weeks."

"She did, huh?" Rand smiled at her energy. "What else did she tell you?"

"Nothing that I did not know." Her native tongue was nearly undetectable.

His pupils were dilated and he had to put the shades back on. "And what would that be?"

"That you and the great captain have no aeroplane to fly. That your company is trying to sell the aeroplane."

"And how did we know this?" Rand smiled for the second time in three weeks.

"El Gordo told…"

"Oh yeah, Uncle El Gordo."

"That is correct. Gordo told me. He called me on the phone to come for you."

Rand peered through dark lenses. "Luz. What the hell are you talking about, my amiga?"

"I have spoken to Gordo about you many times, Rand. Last week he called me and said that your aeroplane is for sale and he put together whose aeroplane it was and he needs someone to fly the aeroplane for him." Luz ran out of breath.

"Wait…? Uncle El Gordo wants to buy the Merlin?"

"That is correct."

"And he wants me to fly it for him? Like a job? And I'd be working for… Uncle El Gordo?" Rand peered at her again, waiting for the real explanation.

"That is correct."

Rand took another step back from her intense gaze. "And where is Uncle El Gordo now?"

"Rand? Why do you start all your sentences with 'and'?" She kissed him again. "You look tired my darling."

He started to get annoyed. "Where is El Gordo? Is that better?"

"He wants to meet with you."

"When?"

"Tonight."

"Where?"

"I do not know yet." Luz didn't recognize the look on Rand's face and she wasn't sure about the beard. But the longer hair… that is a very good change for him. "Where were you going?"

"To kill myself."

She laughed. "It is a good thing I found you then." She saw a strange, serious look cross his face for an instant and her smile disappeared. "I was just trying to find the Lafitte's bar. I did not expect to see you until possibly tonight."

"Su-plize." Rand took a deep breath and realized he'd gone a few minutes without thinking about Reni. He looked up the street and marveled at the beauty of architecture from the Spanish occupation. The blue sky above perked him up like a cup of…

"Hey, Luz. Ya ever hear of Café DuMonde?"

"No sir."

"Come on." He reversed course down Bourbon to St. Louis, looking at Luz every few steps to make sure he wasn't having one of those dreams. He glanced into Pat O'Brien's courtyard with the fountain on the way to Decatur. Café DuMonde stood picturesquely across the street in front of the great levee that held back the gushing Mississippi.

"Rand?" She walked with her arm around his waist.

"Yesss?"

"Are you not happy to see me?"

He pushed her away from his hip to grab her hand and looked directly at her. "Luz. I have had a very bad month. A good friend of mine has died recently...my mother is very sick...and the great captain is also very sick now, too. I have had better times."

They crossed Decatur and were directed to a table on the patio that overlooked St. Louis Cathedral. Rand ordered two coffees and a portion of beignets.

"I have heard about your friend who was murdered."

"How?"

"El Gordo knew about it. What is a bin-yea?"

"It is a doughnut, without the hole and fried in grease, doused in powdered sugar." A reason to continue living. "They're only good when they're hot. Good groceries."

"Good groceries?"

"Sorry. Just an expression around here." His file on her opened to the first night they met. The next morning. Another reason.

Luz wore gold-rimmed sunglasses from Paris. She glanced around as a horse and buggy clip-clopped past with two large tourists on the latter. "I think I like New Orleans. El Gordo has told me much about the history here." The waitress threw down the order and smiled. "Everyone is very friendly so far." At twenty-one, she was a seasoned traveler. Her father had taken her three times to New York on buying trips and also to Spain, California and Israel.

"I am very proud to call it home." Rand took a long sip of rich chicory coffee. "Luz. It seems like you are here on a business trip?"

She leaned on the glass-topped table with a wrought iron frame and became very serious. "Well as you know, El Gordo called me...about you. He has wanted me to come up for some time now, and this was a perfect time because he is very busy and needs help."

"And he wants to buy the Merlin?" Rand asked, just to make sure he hadn't dreamed that part.

"And...yes." She smiled at him. Suddenly a beeper went off under the table. Luz grabbed her purse and pulled out a pager.

Rand had never seen the new digital units. "What in the world...? Let me see that." Numbers across the top read 09-8920128-5. "What's this?"

Luz looked at him tight-lipped. "It's him. We need to find a phone." She stood immediately with game face on.

"We do? I guess breakfast is over." Rand threw a five on the table and finished off the coffee with a big swig. "There's a phone right there."

They walked over to the payphone and Luz dug in her purse for quarters. She dumped two in the slot and dialed the number on the beeper. A pen and a small pad of paper magically appeared and her focus was a hundred percent on her business. She spoke directly into the phone. "Hey." She looked up at Rand. "Yes. He's right here." She looked down and began to write on the pad. "Okay." She hung up. The call took twenty seconds. Rand couldn't believe she hung up so soon.

"El Gordo wants to meet you tonight."

"Tonight? Where?"

"Here." She handed him the pad.

Rand looked at her and to the pad: Esler west ramp 2335-2340. "What does this mean?"

"I take it you know where Esler is?"

"Esler? The only Esler I know is an airport way up in Alexandria."

"Hey! You're catching on!" Luz grinned and planted a big kiss on his confused mouth. "Between eleven thirty five and eleven forty tonight on the west ramp."

His head began to crunch information. It was painful. He stared blankly at the pad. What the fu...? "Five minutes...?"

"Yes. If he is not there by twenty three forty, you may leave." She handed him two hundred-dollar bills. "He said to rent a plane with this."

Rand felt like an idiot at the circus. "Rent a plane?" I can do that. "West ramp at Esler?"

"You got it, my sweet amigo. I need to get going." She hastily put the beeper back in her purse and kissed him again on the mouth. "Maybe I will see you again very soon." She wiped lipstick off his face and hurried across the street and back into the Quarter while he stood still, watching unbelievingly. I must be dreaming. He opened his hand to stare numbly at two pictures of Benjamin Franklin.

Rand pushed hard on the right rudder as the Cherokee Lance climbed steadily up through 1,000 feet. The fuel-injected 300-horsepower Lycoming roared with power. With the propeller spinning clockwise in front of him, the blade on the right side produced more thrust than the left, which naturally caused the airplane to yaw to the left. The pilot's pressure on the right rudder kept the airplane flying straight. His first flight in nearly three weeks gave him a much-needed adrenaline rush. Although he had enjoyed his time in the Merlin with Hotchkiss, he missed being in command, free to fly unquestioned.

The four-hour nap in the afternoon had revived him and Rand actually cleaned up his apartment and fixed the phone before taking a swim at sunset. The night air was smooth as the city lights below the plane made a move on his emotions. He looked down at the UNO campus and Reni returned to the forefront of his mind. He was still unable to process the events fully, unable to cry.

The Lance continued to climb as he lifted the handheld mike to bid goodnight to the tower before leveling out at 1,500 feet. Following the Causeway to the Northshore, he was soon engulfed in the very dark night, glad that his only engine maintained a steady groan. Rand wasn't sure why he was flying to Alexandria, but he was happy to have something to do besides sit sipping bird all night under the curious eye of the bartender. After the lights of Baton Rouge slipped behind his left wing, he tuned in the Alexandria VOR, centered the needle and flew a 300-degree course toward his destination.

 He checked his charts for the Esler communications frequency with a penlight flashlight. The control tower closed at ten and he realized that his landing would be done without aid from ATC. Pulling the throttle to idle, he descended into the dark hole with an alternating green and white rotating beacon. He lowered the gear and flaps before touching down between white runway lights at 23:20.

Rand moved the Lance through the blue taxiway lights that led to the deserted FBO. He circled the plane around to the middle of the empty ramp, shut down the engine, opened the door and jumped to the dark ramp from the right wing. He checked his watch at 23:30. The place was shut down for the night. A sign on the door gave a phone number if fuel was needed.

Rand pulled his leather jacket over jeans and short-sleeved cotton shirt in the clear 38-degree night. The stars were out by the billions and he reminisced about his nights in the Gulf on the drilling rig's heli-pad. There was not a soul in sight within total silence. He checked his watch at 23:34.

The road from town ran uphill to the airport, and he could see headlights approach that were a good two miles away. This has… to be him. Suddenly, the car turned off the highway and continued away from the airport. Now, even if headlights were to appear again right at that very moment, Rand doubted they could make it to him by 23:40. Goddamn Luz. The plan sounded so stupid when he heard it that he wondered why he even made an effort. None of this made sense. He checked his watch at 23:37 and looked at the dark airport road. Nothing.

He took in a deep breath of the crisp air and shook his head before heading for the Lance. He heard a faint engine noise and turned back to the road. But there were no lights. He climbed up on the wing for a better view. Suddenly, and without warning, an enormous sound of rushing air began in the darkness. He saw stars disappear where the sound was. What the fuck...? Rand looked up, looking for... a helicopter?

The huge noise hovered right above him. He could barely make out the silhouette of a small chopper with no navigation lights on. A black Hughes 500 set down on the ramp out by the taxiway. Rand smiled wryly at the operation. He held his ground on the wing as he waited for the blade to wind down but the engine was left at idle and the pilot walked at a fast pace toward the Lance. Rand jumped off the wing as he watched the dark-haired man approach. He was about six feet tall and wore a Mexican wedding shirt with pockets in the front over his protruding stomach. His toes pointed out slightly as he walked quickly over to Rand with a big smile, exposing white teeth under a largish nose. Rand returned the smile. What the...

"Rand Chapman?" The voice was deep but scratchy.

"That's me." He took the strong big hand that squeezed without a shake. "Brophy Wales... Betcha thought I wasn't gonna show." He spoke above the humming engine.

"You got that right. I was getting ready to skedaddle." Rand looked into intense brown eyes.

"Nice work getting here. I have a proposition for you." He watched Rand's attention pique. "I have paid cash for the Merlin today. I need you to go get it for me and fly it to Tampa tomorrow." Wales' eyes searched the darkness behind Rand and checked for passengers in the Lance. "I hear you need a job."

"Yeah, I'm looking around."

"What kind of salary are you looking for?"

Rand was surprised by the question. "Well I was making about four grand a month before," he replied, giving himself a small raise.

Wales handed Rand a cloth sack. "Here's your first month's salary. And pay cash for maintenance and fuel for the flight to Tampa. Park it at General Aviation and take a flight back to New Orleans with cash." He handed him a beeper. "Your number is eight-two." Wales watched Rand's expression remain unchanged as he looked over a unit identical to the one that he'd seen Luz use this morning. "Keep a pocketful of quarters at all times. When I beep you, you will see my number, which is oh-nine, followed by a phone number, followed by a dash and the amount of time I expect you to take to return the call. If you see a one, it means I need to talk to you real quick. Always use a pay phone and make sure no one is looking over your shoulder." Wales grinned. He knew Rand was getting it. "When you call me back, punch in eight-two first, then your phone number without the area code. I'll know which one you'll be in. If I don't answer right away, wait by the phone until I call you." He watched Rand as he inspected the device. "Got it?"

"Got it"

"You have any jet time?"

"Jet time?" He sank a little before answering. "Uh no, just turboprops."

"Well, you will soon. By next week, you'll be flying me around in my Learjet."

"Cool. I can live with that." Rand doubted it, but just the very idea made him want to jump to the stars above. He showed none of this emotion.

"Okay. You know what to do. I'll beep you when you get back. Adiós." He hurried back to the dark helicopter and Rand watched in amazement as the craft lifted off.

Rand slid back into the Lance and started the engine before he turned on the inside dome light. He opened the bag as the engine warmed and his stomach dropped. Hole-E-Shit. There were twenty stacks of one hundred twenties. He taxied to the long runway, pushed the power up to full thrust and the Lance and Rand rushed down the runway with 40,000 U.S. dollars. Learjet? That guy is blowing smoke up my ass.

After five hours of sleep, Rand awoke and made his way out to Moisant. His maroon leather briefcase held $8,000 as he boarded the seven o'clock Southwest to Houston Hobby and the eight-thirty to Midland. The lead mechanic met Rand at the gate and drove him to the hangar, where the Merlin sat in the ready position. Rand felt guilty that he was going to fly her without even asking Hotchkiss. The bill for the engine work was nearly $6,000. He paid the hangar manager in cold cash, counting out three stacks of one hundred twenties.

Because of a high-pressure area dominating Texas and the southeast, Rand decided to forego an IFR flight plan and just go VFR. The seats sat empty and the right seat in the cockpit was too eerie to look at. He felt the ghost of Hotchkiss, unaware that Kiss had passed in the night. He paid cash for the fuel top-off under curious eyes of the FBO manager. Soon he was rocketing down the desert runway with fresh engines.

The Merlin jumped into the sky and Rand couldn't believe he was flying the ol' girl solo. He climbed straight up to 17,500 feet. Four hours later, he descended into Mobile for enough fuel to make Tampa and filed an IFR flight plan for the last leg. The fueler gave him a strange look as they watched this kid pay cash for 200 gallons of Jet-A and reboard the million-dollar airplane... alone.

Rand pushed the empty Merlin through Gulf air and touched down at Tampa International, taxied over to General Aviation and left the door key at the front desk. He got a ride from one of the rampers over to the terminal and caught the seven-thirty Eastern up to Atlanta, connected to New Orleans on another Whisperjet, and drove the SS into the Quarter by midnight. As he opened the car door on St. Philip, his beeper went off. Damn. The numbers read: 09-8929874-10.

He walked up Bourbon to the payphone just outside of Lafitte's. He dialed the number, still numb from a long day. He recognized the voice. "Rand?"

"Yeah. How did y..."

"Tomorrow. Eagle. Zero nine one five."

"Eagle? At Lakefro...." Dial tone. Rand thought they had been disconnected. He reached for the quarters in his pocket. Eagle. At nine-fifteen. That's probably all I need to know. He scanned the ever-present herd of drunken tourists on Bourbon. A man in the middle of the chaotic street leaned on a fifteen-foot wooden cross, preaching the Good Book subliminally to alcohol-soaked brains. Rand stepped into Lafitte's where a man could unwind from a long day in a dark, quiet setting. "Barkeep, please..."

As the old clock in the Eagle Aviation lobby on the far east ramp of Lakefront Airport hit nine-fifteen, a whistle-whine announced the arrival of the beige Learjet before it crossed the perimeter road. Rand's legs began to tremble slightly under dark gray slacks. He stood just outside of the open hangar doors and since it was nine-fifteen, he allowed himself to believe that this Lear was coming for him. The jet taxied onto the tarmac and swung a right one-eighty, thirty feet from the hangar. Rand recognized the same face from two nights ago in the left seat. The man waved for him to come over. He heard the left engine shut down as he approached the strange airplane with only one round window on the left side and a T-tail that shot skyward while the pointed nose tilted slightly downward. Straight wings with silver leading edges and tip tanks gave the appearance of an attack plane. The clamshell entry door opened from the top first followed by the bottom half. Out popped the man with the shape of...Jabba the Hut. Rand could see the gray at the temples today as the meaty hand grabbed his and pulled him into the jet. Rand's heart pounded and he was very glad that he had only one drink at Lafitte's before a good night's sleep. "Nice jet!"

"Get on up there." Jabba wore an I just blew you away grin. His point toward the cockpit indicated that they weren't going to sit around drinking coffee for an hour-long briefing. "No, not there." he laughed. "There." He pointed to the left seat.

Rand blushed with awkwardness as he pulled his long leg from under the co-pilot's seat and bent over to keep from bumping the overhead panel again. The yoke was nearly in the seat and there was very little room to maneuver the legs. He got his foot out of the wedge and restarted the process on the left side. Finally, he sat down in the captain's seat and tried to comprehend how he could possibly fly this strange bird. The instrument panel was half the size of the Merlin, yet all the instruments were there in miniature. The throttles looked like gadgets from a toy. As he heard a small winch lock the doors behind him, he noticed two GNS systems. Rand pushed his head against the windshield to see the nose, but saw nothing but the pavement below...very close. Again, his face rushed with adrenaline. He leaned to the left, head against the glass as if wearing a helmet, but there was no more room as the instructor groaned into the right seat.

"Damn. Tighter than duck pussy." Jabba looked over at Rand for the first time in the daylight. He saw sharp blue eyes. "Hardest part about flying this baby is getting in the seat."

Rand laughed at the comical entrance. "I hope so."

"Taxi us over to the other side of this hangar and I'll give you some 411."

Rand pushed the tiny throttles forward and the nosewheel below groaned as it turned to the left and off the ramp. He realized that only the right engine was running so he pulled back the left throttle to idle, slightly embarrassed. He stopped the airplane behind one of the aluminum T hangars. "Here?"

"Perfect." He watched Rand find and set the brake. "Okay. Today's the day. This is a Lear 23, serial number nine. The ninth Learjet ever built. You and I are gonna fly around for maybe three hours today and then you're going to take a checkride this afternoon. Tomorrow we will start a little trip together. Any questions?"

"Yeah." Rand smiled slightly. "What's your name?"

"Brophy Wales." He held out his hand again with a big toothy smile. "I told you the other night." Wales grabbed the laminated checklist, also half the size of the Merlin's, and handed it to Rand. "The beautiful thing about this airplane is that Bill Lear himself owned this one. He tried to get the FAA to certify it for single pilot use. They wouldn't buy it. So I did. That's why all the switches are on your side."

Rand's head pressed the windscreen lightly as he looked down to read switches that were labeled anti-skid, fuel pumps, anti-collision lights, pitot heat, engine heaters, hydraulic pumps, fuel transfer valves. The fuel gauges were on the center pedestal, as were the thrust reverser indicator panel and the landing gear panel. The gear handle was miniature, obviously meant to be used with the thumb and index finger. Rand held his right leg inward slightly to make room for the throttles that were uncomfortably close. He wondered how long he could sit in these tight quarters. Wales continued the lesson in his right ear.

"This is the closest thing to a rocket you will find in general aviation. Now there are two things that will kill you in this airplane: Too slow and too fast. Too slow down low on approach and takeoff, and too fast at high altitudes... although if you get too slow high, that will also kill you."

"Oh good. I was hoping you weren't going to say lack of experience." Rand continued to look around the cockpit. Jee-sus.

"Experience this. Let's crank the left engine." He reached over Rand's lap to point at the appropriate switch. "Just hold that to start and when the RPM gets to ten percent push the start lever up to idle and watch to make sure it doesn't overheat on the EGT gauge here. When I don't know jackshit about an airplane, I use the redline rule. Whatever you were doing to get to the redline, stop doing it." He saw Rand follow and understand. After the engine started, Wales called ground control and told them they were ready for taxi and a VFR departure to the southeast. Within three minutes they lined up for takeoff on One-Eight Right as Wales read the checklist aloud, pointing at the switches as he went through items. They completed the series as the tower cleared them for takeoff. "Get ready to get blown away." Wales laughed as he acknowledged the tower's instructions and told Rand to push the throttles up to ninety percent on the RPM gauge.

Throttles buried in his palm, Rand hesitated with a blast of acceleration at forty percent RPM and a sweet whine of jet power. Instinct yelled for him to stop at fifty percent after his head nearly jerked off his shoulders, but he continued to push boldly to the ninety- percent mark. When he finally was able to look down at the airspeed indicator, it clicked past 110 knots. Wales laughed out the order to rotate, which Rand did. He felt he was out on the swift moving pavement by himself, no airplane in sight. As he pulled back on the yoke, his head shot off the surface of the planet and the Industrial Canal in front of him disappeared as if a rocket were strapped to his ass. The acceleration force kept his back planted on the seat and he would have been really scared except for the comforting laughs from his co-pilot.

"Je-zus... Christ." Rand looked down to check his altitude. The swamp at English Turn was already visible less than ten seconds past lift-off. He couldn't believe Mr. Altimeter as it motored through 7,000 feet or Mr. Airspeed pushing through 250. He began a turn to the left and over-controlled the ailerons to a rough bank, before recovering smoothly for the rollout on a 120-heading as they shot through 10,000 feet. After he rolled out, Rand glanced back at the silver leading edge and nearly jumped out of his skin as he saw Lakefront Airport resemble a launch pad. A tear slid down his cheek and he turned to get back into flying the jet.

"Okay, Rand. Let's level off at 13,500." Wales knew that Luz had given him good info on this guy. He will be perfect, Gordo.

"Thirteen-five." Rand couldn't believe how sensitive the control forces were. The Merlin needed serious pressure on the yoke before it would bank. The Lear just needed a thought to the left or right and it was there. He pulled back the throttles at 13,500 to fifty percent RPM and the airspeed indicator stuck on 250 knots.

"How about a couple of steep turns to get you accustomed to the..." Brophy felt the plane begin a bank. "Let's try forty-five degrees first and then..." He laughed as the bank indicator read sixty degrees and Rand correctly pushed the throttles up slightly to compensate for the decrease in lift. As the plane sliced the air, the only moving part on the instrument panel was Mr. Clock's second hand. "Steep turn this." Wales laughed.

Rand felt crisp. He knew if he were taking a checkride today, he had better show his stuff...and fast. At the three-sixty point, Rand rolled out with a smooth, even pull on the throttles and a counter yoke push as lift returned. In a seamless operation he kept the bank coming to the left, rolling back into a 60-degree left bank, pulling back slightly on the yoke, and adding power again until another smooth rollout, pushing the yoke forward and pulling the power back. Mr. Altimeter ceased on 13,500.

"I guess I'm a pretty damn good instructor." Wales looked over to him. "The FAA guy giving you the check today will want to see steep turns, a high dive, one accelerated stall, and then it will be back to the field for a V1 cut, an aborted takeoff, an ILS, a VOR approach and a couple of landings."

"Okay." Rand watched Wales pull the throttles to idle.

"Hold thirteen five and when the stall warning horn goes off, just jam the throttles to the firewall and level the wings. It will accelerate out of the stall before you can say holy shit. Go ahead and roll into a 30-degree bank."

Rand rolled quickly into a 30-degree right bank as the nose rose with the loss of airspeed. In less than ten seconds the stall warning horn sounded and Rand jammed the throttles up. He jerked the wings level as thrust pushed him back into his seat and the airspeed jumped into a safe recovery. "Holy shit." He rode a wild animal, yet he had total control, suddenly glad the throttles were as close as they were. Brophy laughed to his right as he picked up the microphone to talk with ATC.

"Yeah Houston, Lear One Three Sierra November requests a climb to flight level three seven zero for a practice emergency descent into New Iberia, over."

"Learjet One Three Sierra November, squawk three three six two and ident."

Brophy plugged new numbers in the transponder and pushed the ident button that illuminated their target on the radar screen at Houston Center. "Identify...this."

"Lear One Three Sierra November, radar contact. I will coordinate with the high altitude sector for your climb, sir. Climb and maintain three seven zero."

"Sector this." Brophy brought the mike to his mouth and dialed in 37,000 on the alerter. "Roger, out of thirteen five for three seven zero." He jiggled the yoke and Rand released his. "Take a break." Brophy held his hand out to present the spectacular view of the Mississippi running out to the Gulf. "Enjoy the view."

They were over the end of the earth, the small Cajun town of Venice and the last paved road before a major series of bayous and swamps. A large tanker pushed up South Pass toward the Big Easy; fishing camps lined the banks amongst tall marsh weeds. Rand spotted drilling rigs on the horizon. He wanted to smile big, but the thought of the FAA checkride reeled him in a tad.

All pilots dread FAA checks. There is no guarantee that it will be fair. The FAA employs pilots that are different from the basic model, usually someone that actually enjoys reading manuals and regulations. Rand knew immediately that the oral portion of the examination could be the trick fuck. The question difficulty seemed to be in direct proportion to hours spent studying narcoleptic numbers. With increased hours, the easier the questions and the examiner. And vice versa. If the pilot performs poorly on any check, a permanent record is kept in Oklahoma City until the end of time. If extreme incompetence is detected, the examiner could walk away with his certificate altogether.

For a type rating in a Lear, it would normally take at least two weeks to prepare, with about fifteen hours of flying and many more hours in the books. It seemed crazy to Rand that he would lay his license on the line this afternoon. And he hadn't even seen the flight manual.

The acceleration pushed them tight against the seat backs and the airplane shot skyward. As they went through 18,000 and into the PCA, Wales had to remind Rand to set his altimeter at 29.92. The Lear climbed like a homesick angel straight to 37,000 feet. Rand watched Wales unbuckle his seatbelt and began to contort toward the aft. "Where ya goin', bro?"

"Here, slap the autopilot on and hold point-eight." He smiled. "Sometimes you gotta trust your autopilot."

Rand looked over at the very empty co-pilot's seat and felt immortal, high above the planet within a dark blue, euphoric stratosphere. Aviation never disappointed. He checked his groundspeed and read an unbelievable 430 knots.

Jabba sat back on the leather bench against the aft bulkhead. The 23 had only that bench, which sat two comfortably, and one more leather seat along the right side. There were two round windows on the right and one on the left. A portable toilet was under the small seat opposite the clamshell entry door. Including the pilots, the airplane could stuff six people on board, but there had never been more than two passengers since Wales bought the jet four months prior. Jabba opened a teak compartment next to his seat and pushed a cassette into the Bose system. Music took over the passenger compartment and danced into the charged cockpit.

Rand looked ahead as the Mississippi defined herself below. He could see Baton Rouge and the Atchafalaya Basin clearly. He heard music from the back of the plane as he sat alone at the highest altitude he'd ever been... and his heart sank.

> Maybe I should have loved you
> All those lonely... lonely nights
> Baby I should have held you...
> But you were always on my mind
> You were always on my mind...

Reni swung out in front of him and he was blasted by the swift reminder not to get too damn happy. Gonna get you Rand.

Wales returned to the cockpit and was glad to see Rand looking comfortable in the left seat. He had tried for months to get Camille to do one steep turn without a meander to a thousand feet off target. Most people are not meant to be pilots. Some are naturals. "Still got us blue side up, I see."

"Yeah, so far. I'm guessing at the power setting."

"Set this." Wales crawled into the right seat, careful not to kick the yoke. "You're down at about point seven- eight."

"Point seven-eight?" Rand looked around Mr. Altimeter.

"Yeah. Point seven-eight Mach. I usually cruise us at eight oh. At this weight and altitude it takes about seventy-five to eighty percent RPM to hold it." Brophy pushed the throttles up slightly and pulled out the small flight manual under his seat. "If you have any questions about the settings, they're all right here."

"Yeah, I'd like to take a little gander at that before I go steaming around with a Fed breathing down my neck." In Mr. Airspeed's small window, Rand saw .77, .78, .79, .80, .81, .82...and a wide red and white barber pole line. "Now excuse my ig-nance, but what does Mack stand for?

"Mack this." Wales laughed. "It's Mach, M-A-C-H. It is how we measure speed at high altitudes. One mach is the speed of sound, and it varies with temperature and altitude. At sea level, where the air is thick, it would take around 750 knots indicated to break Mach 1. At 50,000 feet it would only be around 300 knots." Brophy saw Lafayette come under the nose. "This airplane cruises nicely at around point eight-oh, eighty percent of Mach 1. After that things get spooky. I'll tell you more about that later." Wales checked his oxygen mask and saw that Rand's was also plugged in. "The Fed is gonna want to see a high dive...a rapid decompression drill. The trick is no matter what the hell is going on, get your oxygen mask on first." Wales reached behind his head and gave the mask a slight tug to release it from the hard plastic strap that held it. He smoothly donned it over his face and switched his mike selector to the "mask" position. "Can you hear me?"

Rand heard his voice come out of the speaker above his head. The straps leading to the back of Jabba's head dug into his reddening face. "Looks good on you."

Wales pulled the contraption off his head. "I hate that damn thing." He hung it back on the strap. "At 41,000 feet, if you get a decompression, you have about ten seconds of useful consciousness before you pass out and the jet spirals back to the planet...with your sleeping body. So it is key to slap the mask on before you do anything else."

"Roger that. Mask on first."

"Mask this. Now when he asks you to climb up to a high altitude during the check, you know what's coming. Think about the mask on the way up."

"Roger that."

"Roger this. After the mask is on, switch over to the mask position for your mike and tell ATC you have an emergency and will be descending rapidly. Pull the throttles to idle and reach over and slap the emergency code in the transponder, pop the spoilers and slow down to gear speed of point seven-eight." Brophy pointed at a silver toggle switch to the right of the throttles above the flap handle. "That will kill a lot of lift and slow the plane down fast.

Once you get below point seven-eight, you can throw down the gear without blowing the gear doors off." Wales pointed at the small gear handle. "Now in a no-shit rapid-D, I would forget about that speed and say fuck the doors. They can be replaced. But for the check, take the time to slow and then throw out the gear."

"Got it."

"Get this. Now you're set. Once the throttles are idle and the spoilers and gear are out, just push the nose down to the airspeed redline and watch this bitch come down like a ten-dollar whore." Wales enjoyed teaching. He lifted the mike. "Houston, Sierra November is ready for the high dive."

The speaker answered. "Stand by Sierra November. I'll coordinate."

"Coordinate...this." He pushed the mike key. "Roger." He looked back over to Rand. "Okay, when she clears us... that is your cue."

"Oh-tay."

After twenty seconds, the voice returned. "Learjet One Three Sierra November, you are cleared to descend and maintain one zero thousand feet."

Rand quickly put the mask over his head, snugly on his face and closed the throttles. He switched the mike selector to the mask position, clicked off the autopilot and just touched the transponder to let Brophy know he was thinking about it. He popped the spoilers, waited for the speed to hit point seven eight, pulled the gear handle and waited for the green gear-down lights to illuminate. He pushed the nose over and banked the plane forty-five degrees to expedite loss of lift. The Lear sliced downward through thin air at 14,000 feet per minute. At 13,000 feet, Rand pulled back on the yoke slightly to break the steep angle and something other than cane fields and swamp appeared in the windscreen. Within two minutes, they had fallen 27,000 feet.

"Perfect." Brophy had only seen one other rapid-D done to perfection on the first try. His. "You want another one?"

"Naw. Not unless you do."

"Naw this." Wales reported level to Houston and she switched him over to Lafayette Approach. He asked them for vectors to the ILS at Acadiana Regional at New Iberia. For the next hour they practiced approaches and power settings at the long runway with very little traffic. After four ILS approaches, and two non-precisions over sugarcane fields, the low fuel lights illuminated on the glareshield as Rand climbed out on the missed approach procedure. Wales saw the red light immediately. "Thank God. My ass hurts."

By high noon, Rand had one steep turn, one stall, a high dive and six approaches in the airplane he'd just met three hours prior. The FBO at New Iberia had a small waiting area and as the fuel truck pumped Jet-A into the tip tanks, Rand pulled out the flight manual and began to speed-read through

1,000 pages. The first quarter of the manual was devoted to performance charts on different climb weights and speeds. There were cruise tables to show the range of the airplane at different altitudes and weights. None of these pages needed to be memorized, but the captain should know where to find them. The second quarter of the manual gave a description of each of the systems. There were many changes from the Merlin to the Lear, but his prior knowledge of the complex hydraulics and anti-skid systems made comprehension fairly simple. The electric nosewheel steering system was different and the fuel transfer from the tip to main tanks would take further study. There was a drawing of each cockpit switch and light, with an explanation of its function. Rand skimmed over the text. Many of the systems listed the limitations next to the schematic. There was a limit of VMO or maximum Mach speed of .82, and a big warning box next to it: Never exceed this limit. The pressurization showed a maximum of 8.4 differential pressure in square inches between the cabin and the ambient. Speed with a cracked windscreen was 250 knots. The window heating system was strange and Rand made a note to ask Brophy about it.

The third quarter of the leather book held all the checklists: before engine-start, before-taxi, before-takeoff, after-takeoff, cruise, descent, approach, landing, after-landing and engine-shutdown. The last quarter of the manual was devoted to emergency procedures and irregular operations. On the first page was the procedure for an engine fire and failure in a checklist format. The following pages outlined procedures for smoke in the cabin, landing gear failure, hydraulic failures, and electrical problems. The less severe the problem, the further back in the book it was. The last page was the procedure for a leaking potty.

In the pocket between the two cockpit seats, Rand discovered another small book with a red plastic cover and tabs. It contained just the emergency sections of the manual. When the excrement hit the fan, this book could be whipped out and opened to the appropriate page within seconds.

Rand put the manuals down and felt a tad better about the academic portion of his crash course. The fuel truck had unhooked and he found Wales around the corner next to the restrooms rolling quarters into the payphone. Jabba spoke in rapid Spanish while he dug twenties out of his pocket for Rand to pay for the fuel.

The young girl behind the small counter raised her eyebrow sharply as Rand counted off ten Jacksons before he returned to the plane. He did the walk-around with the flight manual open in his left hand, checking the tires, oil, brake lines, engine intakes and fuel vents as per the instructions. He set the book on the potty seat and made the same rounds again without manual aid.

Rand crawled back into the cockpit and shadowboxed with the engine-failure and shutdown procedure and instant restart in the event of a flameout. He looked over the switch-description page and the new cockpit started to feel cozy as his confidence level rose. He read that the engines were made by General Electric and had the model number CJ 610. The service ceiling of the plane was a shocking 41,000 feet.

Jabba came out of the lobby forty quarters lighter in the big front pockets of his Mexican wedding shirt. He closed the entry door and crawled up to the right seat. "Your checkride is at three o'clock."

"Roger. Where?"

"Right...here." Wales opened the big binder to the tabbed pages and handed it to Rand. Little Rock, Arkansas-Adams Field. He handed Rand the High Altitude Chart. "I'm sure you know how to file an IFR flight plan."

"Oh sure."

"File us before we crank engines at forty-one."

"Forty-one?"

"Flight Level Four One Zero. We ain't fuckin' around. We'll fly over to Lafayette on one engine and shoot an ILS over there. Then we'll get the other one spooled up and sail to Arkansas." Jabba put his big arm around Rand and smiled devilishly. "I got a surprise waiting for you after you pass the check."

"Surprise? For me?"

"It'll take your mind off all the bullshit that's happened to you. And even your mother is going to see blue sky."

Rand snapped his head toward the big man with the warm, kind smile. "My mother? How do you know about that?"

"Know this. I know."

As they executed the missed approach, Rand realized he was over USL, the campus where his journey off the beaten path began. He compared his progress with that of the paved road and realized that he wouldn't trade paths for anything. "Gear up... flaps up... max power," he commanded.

Wales looked down at the river to reminisce about his past life in the tiny bayous below. This day had been a mental vacation for him, away from the constant logistical problems that Mr. Cathey had created for the past six months. Today, he was able to concentrate on something other than the guns and the Cartel and the governor and the judge and his attorneys and the CIA and the DEA handlers. He took a deep breath as the sky darkened for their entrance into the stratosphere; his personal untouchable hideout until the inevitable descent back to the cutthroats that lurked on the planet's surface. He looked over to Rand, still flying without the autopilot, and gestured toward the vast expanse outside the windscreen. "This...is Learjet country."

"It's getting dark again." Rand wondered where he was going to find strength for a checkride in less than two hours.

Wales knew that Rand had to be saturated with information. He saw his young student's energy starting to flag. Time for a booster shot. "If you had gone to Flight Safety or SimuFlight for training instead of the Brophy Special, they would have spent a whole day explaining what I'm about to tell you."

Rand told himself to suck it up. As with all long days, he began to concentrate on longer stretches of time. Tomorrow...next week. It was a method he had learned on the rigs, unloading pipe boats for twenty straight hours. Mind over matter.

"See that red barber pole on the airspeed?"

"Yes."

"Never exceed that."

"Okay."

"Mach tuck is the motherfucker of a straight wing jet." He pointed with his thumb toward the wing. "At about point eight-four that wing will separate the relative wind so that it blocks the relative wind across the T-Tail." Wales looked left. "When that happens at 41,000 feet, this bitch goes end over end, breaks into little pieces and your day is a disaster."

"Shit."

"It took the Feds two years to figure out why these Lears were disappearing from the radar at high altitude. They finally realized that pilots were popping the circuit breaker for the overspeed horn and test-flying the envelope." He looked into Rand's baby blues. "I know you're a hotshit pilot. But don't go there."

"Roger that."

Wales clapped his big hands together. "Final chapter. Descents. It's simple. Three for one. It works on every jet from the 747 to the 727 to this. A power-off descent takes three miles to descend 1000 feet. For 10,000 feet, thirty miles. For 20,000 feet, sixty miles. For 30,000 feet, ninety miles. For 40,000 feet, 120 miles. For 45,000..."

Rand waited for the mileage number before he realized that Wales wanted him to answer. "Ohh...Let's see...135."

"See this." Wales casually pointed at the DME from the Little Rock VOR. It read ninety-two and clicked down fast.

"Shit." Rand looked ahead and saw the Arkansas River winding from west to east. "Let's get a descent going."

Wales picked up the mike. "Memphis Center...Learjet One Three Sierra November ready for descent."

A male voice replied. "Oh sorry, Sierra November... Descend and maintain one zero thousand feet. You gonna have enough room to get down?"

"Affirmative." Wales watched an exhausted Rand pull the throttles back to idle with the first look of bewilderment he'd seen on his face all day. "You gotta watch these controllers. They forget how high we fly. Usually got to ask them to start down."

Rand recalculated his descent at eighty miles out and just coming through 38,000. Shit. Green rolling hills took up most of the windscreen and he saw the multiple runways in the open space just south of town. He thought about using the thrust reversers to help him down before he spotted the silver toggle switch of the spoilers. Aha. "Whaddaya think about spoilers?" He looked to Wales with sudden urgency.

"Spoil this. You figured it out." Wales smiled again. "You will get a two for one out of 'em." He watched the hand click the switch.

The spoilers popped from their flush position on the wing to straight up. The instant loss of lift nearly took Rand off his seat as the seatbelt kept him seated. "Whoa!" He grinned. "Smooth as granite."

Wales laughed. "Granite this. Next time when you go for the switch, start trimming the nose back just before you hit the spoilers...and vice versa. Try it again."

Rand proudly taxied onto the ramp at Little Rock Air Center. The high-pitched whine of the two CJ-610s died soon after he sent the engine switches to the cutoff position. Next to the entrance of Little Rock Air Center stood a burly, unshaven man who made silent eye contact with Jabba. Wales jumped out of his seat and waddled across the ramp to meet him. Rand tried to picture the big lug as the FAA designee, but it didn't compute and Wales offered no introduction. Rand moved into the lobby.

An older man, around seventy-five, with a stoic posture and a thin crop of hair combed straight back stepped over to Rand with dignity. "Are you with Mr. Wales?"

Now, this guy looks like a pilot. "Yes sir."

"Good. I'm Tack Marshall. I'm a little early."

Rand's palms began to sweat as he shook the check-pilot's hand. "Nice to meet you, sir." He had hoped to take a break for awhile, maybe drink a Coke, take a smoke. That wasn't going to happen. "Are you from Little Rock?"

"No, I just flew in from Miami. I'm an old retired Eastern pilot." He regarded Rand through bifocals. "I met Brophy on a flight a couple of months ago while I was pass-riding from Washington to Miami."

"Oh, I see." Marshall was the classic airline pilot. The man stood so straight and tall that Rand adjusted his posture to match. "Which airplane did you fly at Eastern?"

"Well, I started as a co-pilot on the DC-3 back in 1947. I flew the Constellation, the Martin, the DC-8, DC-9, the 727 and finished up on the new French airplane, the A-300. They finally kicked me out cause they said I'm too old." The blue eyes were as sharp as any twenty-year-old. "Now, I'm out here looking for anything to keep me in flying and out of trouble. I lucked out and landed a designation with the FAA." He laughed slightly at himself. "Don't know too much about these Learjets."

That makes two of us... Rand didn't add.

"The FAA was kind enough to let me go to school for three weeks on the Lear, so I'm rated in it. But that's about it."

Wales pushed through the door shadowed by the larger, unshaven man. Rand casually checked him out, and definitely spotted a gun handle protruding from the middle of his back, above his belt.

"Hello, Tack! I see you've met my hotshot captain." Wales laid it on thick. "Wish I could fly as well as he does. When's the next Whisperjet to Miami?"

"There's no non-stops from here. But the next one to Atlanta is at five."

"Perfect." Wales finally let go of the older man's hand. "You want me to play co-pilot or will you?"

"It doesn't really matter." Marshall loved to fly. "But I'd be glad to do it."

"You got it." Wales moved them all to the deserted area around the payphones. He glanced around as the large man subtly blocked traffic and reached into his pants pocket. "Thanks for coming up here." Brophy handed Marshall ten Ben Franklins. "Take good care of my airplane." He winked quickly at Rand. "I gotta run."

Marshall wanted to bow to Wales. "Oh, this is too much, Brophy."

"Not when you add in the airfare." Wales smiled with knowledge that the man still flew free with his old airline. "Don't worry about it."

The retired captain slipped the cash into his pocket. Aviation had been relentlessly good to him. "Thank you. You are much too kind." Wales handed Rand another beeper and headed for the parking lot, followed by his shadow.

Marshall found two chairs around the weather-briefing table in the pilot lounge and began to fill out the FAA forms. He checked Rand's medical certificate and airman's license before asking him to retrieve the Lear's Flight Manual from the plane, causing a quick sinker in the younger pilot's gut. Shit. Hope this guy doesn't dig too deep. Rand returned with the book wearing the façade of a man who'd been studying it for weeks and sat down at the table comfortable as a murder trial defendant.

As a check-airman at Eastern for twenty of his thirty-three years on their property, Marshall prided himself on being a pilot's pilot. As far as he was concerned, they could throw the book out of the window. A man was either a pilot or not. He was a pioneer, and it seemed to him that guys who couldn't fly were the ones who spent their careers writing manuals and trying to get promoted to chief pilot or any non-flying positions. Still, there were some things in the book that needed to be known. Marshall opened the manual. "Rand, can you tell me what your envelope is at 41,000 feet on a standard temperature day?"

Rand appeared calm as his gut churned and his palms sweated. He slid the book toward him and opened the cruise section to the page showing the envelope graph. After following the lines to 41,000 and crossing to Standard temp, he read the numbers. "Two forty-seven to two sixty-three."

"Do you find anything disturbing about that?"

"Let's see... sixteen knots." Taking his time, Rand explained slow speed stall and Mach tuck before wrapping up his conclusion expertly. "Really need to be aware of turbulence up there."

"Very good answer." Tack looked under wavy hair into eyes similar to his own. He wished he were Rand's age again, an entire career ahead. "Now tell me. What is the maximum speed at which you may lower the gear?"

"Two hundred and sixty-five knots indicated or point seven-eight mach."

"And the flaps?"

"Two-twenty for eight degrees, one-eighty for full."

"What would you do if you were just climbing out after takeoff and the left engine made a tremendous noise and exploded?"

"Well, I would pull the left throttle back to idle and move the engine lever to cutoff. Then..."

Marshall put his hand up to stop him. "Good. Let me just add this: Fly the airplane." He peeled the glasses from his face. "Fly the airplane. I've seen guys get so caught up with the emergency that they forget to fly the darn airplane. There have been so many accidents because guys get distracted. A couple of years ago, we had an L-1011 coming down to Miami from LaGuardia. When they went to put the gear down, one of the green gear lights had burned out. The captain elected to go out over the Everglades to cycle the gear. There they were at night monkeying around with the twenty-cent light bulb while none of them watched what the airplane was doing. Turned out that they all thought the autopilot was still engaged when it was not. They killed 200 people when they crashed into the swamp."

Rand had heard about the crash. "Wow. Unbelievable."

"Now, how much time do you have as co-pilot on this plane?"

Rand suffered another sinker. "Uhh...none."

"Good for you. I always hated being a co-pilot. I'd rather be a captain on a J-3 Cub than co-pilot on a 747." The man never loosened his tie and his coat remained crisp on his straight back. He rose. "Now, I've never flown the 23 models before, just the Learjet 25. Let's go scare the hell out of each other." He strutted out to the waiting plane, took off his jacket and sat in the right seat, the tie still tight.

For the next hour, Tack Marshall enjoyed the beautiful day in the wonderful flying machine. He gave Rand the required V1 cut and two approaches followed by a high-dive. When they leveled at 10,000 feet, Rand took off his oxygen mask. Marshall had seen enough and held his thin hand out and over to the left seat. "Congratulations, young man, you are the world's newest Learjet captain." he smiled. "Great job. Now, if you don't mind, I would like to shoot a few landings."

"Help yourself." Rand felt a thousand pounds of pressure release from his chest. Euphoria instantly replaced tense apprehension as he handed over the yoke to the man who loved airplanes.

The veteran pilot savored each second of stick time as he would sips of fine French wine. He flew with aged hands that had captained thousands of planes over millions of sacred miles before signing Rand off an hour before the five o'clock to Atlanta. By midnight, he lay in bed under a full Miami moon. A gentle breeze rustled banyon leaves as Tack Marshall slipped contentedly to peaceful sleep.

Rand had the linemen put the Lear away and felt the joy of accomplishment in securing his first type rating. He looked for a suitcase that wasn't there. He pushed the glass door open and the young receptionist yelled his name before handing him a note. It read: Excelsior Hotel downtown. He grabbed a taxi and sat drained as the driver made his way through the spread-out streets of downtown Little Rock. Rand noticed the governor's mansion and the dome of the capital building before he threw the black man a cool twenty. He felt strange checking into the hotel empty-handed and alone.

After purchasing a toothbrush, toothpaste and comb from the hotel gift shop, Rand entered a suite that Wales had secured. He lay on the bed exhausted, yet charged. He looked at the phone to share euphoria. And real life attempted to backhand him across the face. The creepy claustrophobic hotel feeling started to make him think about... "No!" He jumped to his feet and stripped naked before entering the sweet hot shower. He redressed into the same clothes. The phone rang as he laced his tan shoes. "Hell-o."

"Did you have to suck his dick?"

"Just once. It went real good. You're the instructor of the year."

"Instruct this." Wales was instantly Rand's best friend. "Good job. And all good deeds are rewarded. Look in the drawer under the phone."

Rand opened the drawer. "Whoa." It was filled with twenties and he spotted a few Ben Franklins.

"When the mall opens in the morning, take your co-pilot to buy a suitcase and fill it with enough to last for at least two weeks. We have work to do."

"My co-pilot?"

"I told you I had a surprise for you." Wales smiled from his suite on the top floor. "Sit at the far end of the bar downstairs and you can meet in ten minutes. You will need a briefing before you go flying tomorrow." He smiled again. "Expect to move in the afternoon. I will find you around noon." The line went dead.

Rand put the phone down and pulled paper from the night table. There were 400 Jacksons and fifty Ben Franklins. He piled them on the bedspread and inhaled the euphoric waft of fresh cash and tossed two handfuls in the air. "Shit hot!"

Rand passed the piano player as he entered the dimly lit lounge amid steady chatter of the seven o'clock crowd. He looked toward the end of the bar, but there were only well-dressed older couples waiting for tables in the adjacent restaurant. Two end stools became vacant and he sat down to search the crowd for…my co-pilot. He wondered what type of captain he would be as he ordered a word with the bird.

A hormone-agitating thread of perfume entered Rand's system at groin level as a figure in a dark blue dress slid onto the stool next to him. This co-pilot may have to wait a spell. Outlined in candlelight was shiny dark hair, full lips painted red, and a spectacular come-to-mama bosom. It took a long second for Rand to recognize her as she turned toward him. Her sapphire eyes beamed excitement, partly because she also had passed a checkride today for her U.S. private pilot rating, and partly because tomorrow she'd be starting her new position in the company.

"Hello, my sweet captain."

13. Instant Captain

The sun cooked the rotating planet as noon approached the mid-Atlantic. The Chinese snored under a full moon, as did Vietnamese rice farmers within their scarred countryside. Time's paintbrush swept an unfinished masterpiece for future historians to marvel in finger-pointing fascination.

Rand woke in an avalanche of down pillows after a long deep sleep. He checked the bright silhouette around a thick white blind and tried to believe where he was and what had transpired yesterday. Luz...a pilot? My...co-pilot? As he went over her story of what was happening in the rugged woods of western Arkansas, Rand tried to picture the flight school she described, where she evidently logged forty hours of flight time in just over ten days. She also had passed her written test with a near-perfect score. They had proudly displayed temporary airman certificates to one another during a round of cocktails; his with LRJET printed boldly under ratings and hers with Private Pilot, multi- and single-engine ratings. He needed this quiet moment to absorb information that had been presented with birds flying over a hundred-dollar dinner. He sweated slightly as he recalled what Wales had authorized her to divulge.

"Tomorrow you will see the beehive," Luz had whispered to him in the noisy bar.

"Beehive?"

"Yes. Mena."

After three birds removed the monkey wrench from his aching lower back, adrenaline had flowed smoothly through Rand as he celebrated his greatest day in aviation. "Mena. Who the hell is Mena?" He nearly slurred.

"Ssshhhh."

Rand reeled back. "What?"

"Never talk about this too loud. Mena is where our operation is based. It is where we are training the Contra pilots to defeat the Sandinista Army."

"The Nicaraguans?"

"Exactly."

"Oh good." Rand whispered. "I thought we were running drugs or something."

Luz pulled back, unsure of how much Brophy had told him. "You will have to ask El Gordo about that." She tried to understand the blank stare he now gave her.

"How many pilots are we talking here?" Drugs. I knew it. The entire day was a drink of water from a fire hydrant.

"Dozens. Fifty maybe."

"And you? You were part of this flight school?" Rand raised an eyebrow.

"I was the first one to graduate." She was proud.

"So can you fly?"

"You will find out soon enough." She'd definitely been bitten by a huge flying bug. "I love it." Her eyes sparkled in the light of a bar candle. "El Gordo told me to tell you that he only had to give my designee two Ben Franklins. But he gave your guy ten." She laughed as he mocked huge surprise.

"Oh, so that's what you are. I will make a note of your behavior. You can be very smart." He reached to his shirt pocket for his pen.

She put her hands around his neck. "It has been a long time, my captain." She felt him pull back slightly and a warm flash bolted across his back where she held him.

Someone had slipped a quarter into the juke. The first song of ten selections broke the quiet chatter. Willie Nelson's voice chilled the new captain.

> Maybe I should have loved you
> All those lonely, lonely nights
> Tell me
> Tell me that your sweet love hasn't died

"You hungry?" Rand quickly stood and carried his drink while Luz walked beside him into the dining room. They were escorted to a white linen tableclothed booth. He let her slide around the red padded seat before he sat to face the door. "Now. I'm trying to envision a flight school out in the woods of western Arkansas, teaching a rebel air force to fight a war against the present leaders of Nicaragua."

"Okay."

Rand half-expected her to tell him how absurd the last statement was. She peered at him as if to ask for more. "And does the FAA know about this flight school?"

"I doubt it."

"You doubt it." He was the prosecution. "What type of airplanes did you train in?"

"A Cessna Titan and a Cessna 182."

"And who was your instructor?"

"A guy named Nevada signed me off, although my instructor was a guy named Vermont." Luz answered loyally.

"Nevada and Vermont? The Vermont guy…was he an American?"

"Oh no. He is Nicaraguan. He does not speak English. I believe Nevada is an American."

"Ah-ha. And the designee gave you two checkrides… today?"

"Yes. The one in the Titan for about an hour and just three touch-and-go landings in the 182."

"Are the other guys also going to get FAA certificates?"

"I doubt it. No. They do not speak English."

"How many airplanes do they have out there?"

"Five Titans and the 182."

"Where?"

"There is a field out there northwest of Mena. It is hidden deep in the hills and it looks just like the mountains of Nicaragua. The place is called Nella." Luz looked around quickly. "But I took my check from a designee in Mena. El Gordo had me fly the Titan over here after the check."

Rand had stared at her for a long three seconds. "And who's paying for all of these airplanes… and the training?"

Luz scooted close to him in the booth. "This is where things get a little crazy. There is a new law that prevents the support to the Contras from the U.S. Government. It is called the Boland Amendment. The CIA is taking it upon themselves to bring the rebels back into power."

Rand comically saw himself spit his drink half way back to New Orleans. The See-Eye-Eh. "Back?"

"That's right. This is the same party that was thrown out with Somoza."

Rand's radar had swept all day, trying to figure the strange activity. Like most of the world, he had just learned there was an intelligence agency, filled with spies, run by the government. "The CIA is running this?"

"No. That is the technical question. They are overseeing the operation. Advising."

"And paying for it?"

"I do not think so. This is what El Gordo has been working on."
"With drugs?"
"Rand, I really do not know all the details."
"Okay. One last question. Who were the other instructors at Nella?"
"Who were they? A guy named Montana and another named…Kansas."

    With birds buzzing his brain, Rand had been intrigued by his new co-pilot's revelations. But now, in the light of day, suspended in an impossibly soft bed, he remembered the old cliché: If it's too good to be true…

    Rand showered and met Luz in the lobby for their trip to a downtown mall to shop for a suitcase and a week's worth of wardrobe. Two hours later, with new Tumi in hand, Rand wore a new pullover golf shirt and pre-washed Levis as they entered the Excelsior's lobby. Luz carried a new briefcase. The beeper went off and he found a bank of payphones behind the lobby bar. He fished a dime and dialed the number from the pager.

    After one ring, Wales picked up. "Finished at the mall?"

"Yes."

"Air Center at one five zero five." Dial tone.

    Rand again thought for a second about redialing as the hammer hit him over the head. Get a clue. They were already packed and he stuffed the cash into the new briefcase. At three o'clock the new duo was on the ramp with a fully fueled Learjet. Rand had a warm body in the right seat to make his flight legal and he told her to get the ATIS.

"Okay, my captain. I will get the ATIS."

    Rand shook his head and hoped this career wasn't going to be him as Ricky Ricardo and Lucy as his co-pilot. He shook his head with slight disbelief as she searched for the radio in the strange cockpit. He'd never seen any pilot with lipstick.

    Luz finally found the radio on the center console between the two seats. "Oh there you are." She checked the Adams information page and dialed in the correct frequency.

    Rand cut his eyes behind a new set of dark wrap-around shades. He had figured that if he was going to be a spy, the least he could do was look like one. The sight of Luz in this cockpit was light-years from resolution in his squeaky brain. He watched her daintily pull a hotel note pad from her purse and place it on her kneeboard before the purse disappeared into a tidy hole behind the seat. A fucking purse… in the cockpit. She began to write the ATIS clearly on the pad.

    Rand was amazed that this seemed to be no big deal to her. He was very glad that the plane was designed to be flown single-pilot with all the essential switches buried under his left thigh. "Okay, Luz. I will work the radios until we get to cruise. There is a different terminology in the IFR world. I will try to teach phraseology as we go along." Rand was a thirty-handicapper giving swing lessons. "I will handle the jet mostly for now as I introduce your duties." He looked at her as she smiled at him. He drew his head back to overcome the shock every time he saw her in his cockpit and bumped his head on the windscreen. "Today, just after takeoff, I'm gonna call for gear up and flaps up. When I do, I want you to grab this gear handle." He reached over to put his index finger on the small handle. "Pull it out slightly and move it to the up position." He watched her stare at it. "Then, take this flap handle and move it to the zero position." He pointed to the handle that was now at zero and shadowed his hand from the eight to zero position. "Got it?"

"Yes, my captain. This is like the Titan." The purse was back on her lap and she dug to China in it. She came out with dark French glasses with pure gold rims. She placed them on her face. "Ahh. This is much better." She looked past her captain's cynical eyes. "Oh, here's El Gordo. He is with the governor's brother."

Rand turned to see a Mercedes sedan parked at the gate. He saw Jabba close the passenger door and begin his waddle across the ramp as the driver drove away. Wales wore dark gangster Ray-Bans and another Mexican wedding shirt with a large open collar; front pockets weighted with quarters. As Wales climbed the steps, Rand cranked the right engine and called for taxi. "Roger sir, Runway Four Left." Rand acknowledged with the ground controller and rechecked his chart for the correct taxiways.

Wales knelt next to the potty seat and stuck his head into the cockpit. "Let's just launch VFR to the west, over to Mena. It's about a hundred miles. Sixteen-five is a perfect altitude anyway." Wales smiled at Luz. "Have you ever seen a better looking co-pilot in all your life?" He grabbed Rand's right shoulder before he retreated to the rear.

Rand rechecked all the switches mentally as the entrance to the runway neared. He hoped he hadn't forgotten anything when he remembered that there was a checklist for all that stuff. Yeah, the checklist. A great relief hit him. "Luz? Will you grab that checklist and read from the left side. Make sure I answer correctly, exactly what is printed on the right side." Rand watched her grab the laminated list as if it were a moon rock. "Hey, why don't you put the flaps down to eight degrees."

Luz methodically moved the flap handle to the eight-degree mark. "Okay?"
"Perfect."
"The before-takeoff checklist?"
"That's the one."

"Flaps?"

"Eight degrees and set."

"Anti-skid?"

"On and checked."

Luz looked for the anti-skid. "Where is that?"

"They're all over here." Rand pointed to the switches out of her view on the left sidewall.

"Oh, okay, let us see. Anti-ice?"

"Off."

"It says here 'on slash off.'"

"Yeah, well, we don't need it today." Rand motioned with his right hand to keep it rolling.

"Okay. Navigation?"

"It's set."

"Pee-tot heat?"

Rand laughed. "Hon, that's pronounced pee-toe."

"Pee-toe heat?"

"It's on."

She looked over. "What is this pitot heat?"

"It heats up the airspeed probe outside, so it doesn't freeze up if we go through ice in the clouds."

"Okay. Thrust reversers?"

"Armed for abort."

"Spoilers?"

"Confirmed down."

"That is it."

Rand felt like he'd just pulled a tooth as he picked up the mike. "Adams... The Learjet One Three Sierra November is ready on Four Left."

"Roger Sierra November. Are you going VFR?" The controller seemed surprised.

"Affirmative. We will depart to the west."

"Okay. You are clear for takeoff."

"Cleared for takeoff on Four Left, Sierra November." Rand hung the mike on the holder to his left. He moved out onto the runway and cut his eyes at Luz. "You ready girl?" He glanced at her again before switching on the strobes and landing lights as he guided his rear end over the centerline and advanced the throttles up to ninety percent. He felt delicious power as the jet began to rocket down the runway; the intoxicating rush of gravity forces were as strong as the day before. In a blink, the plane moved through one hundred knots. He glanced quickly at the engine gauges and briefly at the airspeed indicator as it went through 105. He pulled back and the jet launched at a 25-degree angle.

"Gear up, girl." He swallowed. "And flaps up." There was no movement from his right as the jet pushed through 1,000 feet. "The gear?" No response. Rand finally reached over and raised the gear and the flaps himself. He wanted to laugh when he saw her neck bent to the right, mouth open. Gravity forces pushed her back into the co-pilot's seat as the green trees of Arkansas shrunk out of view like she'd been shot out of a cannon. Rand instantly remembered his first shot out of the Merlin, but he'd expected it...and it wasn't a Learjet either. He laughed.

"Ay yi..." Luz mumbled in Spanish. "Magnifico!" She looked at Rand as if they were sitting in the back row of the Concorde. The Lear smoked out of 5,000 feet at 250 knots. As Rand ran the speed up to 300 knots at 10,000 feet, she tried to fathom that she was now traveling twice faster than the Titan cruised and climbing at 4,000 feet per minute. Ay yi.... At 15,000, she finally looked over to Rand as tears streamed down her cheeks. "I can not believe this." She turned as Wales poked his head into the cockpit and Rand leveled off at 16,500.

"Whaddaya think about my little baby?" Wales saw the tears. "What happened?"

"I am sorry, I had no idea about this plane." Luz dug in the purse for a Kleenex.

Wales looked at Rand. "You didn't brief her?" He shook his head, grinning.

Rand laughed. "She'll be fine." The captain was more concerned about the briefing she had given him. Rand saw that he was already just forty-five miles from Mena and he pulled the throttles to idle before pushing the nose down. He wondered what evil creatures lurked on the surface below. "Starting down." He moved the pressurization to sea level.

"Starting down... already?" Luz looked over to the DME. "Ay..." Rand and Wales laughed aloud as she enjoyed being blown away.

Brophy turned serious. "Rand. After you land, taxi to the north side of the field. There will be a large gray hangar. Taxi with enough steam to coast into the hangar with both engines shut down. They will close the door behind us."

"Okay, Batman."

Inside the hangar, Wales popped the door. "Go ahead, give him a big kiss for that landing." He grabbed Rand's shoulder again. "File us a flight plan for Pueblo, Colorado."

"Roger that."

Luz looked at Rand with glazed eyes. "That was the most beautiful experience of my life. I will promise to be a better co-pilot for you next time, captain sir."

Rand left Luz in the cockpit to familiarize herself with a hundred switches and moved to a small hangar office to place an 800 call to the FAA briefer. He was immediately put on hold. Rand looked around the strange hangar. Dozens of crates were stacked against the back wall. He spotted an older couple who paced with furtive glances, puffing on Marlboro reds. He saw the same large guy that had met the plane in Little Rock come down the stairs and exit the hangar with a satchel in hand.

Rand filed a flight plan for Pueblo at 39,000 feet and moseyed over to check out the crates. One had been pried open. His heart threatened seizure as he saw the cool handle of an M-16 rifle. Hole-E-Shit. His face flushed with estimation of a thousand guns and stepped back.

"Can I help you?" It was the older man with hard creases in his face and neck. The glasses he wore were slightly rose-tinted.

The nicotine smell made Rand back away slightly and his scrotum told him that danger was very near. "Help me? I'm beyond help," Rand quipped. "Naw, I'm just waitin' for Bro." The man didn't change expression. "You work around here?"

"I wouldn't go too far from your plane. Please don't go snoopin' around my hangar."

"Oh, sorry. I think we'll be leavin' soon." Rand smiled. "Sorry." He watched the man return to another small, enclosed office with a tiny window he hadn't noticed before.

Brophy came back down the wooden stairs from the loft holding a maroon Samsonite. "Ready?"

"Yes sir."

Wales threw the bag in the back of the plane just as an Alfred E. Newman double appeared from the ramp. Brophy's face stiffened slightly with the surprise visit from Mr. Cathey. They stepped outside together. After four minutes, the hangar door slid open with a small lawnmower-engine assist. Everybody except Alfred E. followed Brophy's order to push the Lear out of the hangar. A fuel truck appeared and topped off the tanks. Wales looked at Rand. "Let's go flying."

"Thought you'd never ask." Rand wanted to be dumb as possible.

Twenty-two minutes later, as Rand leveled off at Flight Level 390, Luz turned to him with eyes agog. "I am living a dream. This is in no way a real experience. We are at thirty nine thousand feet?"

Rand smiled at her. "Yes ma'am."

"Did your Merlin fly like this?"

"Nowhere close. We topped out at about 20,000 and top speed was about 340."

"Rand!" Wales yelled. "Can you step back here?"

He turned around. Fuck... no! And leave her...up here by herself? "Uhh..." He pointed at Luz behind her back, but Wales smiled and waved him to come on.

"Okay, hon." Rand gave instructions as he climbed out of the left seat. "The autopilot's on and the navigation is tracking direct to Pueblo. If the controller calls us, let me know." Don't touch a fuckin' thing he didn't add before moving to the aft next to Wales.

"How's it going?"

"We're still airborne." Rand looked out the window for comic effect.

Wales smiled behind gangster Ray-Bans. "We're filed for Pueblo?"

"Yep."

"Start the descent to Pueblo and when you get below 18,000, cancel IFR and shoot over to Santa Fe.

"Okay."

"Land there and taxi to the east ramp. I need to make a phone call."

"Okay."

"Then file us for Bakersfield and top off the tanks." He took off his glasses. "By the time you get fueled, I will be ready. When we get to about 10,000 in the descent into Bakersfield, I want you to cancel IFR again. Look on your chart around Santa Barbara and find the Santa Ynez airport just northeast in the mountains.

"Okay."

"Drop me off there and swing down the hill and park at Signature Aviation at Santa Barbara. Check into the Biltmore in Montecito."

"Montecito?"

"You've heard that money talks and bullshit walks?"

"Yeah."

"There is a lot of talking going on in Montecito."

"I will check in with you sometime tomorrow." He handed Rand another beeper. "This is a big meeting I'm going to tonight. Serious power brokers."

"Yeah?"

"It doesn't get any higher. You know they want to hang this fat boy in Florida."

The rest of the day was clockwork. Wales stuffed the payphone with quarters in Santa Fe and left the suitcase in the airplane while a lineman pumped Jet A into the tip tanks. The stop took twenty minutes before they launched further west.

A high-pressure area hovered over central California on the descent into Bakersfield as Rand and Luz scanned desert mountains and Death Valley. Rand punched Santa Ynez coordinates into the GNS and the controller seemed surprised when Luz cancelled the IFR plan. She was trusted with dialing 1200 in the transponder for VFR flight as Rand leveled off at 16,500 for five minutes before pulling the throttles to idle for the descent into the short valley runway at Santa Ynez. Wales ducked into a Suburban as Rand restarted the left engine. The Lear ate most of the 2,800 foot runway and jumped over the coastal mountains to a panoramic view of the Pacific. In one short day, they had easily moved from the hills of Arkansas to the California coast.

Rand shook the yoke to indicate he was handing Luz the airplane. "Hold 230 knots and about a 200 heading." Rand instructed calmly.

"Yes, my captain."

She banked toward the coastline, which surprisingly ran east and west at this point in California. Also to Rand's surprise, Luz actually had a good set of hands. Rand reached over and took her hand. "Slow, easy turns, barely feeling the adjustments, girl."

"Okay my captain. I will try." Luz made a cool 30-degree bank before she rolled out softly to the south.

"Beautiful!" Rand smiled big at her and caressed her soft neck. He pulled her toward him and kissed her cheek. "And you are beautiful."

"This is a dream, my captain."

Rand worked the throttles and talked her through the approach and landing at Santa Barbara. The FBO put the Lear to bed and called a cab from the elegant Spanish-style terminal building. A red taxi pulled up and the pilots threw their bags into the trunk. The driver was deeply tanned. "Where to… dude?" The voice was breathy and eyes were at half-mast.

"The Biltmore in Montecito."

"Cool. Not a problem."

14. Inside Job

The Maestro's second home featured one bedroom, a full bath, living room, dining room, office, galley and a two-man cockpit. After cruising at 41,000 feet for the past three hours, the $25 million chariot touched down softly in twilight on Runway Two-Five at Santa Barbara Municipal. Dual, aft-mounted Rolls Royces taxied with a song of sweet success after a .86 Mach push from deep in the heart of Texas to the rich Mediterranean climate of Santa Barbara. Tax-deductible remains of pheasant and caviar were stashed within the waste system of the new Grumman Gulfstream III as the Maestro peered through his large oval window to the green coastal mountains, searching the ramp for familiar jets under corporate umbrellas.

His Skull and Crossbones orchestra was a yet-unknown collection of all-stars, drawn from the ranks of fourth generation Ivy League lawyers, bankers and chief financial officers. Their legal capture of key government seats to strategically manipulate green lights for huge insider corporate deals would produce a symphony of wealth.

It was the new regime in Nicaragua that was causing deep concern for the Skulls Ohio delegation. The exile of their dictator was beginning to threaten the cheap labor that they had enjoyed for decades. The high profits from rubber trees for the tire industry of Ohio were beginning to skid and the profits from imports of sweet fresh fruit were beginning to sour. Countless billions were in danger without the dictator there to keep workers in line. The new leaders were improving education and healthcare dramatically. The literacy rate was climbing. Obviously, if something weren't done, cancer would someday invade in the form of organized labor. That can not happen.

Over the past ten days, the cream of corporate jets had connected the Maestro's home base in White Plains, New York to oil deals in Bahrain to Shanghai to Alaska to the Permian Basin. On this trip to Santa Barbara, the Maestro began to re-focus on other areas of wealth maintenance.

The Gulfstream's captain and first officer dragged with jetlag while the Maestro had adjusted nicely on his king-sized bed, under perpetual care from his young Japanese attendant. He had showered after dinner and had slipped into a comfortable pair of Wranglers. The new Texas façade called for eel-skin Tony Lamas boots.

He was in fine form as he descended the forward airstair into dim light. With Rolls Royces winding down, the Gulfstream's lone passenger crossed red carpet to duck into the back of a black Cadillac limousine. The limo and its non-verbiage driver moved quietly to the 101 and slipped into Hope Ranch through a coded iron gate to a mile-long driveway, past horse stables, the caretaker's residence and pool house to the main residence. Doors opened and closed silently behind him until he reached the massive ocean room with opened French doors and Italian rugs. One man stood on the lanai, peering into the fresh night. He wore a traditional Mexican wedding shirt.

"Mr. Wales."

The smuggler turned and entered the room to shake a manicured hand. "Maestro." The men took padded leather seats.

"Mr. Wales, let's get started. It is evident that we both have a problem." Soft palms clasped together. "We have allowed the importation of destructive drugs into our great nation. From what I have gathered, you were a main facilitator of transportation." Wales nodded. Cathey had advised him to listen very carefully to this man. "My problem lies, quite frankly, within another area of your arena."

"My arena?"

"Nicaragua. Our intelligence has discovered"...the ultimate tool to scare the bewildered herd..."that Communists are trying to get a foothold in the region." He paused to drive home his point. "It wouldn't be prudent to let this happen to our national security."

Wales almost laughed aloud. "Of course not. What can I do?"

"Your cooperation to date has been noticed and appreciated. I have arranged your requested meeting tomorrow in New Smyrna Beach with another airplane broker who has a C-123 for sale. You will offer him an even swap for the plane and the Merlin."

Swap this. "That's not a very good deal."

"Mr. Wales, I believe that you are not in the best position to negotiate for a few dollars."

You arrogant fuck. "And what am I guaranteed in this deal?"

"You are guaranteed that there are no guarantees. But I can tell you this in confidence: If you play straight with us, there will be no jail time for you."

Guarantee this. "That's what I keep hearing."

As Wales departed, another limo, non-verbiage driver and passenger made its way toward the West Coast compound. The Maestro quickly shifted to his financial numbers. Using well-placed Skulls, the Maestro had directed an obscure bill to pass Congress that allowed savings and loan companies to reduce the legal home-loan assets from eighty percent to sixty percent. All loans at S&Ls would continue to be guaranteed by the federal government though taxpayer contributions. He had dispatched Skulls to Texas, Florida, California and Colorado to organize developers for commercial buildings. The VP's son just happened to make investments in two federally backed S&Ls, one in Florida and one in Colorado. Miraculously, new grandiose projects were funded without a federal inspection of feasibility. Miraculously, the developers were paid in advance. Miraculously, the developers lost interest in their projects and fled with the advances, forcing the S&Ls to take back investment properties as real estate-owned, or REO.

The Maestro's next appointment was from the Appraisal Institute of Chicago. The credentialed suit was scheduled to meet tomorrow with a California Skull, deeply invested in three S&Ls. A million-dollar briefcase would convince him to assess the REOs in a prudent manner for the S&L's audit team. This would contribute to the transfer of a half-trillion of taxpayer earnings into the coffers of the new dynasty; enough to pay every public school teacher in America $80,000 for five years! Instead, more GIIIs, yachts, ranches, palaces and elections would be bought for the oligarchy that would soon control the world. The Gulf of Ka-Ching began to spread.

But it was the Master Plan that absorbed most of the Maestro's enthusiasm. The new frontier of black gold in the Permian Basin of west Texas held the keys to the kingdom. In 1951, the insightful last generation of Skulls had voted to slip a dozen members and their families into Good Ol' Boy country to become Good Ol' Boys, a formidable task for soft-palmed Yalies. Posing as wildcatters, this faction, under the discreet direction of the Skulls' Wall Street branch, had maneuvered into control of key oil drilling companies and supply outfits.

The VP had been in the first wave dispatched to the Permian Basin. Ludicrous as two men in a bull suit, this group had learned to throw money, backslap and talk like Texans. Yet all similarities ended when they boarded private planes to vacation in Kennebunkport and Palm Beach before returning to Yale, Harvard Business School, and hard-to-find military placements. Before long, under piles of cash, they would all start running for office, from West Texas to Miami. Other Skulls had sights set on National Security, Attorney General, the FBI, Securities Exchange, congressional seats from Alaska to Florida, and perpetuation as Director of Central Intelligence.

The Skull business branch had reached CEO positions at large northeast banks and was expanding strategically toward the endless Black Gold mines of the Middle East. The judicial branch had produced a dozen strategically-placed life-members on federal benches. The key political branch was proceeding on schedule with the ascent of a Connecticut Skull into the office of VP. They were just a heartbeat away from a position to appoint members from the Supreme Court to court jester. The legal unarmed robbery of America was in progress.

Something's happenin' here.
What it is...
ain't exactly clear…

15. FREEDOM FIGHTERS

The stoned cabby drove slowly as darkness began to veil paradise. On the 101, Luz could see the lights of Santa Barbara stretch into the hills. She reached for Rand's hand and once again felt his palm sweat. He stared blankly out of the window to his right. The driver exited toward the ocean and meandered through a thick stand of Eucalyptus before turning up the beach road and under the covered entrance to the Biltmore. As he handed the cabby a twenty and told him to keep the change for an eleven-dollar ride, Rand struggled with a decision. He wasn't ready. He wanted to get separate rooms but that didn't seem right, either. The decision was made for him.

"There's only one room left, sir. A Mr. Wales made a reservation for you." The receptionist looked over an index card. "And it's a good thing. We have been sold out for two weeks."

Rand peeled off three Franklins and got back a fifty. A bellman led them into a room with a huge bed and a sweet balcony that allowed audio from the crashing surf beyond the manicured lawn and swaying palms. Rand slipped him a five for the effort. Luz reluctantly turned to Rand in awkward silence. He looked away as anxiety entered his gut. "Drink?" He turned back to her with a slight smile.

"Yes." Luz stood frozen in the middle of the room.

"Whaddaya think? At the bar or here?" Rand opened the sliding glass door and was barraged with flashbacks from a very sweet day in Destin. Don't go there.

"It does not matter."

Rand closed the door quickly and moved away from the window. "I think the bar."

"The bar will be good." Luz watched him fidget toward the door. "I will meet you down there. I would like to first take a bath." She eyed the sunken marble bathtub with golden fixtures and luxurious soaps.

"Okay. See ya in a few."

Rand was on his third bird when Luz came down. She was relaxed and again her perfume attacked. He couldn't believe that he did not want to go there. *I am one… fucked-up… puppy.* "Hello, you."

"Hello my captain." Luz counted three plastic stir-sticks on the varnished bar. "How are you?"

Rand's eyes locked on her full lips. But something held him by the back of his collar. Something damn strong. His hand trembled as he took a big sip. "What a day, huh?"

"It was a great day. A long day, too."

"All great days should be long." He smiled until he remembered where he'd heard that before. "One more." Rand pointed to the drained crystal. "Oh, and…" He looked over to Luz.

"I will have a California Merlot."

The bartender pondered the Merlot selection as he reached for the bottle with a bird on the label. "How about a V. Sattui?"

"I have never heard of that one."

A guitar had been playing softly on the sound system. Now the instrumental was over and a new song began without introduction. It was a big hit nationwide.

Bam. He glared into his new cocktail.

Luz watched the bartender pour the wine and noticed Rand didn't wait for a toast to begin on his fourth bird. She took a sip and Rand continued to stare down at the bar. "I am very tired, my captain. I think I will take this up to the room."

"Okay." He snapped out of a trance with visions of a deep gash across the throat. *Shit.* "I'll be up in a few." Two more bird strikes and he stumbled up to the room to pass out without a touch to the body that slept beside him.

Rand and Luz were studying the Lear's flight manual in the quiet Biltmore restaurant when his beeper went off. He stood instantly and found a payphone in the airy lobby. He dialed and got a quick answer.

"Are you in the lobby?"

"Yep."

"You wearing a blue shirt and tan shorts?"

"Yep." How'd he know...that?

"And sandals?"

Rand wheeled around and saw Jabba at the next phone looking down at his feet. "You bastard." He hung up the receiver. "What's goin' on?"

"We need to take a walk."

"Luz too?"

"No."

Luz paid for breakfast and approached the two men. "Buenos días, Gordo." She planted a kiss on his cheek.

"Buenos dias. I need Rand for a stroll." Wales led him through the lobby and over the palm-filled lawn to the beach across the street. They reached the sand of Butterfly Beach and proceeded due west. "How's things?"

"Good."

"Your girlfriend was murdered?"

"Yep." Rand looked to the horizon across Santa Barbara Channel.

"Did you know the guy?"

"Never met him."

"Can you get past it?"

"Fuck if I know."

"It's a test." Wales set a slow pace on the packed sand.

"What's a test?"

"This bubble." Wales held his hand to the sky. "This little teeny planet in a mass universe."

"Yeah, it better be."

"Ten percent is my best guess."

"Okay, I'll bite."

"Ten percent of your life is what you control. But ninety percent of you... is how you handle the ten."

"I like that."

"Like this. Did you kill her?"

"No."

"It wasn't your fault. It wasn't your plan. This is all... about God's plan."

"What?" Rand missed a step. "Don't tell me that you are a... Bible thumper."

"Don't tell anybody."

"You?" Rand had a step to make up as Wales continued at a slow pace. "Can't be."

Wales smiled knowingly. "It's the only explanation that makes sense."

"What about all the sins...? All of your... sins?"

"If you think that you have to be without sin to follow Christ, you have no idea what it's all about."

"Really?"

"Really. I can tell you right now that God has a plan for you here and that if he didn't, you would not be here." Wales patted him lightly on the back. "What have you done to get yourself on this beach, to get yourself born on this planet, to get light from that sky?" He pointed up.

"Nothin'."

"Exactly. Now you can accept things that you have no control over or you can be afraid and angry. But I have a strong feeling that you will play the game without fear." Wales repeated advice his father had given him.

"Game?"

"Your game is on. You can let this shit you can't reverse eat you up. Or... you can spit it out and start a new game."

"Sounds easy."

"Look around my friend. You have been blessed."

Rand caught a positive wave. "I have?" He looked to the blue Pacific crashing to the beach and thought about the Lear he now commanded and the money he had suddenly...and Luz.

"And my brother, we got a game going."

"We do?"

"What I'm about to tell you is not to be repeated except to Luz."

"Okay."

"As you know, I have been working with Uncle Sugar to help the freedom fighters down in Nicaragua." Wales searched the beach for potential assassins. "You know the difference between freedom fighters and terrorists?"

"Uhh, no."

"Freedom fighters are terrorists on our side."

"Okay."

"There is another side of the mission that I have to share with you." He looked to the sky. "I am also working with the DEA to bring down the biggest cocaine ring in the history of the planet."

"Oh good. The DEA and the CIA."

"I want to assure you that this operation is with the concurrence of the U.S. Government." Wales kept his head up with active eyes. "I've got the Medellin cartel lined up like ducks at the arcade."

"Medellin? Colombia?"

"Right. Now, you must be aware that these folks are downright ruthless. They would kill me without any hesitation."

"And me in the process?"

"Yes."

"That would suck." Rand loved the sound of waves.

"I am giving you a path out. You can get out of town right now and I'll fly back with Luz. I'll give you an additional $10,000 and you can be on your merry way. No questions asked."

"Hey, I got a question. Don't we have an army for this kind of stuff?"

"Question this. This ain't about national security."

"It's not?"

"Knot this. This is about world domination and wealth."

"Huh?"

"When the CIA gets involved, it's usually for reasons that can't be explained to the voters or to destabilize a potential power. If all the factions are fighting against each other, it's hard for them to become a threat to the U.S."

"Okay."

"But this little mission is suspicious. I don't believe for a second that Nicaragua is a threat at all. I know the place. Even the guys we are training don't believe this bullshit."

"What is it then?"

"I'm not sure, but I suspect a business problem with labor and imports. This is our game, the simple one you played as a kid: connect the dots. You remember playing connect-the-dots?"

"Of course."

"Course this. Connect the dots and get a picture of big Fat Cats."

"You know these cats?"

"Getting clearer everyday." Wales looked at the horizon to seven cash-producing oil rigs that fouled the pristine scene as they reached the hard-packed sand where the tide had retreated.

Rand couldn't believe his eyes. He'd just spotted the big guy from Adams and Mena, strolling the beach to their right, away from the water. "How'd he get here?"

"Good. You are observant. Shadow can be trusted like a brother. He is always close by. If somebody's tailing me, he'll get 'em first. You will be moving him around once we get into the operation. We go way back." The surf crashed soothingly against the rocks where the beach ended and they turned around. Shadow walked casually on the shoulder of the beach road.

"So what's up with the Merlin?"

"I'm working on a trade with a guy in Florida. We'll be leaving soon to close the deal." Wales realized once again that his mind was saturated with logistics as he balanced life-threatening information in his head. "I got a C-123 lined up."

"What's that?"

"It's a Vietnam era cargo plane. The spooks love 'em. Two Pratt & Whiney radials inboard and two CJ-610s outboard."

"Like the Lear's engines...on a cargo plane?"

"Exactly. Gets out of a tight field with all four running until you clear all obstacles. At cruise, you shut down the jets and run on the Pratts." Wales surveyed the ocean's surface and the constant string of jets climbing out of LAX in the crisp blue sky. He figured that the 747 with red JAL paint was headed for Tokyo and the blue paint twenty miles in trail was Korean Air, starting a long trek on the great circle to Seoul. Rand had seen none of the planes that were five miles above. "The C-123 was Air America's best plane."

"Air America?"

"The paramilitary that ran the secret war in Laos, funded by opium trade, used the 123 out of the short fields. They called the outfit Air America. Guys like you and me. It was obvious to the boys doing the work but there were few reporters snooping around in the jungles of Southeast Asia for a good story. The same government boys that ran that operation are jumping on the situation down in Nicaragua. Brophy smiled. They crossed the lane to where the Biltmore challenged salt air with a ton of white paint. "So, are you in?"

"Let me think about it...yes." Rand smiled.

16. Live Boy or Dead Girl

A bang of coins hit the bottom of the Pac Bell sack. "Damn." Rand heard the echo from the adjacent area that housed five payphones in the lobby of the Biltmore as he waited patiently for Luz to finish dressing. The afternoon had been a sweet one for Rand and Luz as they slept in ocean air that streamed through open French doors. He heard another bang of coins hit the bottom of the sack. "Damn." The Pacific Bell technician dialed a number. "Jim. It's Pete. Look, I'm over at the Biltmore. I can't believe it, but every one of these phones was inop because…they're all jammed with quarters." There was a short pause. "I just emptied it this morning with the same problem. Somebody's making some serious phone calls out of here."

Rand smirked with knowledge of the guy's big mystery as Luz walked across the lobby. She kissed him passionately on the mouth. "Hello, mi amor."

"Buenos tardes." Her dress was low-key, and she wouldn't turn heads on the street, but once any breathing male took a look into the eyes…and down to the come-to-mama bosom…he would be lost forever. "You look rested."

"I love the Estados Unidos. That is the best bathtub I have ever seen."

"The bathtub, huh? All this and it's the bathtub that you love." He smiled at her. After his walk of enlightenment with Brophy, Rand had returned to the room with a swirling head of new knowledge. A game… a test? He plugged in the new data and it changed his output. Perhaps Reni was simply finished with the game and had moved on to another. A new comfort of her faith was suddenly a great relief and he had slept for an hour as a fresh breeze blew into the room. When he awoke, Luz was on the patio in her bikini, patiently reading a novel written in Spanish. Rand lay between silk sheets and felt life return. A great weight had been lifted as he took in all the miracles that had been presented: The ocean surf in the distance, the palms clapping, the glorious blue sky, the ceiling fan. He stretched and called to her. "Luz?"

"Jess?" She pulled her shades off to look into the room. "Are we finished napping?" Luz entered and took a seat on the edge of the bed.

"I hope not." He ran his fingers over her hand. "Would you like to jump in?"

Her dark eyes opened slightly. "Are you now ready for me?"

"Ready?"

"Are you finished with the ghost?"

"Ghost?"

"I know you are thinking about her." She pushed his hair back with her fingers. "It is only natural." She saw his eyes absorb her words. "It may not go away, Rand. And you may have to live with it for a very long time."

"I have been holding a lot inside. I can't seem to get it out," Rand conceded, as he soaked in her beauty. "I am afraid to be crushed again." He looked away. "You are so beautiful, Luz. It's been less than a month. No, a month ago yesterday."

"Do you feel guilty?"

"I'm not sure what I feel. I'm afraid to go forward."

"Do you want to go forward?"

"Of course."

"Come with me." Luz took his hand and led him to the large marbled bathroom. She ran water into the enormous bathtub, poured bath oil into the water, added bubbles and lit three candles on the white marble counter. She sat on the small padded stool and motioned him to come over. She slid down his shorts and her hand parted his thighs and patted his rear. The tub filled quickly and she ordered him in as her bikini fell to the floor.

"I'm feeling better already." Rand smiled. His gut was still a little tight. He followed her into the warm water.

Luz turned the faucets off. Only the movement of the water and the birds beyond the opened sliding door broke the silence. She moved behind him and sat with her legs spread around him and told him to lean back on her. She rubbed the tightness from his chest and stomach. Luz felt his breathing slow. She held him gently in a time warp and he neared sleep. "Relax." The candles flickered in dim light.

Rand felt peace. He began to think about his future and the fortunate turn of events. He felt this girl loving him and realized it was she who saved him. Her warm breasts on his back and her strong hands dissipated tension. The oil generated smooth blood flow and he felt a triumphant return of life underwater. He breathed easily for the first time in over a month and suddenly her hands massaged him to glory. A negative thought rushed his head but he shooed it away and took another deep positive breath.

Luz was alive. She kissed him on the neck and bit lightly on his lobe before she stood as he slid to the back of the tub. Rand's heart thumped fuel to his rocket. All systems were go as he viewed and anticipated. She lowered herself easily onto him. Her nipples stiffened as he slid inside her. "Ohhh..." She kissed him tenderly on the lips as they froze, belly to belly, chest to bosom.

"Shall we...?" Rand looked toward the bedroom.

"Yes." She led him by his tip to the bed and rolled to her back, pulling him down on top of her. "Yes?"

"Hell yes."

Her face was naturally blushed when she found Rand in the lobby. They made their way via cab to Stearns Wharf for a quiet dinner over swells of the Pacific and a majestic California sunset. The million-dollar homes of Santa Barbara's Riviera lit up the hills above giant palms and locals running the beach path. The Sunset Kidd, a forty one foot Morgan, slid past the wharf under sail with a dozen wine-sipping guests.

"You are the most beautiful co-pilot a captain could ever ask for." Rand wondered how long this gig could possibly last. He knew that Wales was brilliant to concoct such an incentive for him to stay. As they finished dinner, the beeper sounded and Rand read the row of numbers. He found a payphone and dialed.

"Signature zero six one five."

"Okay." Dial tone.

Rand deadsticked the Lear from 37,000 feet and sashayed around towering cumulus into New Smyrna Beach in late afternoon Florida humidity. On the ramp of a secluded west hangar on the World War II practice field, a C-123 sat with her aft loading ramp extended. The Merlin was parked adjacent and Rand's gut sank with a jolt of a former life. Wales jumped forward to see the camouflaged Vietnam special. The squatty plane looked like a small C-130 but it was even more box-shaped. The inboard engines were radials and the propellers shone in fading light. Two GE-610 jet engines outboard of the props were camouflaged within dark green pods. "There she is...The Fat Lady."

Rand cocked his head slightly. "Fat Lady?"

"Fat this. When she sings, it's all over for the cartel." A man in his late sixties, tall and distinguished, stood next to the plane and shook Brophy's hand as he popped from the Lear. "We have a deal." Brophy was stiff after the coast-to-coast hop with a refuel at Lubbock.

"That's what I hear." The aircraft collector had been contacted by the New Dynasty that had expanded into Florida with another Skull assigned to the high electoral territory. The older millionaire, who had sold many backache pills in his day, had been a big hit on the air show circuit with the 123 for two years, but it was a pain to keep up with the maintenance and parts. He loved the lines on the Merlin and could actually use it on occasion.

Brophy moved toward the Fat Lady like a three-year-old who had just bought a train…a real one. As Rand stepped out of the Lear, he noticed that the seller looked rather sad. Owning an airplane is not like owning a boat. It is never a happy day when you sell one. "Hey. Rand Chapman." Rand shook hands and exchanged names. The seller's eyes nearly poked out as Luz stepped down from the Lear.

Rand turned to see his co-pilot's navy pants and a white pressed cotton shirt. Her full French bra was exposed as she exited the plane bent over; a gold chain vanished into soft loveliness. She bounced out of the plane.

"Luz, this is Harry."

"A pleasure to meet you sir." She took Harry's hand and the man remembered the day when he could command such a gal. "I want to see the new plane."

"Okay hon." Rand received a kiss as she hugged him around his waist.

Harry's face was aglow. "Don't tell me that's your… co-pilot." He watched the pants move toward his former airplane. *I'd have kept that plane if she wanted to fly it.*

"Yeah, it's a tough way to go through life." Rand smiled with a gander of puffy white cumulus. He drew in a deep breath of orange blossom.

"What's he want with the plane anyway?"

"Hell if I know. I'm just the bus driver." Rand walked up into the cargo area. Past the ramp he could see the Fat Lady's cockpit three steps up. A flight engineer's seat swung from the bulkhead behind the two pilot seats. There were strange electric pumps and hydraulic lines exposed in the cargo area.

Wales smiled big at the threesome as he re-entered from the walk-around. "Okay. Sold." He looked at Rand. "You like it?"

The boxcar lines were hard to get excited about. "Yeah. Really sexy." He smiled in jest.

"Sex this. Go file us a flight plan. I'll be right there."

"Da. Where to boss?"

"Boss this. Port Columbus Airport in Ohio. I got school tomorrow." Wales watched his pilots depart for the Lear before the title transfer. After ten minutes, he was back on his bench seat. In darkness two hours later, the Lear touched down on Runway Two-Eight Left at Port Columbus. Wales came forward. "You see Lane Aviation over there?"

Rand taxied slowly after turning off the long runway. "Yeah."

"Taxi in there and stay away from this outfit over here." A sign on the smaller hangar read: E-Sonics. "The guy that used to own this plane owes them some cash."

"Okay, boss." Rand taxied up to the hangar and Wales was the first one out.

"Check into the Great Southern Hotel downtown." He produced another digital beeper. "I'll call you in two days, but be ready to move at any time." The cool temperature exposed his breath. Wales looked toward the plane where the co-pilot tidied. "You sure you'll be okay?" He patted Rand on the shoulder with a big smile. Shadow waited for him behind the wheel of a black sedan at the FBO entrance. Jabba waddled over and the tail lights disappeared into darkness.

A cab delivered the two pilots under the awning of the century old Great Southern. Marble lobby floors and towering carved pillars bespoke elegance as Rand conducted a debrief in the lobby bar before they checked into their suite. Luz squealed when she saw another huge bathtub and they soaked in oiled water for a half-hour. She toweled down and made him lay face down on the bed.

"I will rub your stress right back to California, my captain." She discarded her towel and sat naked on his lower back. Rand was in an orbit around the dark side of Pluto when the phone hyper-spaced him back to the planet at oh eight-thirty. "Hello?"

"They got it."

"Got what?"

"What this. They got the Lear."

"How?"

"It's a small airport. Get out there and see what's going on."

An hour later, Rand and Luz found the plane at the small avionics facility. Rand entered the office of the electronics specialists and introduced himself to the owner. "What's the deal with the Lear?"

A tall bald man was red around the cheeks. "What's the deal? I'll tell you the deal."

Rand stepped back and shot his eyes at Luz. What the fuck?

"I put over $100,000 of equipment in this plane two years ago. Guess how much I got paid?" He looked at Rand for a quick answer.

"Beats me."

"Not a goddamn penny. I've been looking all over the world for this goddamned plane." He pointed toward the small hangar. "There's your goddamned plane." The guy stormed out of the lobby and into his office.

Rand and Luz approached the Lear and peeked into the cockpit from the entry door. "Oh shit." Rand stepped back and let her see.

"Gordo is not going to be happy." The entire avionics package was gone: Both GNS units, both communication radios and both navigation radios. It looked like they had used a power saw. Gaping holes in the cockpit were filled only with cut wires, standing skyward with nothing to power. She looked back into the cabin and saw that the cassette player and three speakers had met the same fate. "Ay yi yi." She turned as Rand's beeper sounded.

Rand approached the human volcano. "Can I use your phone?"

"Fuck no, you can't use anything around here. Take your fucking plane and hit the road. If you can get radio clearance." He followed the two to the front door and slammed it behind them.

Rand spotted a payphone between the two hangars. He quickly dialed and Wales picked up on the first ring. "Well?"

"Uh, they got all the radios." Rand didn't feel he was being real informative.

"Radio this. Stay there and wait for the sheriff to arrive. Just tell them what you know. That you parked at Lane last night and this is a huge surprise."

"Okay. Hey, they're pulling up now." Rand saw the police unit park and two officers approach the hangar. He hung up and entered the office behind them.

"What's going on here, sir?"

With little respect for the two badges, the volcano erupted. "I've been looking for that plane for two years!"

"Sir." The officer interrupted. "Turn around and put your hands behind your back."

"You can't arrest me. This is a civil matter."

"Sir! I said...Put your hands behind your back. You are under arrest for grand theft."

"Me? You need to arrest them." He pointed to Rand and Luz.

Rand watched as the law manhandled the owner against the wall and snapped handcuffs on him, glad not to be in his shoes. Whoa. They moved him out into the police car. He looked at Luz. "See girl. Crime doesn't pay."

The partner snatched the radio equipment and they drove away with the owner alone in the cage. Rand's beeper went off again. He looked at the phone in the now empty office. "Oh well." He picked up and dialed.

"What happened?"

"They busted the guy and dragged him out of here." Rand cut his eyes at Luz.

"Bust this. Good." Wales peered out of the window that overlooked Rickenbacker Air Force Base. A C-123 was parked on the ramp and his instructor waited outside. "Head on back to the hotel and I'll call you later. I got an Air Force weenie trying to teach me how to fly here. I might have to kick his ass before it's all over."

Rand laughed as the line went dead. He and Luz headed back to the Great Southern. At seventeen-thirty, the evening news came over the screen while the two lay naked. Moving lips read a story to the camera about the Freedom Fighters in Nicaragua. And Rand doubted every last word. Go… on.

Out at Rickenbacker, the Air Force major watched in amazement from the right seat as Wales flew his eighth perfect approach of the day. His student had retained every morsel of information from the two-hour ground school and briefing. The amazing pilot was at an unprecedented level after one day in the accelerated course, making the instructor's recollection of his own training pale. The major had found the whole setup unusual and was told by the Adjutant General not to bother with the routine mountain of paperwork. And when the Adjutant General spoke, there was no recourse. He was the most powerful military man in Ohio and commanded all of the state's National Guard. If he wanted a gorilla to fly an F-4, a gorilla would fly an F-4. If the Maestro whispered to the Governor dot that he needed a guy trained covertly in a C-123, and the Governor whispered that to the Adjutant dot, there would be training provided by a qualified C-123 instructor. The major would sign off the big civilian the next day without ink but with admiration for a superb pilot with a photographic memory. A civilian?

The phone rang in the suite the next afternoon. "Outside in twenty. We're going flying."

Rand and Luz packed quickly and checked out with fifteen pictures of Andy Jackson going to the desk clerk. They stepped under the awning as a stretched Cadillac stopped and the trunk popped open. The driver stashed the bags into the trunk and Wales sat on the rear seat as they crawled in behind tinted windows.

"You're looking at the world's newest Fat Lady captain." Jabba smiled. The limo proceeded down High Street to the next block and stopped. "Hang on for a sec. I'll be right back." Wales jumped out and waddled through hot dog vendors to the revolving front doors of the Franklin County Government Building, which took up the entire next block across the street from the Great Southern. Three minutes later he appeared with a man in a dark suit. They disappeared behind a twenty-foot bronze statue of Benjamin Franklin in the plaza north of the courthouse. Wales came to the limo and jumped in. "Let's go to Port Columbus," he instructed the driver as he laughed in amazement. "That was the D.A." Wales looked back at the statue. "His panties knotted with the quick arrest of the E-Sonics guy. Funny how people calm down when you stack Franklins in their palm." He laughed with irony. "Right behind ol' Ben himself."

Rand opened the door of the Lear and the radios were all back in the proper places. "How'd this happen?"

Wales smiled big. "This is Franklin County."

Brophy slept on leather as Luz shot the Lear through 10,000 feet. "Now I can let it rip." She lowered the nose slightly and accelerated smoothly to 300 knots. Her hands were steady and through 30,000 feet she focused primarily on the Mach indicator. As 41,000 came, she leveled the plane, pulled the RPM to cruise and flipped the autopilot paddle to engage. The glow of instruments on her face illuminated pure energy of flying a Learjet. Two hundred miles ahead, the earth's curvature finally allowed the glow of Memphis to be seen as they approached at 490 knots.

Rand moved his hand over to the co-pilot. She squeezed it tightly. "Life is good up here." He leaned forward to see the dark Mississippi snake through a cluster of Memphis lights. Each light represented a human life below, a million smiles and a million tears. He leaned over and kissed Luz before he picked up the microphone. "Memphis Center, the Lear One Three Sierra November requests direct Lakefront."

"Sierra November. You are cleared direct New Orleans direct Lakefront, maintain flight level four one zero."

"Thank you, sir." Rand began to brief Luz on the approach to Baton Rouge. Wales had made it clear not to disclose the destination to the federal controllers. If the FBI, CIA, DEA or Cartel wanted to follow Wales, they would need more than one unit. Two hundred miles from Lakefront, the lights of the crescent were visible, as well as Baton Rouge to the right and Gulfport against the dark Gulf to the left. At 140 DME from New Orleans, Rand asked Houston Center for lower. They were only fifty miles from Ryan Airport.

"Lear One Three Sierra November, cleared to one zero thousand."

Luz disconnected the autopilot and descended at .80 to 30,000, where she picked up 310 knots. Smoking out of FL180, Rand picked up the mike with Ryan in sight just east of the Mississippi. "Houston, the Lear One Three Sierra November is through Flight Level One Eight Zero and would like to cancel IFR."

"Sierra November, you say that you want to cancel?"

"Affirmative, sir. Cancel IFR."

"Okay. Learjet One Three Sierra November, IFR is cancelled, squawk 1200, good night sir."

"Good night."

Luz popped the spoilers and turned to a steady 40-degree bank. The jet came down like an Otis with a broken cable. "You make sure that I do not mess up."

"Count on it, lady." Rand saw her strong arms fly steadily and hoped they would spend this night together.

The spoilers made a slight vibration that woke the slumbering bear in the rear. He moved forward. "Here already?"

"Yep." Rand found the field again after a 360-degree turn and a screaming descent through 12,000 feet. "Don't forget about the 250 limit at ten."

Luz pulled back on the yoke and the speed started to bleed with spoilers extended. They were fifteen miles from the airport, directly over downtown Baton Rouge. "What is happening to the windscreen?" A thick frost began at the corners and moved toward the center.

Wales spoke up from the rear. "This has happened before. Certain temperatures create a fog on the windshield and there's no way to stop it. I told you she was a bitch."

Rand grew concerned as his windscreen continued to frost. "What did you do about it?" He checked his fuel. There was only about thirty minutes worth at this altitude.

"Not much we can do. It's like a beer mug that's been in the freezer. You take it out of freezing temps into warm moist air. It was a design flaw of the early Lears." He smiled big behind them. "How do you think I got her so cheap?"

"Cheap this." Rand rolled in the ILS frequency for Runway One Three at Ryan and the tower frequency to report base and final. In haste, he entered 119.25. The correct frequency was 119.20. The air traffic tower had closed for the night an hour earlier, a repercussion of the air traffic controllers strike against the new administration. "Luz. I got you set up for the ILS to One Three." He looked over to check her windscreen and saw that it was completely frosted over, as was his. The blower from the hot engine bleed-air that was designed to heat the window only created a silver dollar-sized hole in the frost on each inside corner of the curved windscreen. "I'm getting something here." He saw the identical small hole on her side. "And you've got the same thing over here." He pointed to hers. "You just shoot the ILS and I'll tell you what I see through this little hole."

Wales stayed up next to the potty seat on one knee. He'd called Learjet on this problem and their answer was they didn't have an answer. The next series of Learjets were upgraded to an effective window heat system.

Rand ran through the before-landing check and made his last radio call. "Ryan traffic, Ryan traffic the Learjet Three Sierra November on a two mile final to Runway One Three at Ryan." He put the list down and peeked through the hole. "Okay Luz. I'm starting to pick up the runway." It was clear outside with unlimited visibility, yet they were nearly blind. Through 400 feet, Rand was bent over to see the approach lights through the peephole. Luz stayed on instruments as Rand crosschecked her performance. She had it wired. "Excellent, girl. Keep it coming." At 200 feet he could see the centerline of the runway. "Okay...look outside."

Luz leaned left to see the runway through her hole with no peripheral vision. "Ay yi yi." Landing a Lear is nearly automatic: The pilot holds a constant attitude and power until the flare. When the power is sucked off just above the runway, physics cause the nose to rise naturally. If the pilot does not interfere, the wheels should roll onto the pavement. Rand watched her get above the runway and pull the power. The plane rolled on and Luz smiled big...and pretty.

"Atta boy, girl." Rand leaned to his peephole. "The hard part is going to be taxiing."

Wales popped the top portion of the door outward. The little hole wasn't doing it for him. He needed to see who might be waiting. In the dark night, the left engine screamed into the cabin as Brophy yelled to shut it down, which Rand did. The Lear taxied with just the right engine. Wales yelled to turn at the next taxiway and guided them to the empty ramp where he could see Shadow standing next to his Mercedes. "Whoa boy." The plane stopped and Rand shut down the right engine.

"Very nice, young lady." Rand kissed her on the cheek. Her shoulders were tight.

"Gracias, Capitan." She followed Rand out of the tight cockpit onto the ramp.

Suddenly, a single engine plane taxied toward the ramp in a hurry and Wales took a position close to the nose for a possible attach and yelled to Rand and Luz. "Get in the car!"

Rand got behind the wheel. He saw Shadow reach behind his back to grab the .44 and hold it below his waist in his right hand behind the nose of the Lear. Oh shit. "Oh shit." He saw that Luz remained calm as she slouched down slightly, as if this wasn't her first time in such a situation.

The Cessna 172 stopped on the ramp and shut down the single engine. The door opened and Shadow, still out of view behind the Lear, brought the gun to his waist with both hands.

A skinny young man stormed out of the Cessna and toward the Lear. He was alone. "You nearly killed me!" He screamed in a Middle Eastern accent. "I was on final and you missed me by ten feet! Max-ee-mum!"

Brophy calmly walked toward the man. Shadow wasn't so sure. Wales held up his right hand to him and the gun was back below the waist. "We saw you."

"You saw me? I did not hear you on the tower frequency."

Rand sank in the car. He realized instantly his huge mistake and got out to apologize to the guy. "Shit." He walked toward Wales and the terrified.

Wales remained calm as he spoke. "Like I said, we saw you. I was going to come tell you that it was you on the wrong frequency. They just changed the procedure."

The pilot took a giant step backward. "They did?"

"Yeah. You gotta remain on Houston Center frequency while in the traffic pattern now. It is a good idea to monitor both frequencies, though."

Guilt transferred. "Oh." He melted. "I am very sorry...sir."

"Don't worry about it." Wales deadpanned. "I think it is a bad change and think they will change it back to the old way soon. I was going to write a letter to the FAA."

"Are you going to mention me?" His voice rose into high pitch.

"Aw, no. I'll keep this as our secret."

"Thank you, sir. Thank you." He humbly returned to the 172 and taxied into darkness.

Rand was now the embarrassed one. "Shit. That was my fault."

"Fault this." Wales smiled as he pulled the suitcases off the plane and into the Mercedes. He laughed as Rand whistled through his teeth. One day....

Wales wheeled through Baton Rouge picturing a detailed map of every payphone in the area. A freight train approached the intersection ahead on Airline Highway as the crossing barrier came down. He peeled off down the parallel road and sped to the next block to cross the tracks a hundred yards ahead of the train. "Train this." He shot down a narrow street before a stop at a small office building. He left Rand and Luz in the car while he dropped twenty quarters in the slot of the shaded phone. He spoke directly with Vilez. "The Fat Lady is coming. Round up product."

Rand sat in the back alone as they entered a neighborhood with manicured lawns. Wales pointed to a big home on the left. "That's Edwin's crib. There is some clean money in this neighborhood," he added. "Live boy or a dead girl." Wales laughed as he wheeled the corner onto his quiet street.

"What?" Luz looked puzzled. Rand grinned.

"That's what our colorful former governor said when someone asked him whether he could possibly lose the 1976 election: Only if they catch me in bed with a live boy or a dead girl. He was re-elected by a landslide."

Wales pointed out a black government sedan parked in front of the house across the street and three doors down. "Hello, copper." The garage door opened and closed behind them. They all moved into the kitchen of the ranch-style house as Debbie Wales, in tight jeans and a sweatshirt, stepped toward Brophy for a lingering kiss on the lips. "Hey, babe."

"Where are the kids?" Wales looked behind her.

"They just got to sleep." She saw Luz and let go of Brophy to hug her and kiss her cheek. "Hello, you. Who's this?"

"Debbie, I'd like you to meet Rand."

"You like crawfish, Rand?" She held out her hand.

"Love 'em." Rand took her palm warmly. "Nicetameetcha." He was impressed that Wales had scored such a beautiful young wife. While the pilots peeled, pinched and sucked mudbugs at the table, Debbie peeled a couple letters from the pile of mail she had collected and read the good and bad news aloud.

Rand and Luz shared the guest bedroom and were awake at five in the morning. Luz made coffee before the threesome backed out of the driveway, passed another black sedan and made their way out to Ryan. Wales turned to Rand. "Today's the day."

By six-thirty, Rand had pushed the throttles up to take-off power. The Lear rocketed to 37,000 feet. Once the plane was established in cruise, Wales asked Rand if he wanted a break.

"Sure." He went back to the rear seat. "What's up?"

"Up this. Here's the deal." He looked out over the Gulf. "The mission has begun." He looked for confirmation.

"Okay."

"We're taking the Fat Lady down to Nick tomorrow night. Drop me off at New Smyrna and head over to Lauderdale. Check in at the Bahia Mar on the strip. Camille and I will be taking supplies to the Contras out in the jungle.

Then it's over to Managua, where I'm going to load up with powder before returning here. If I'm not back by Saturday… things have probably taken a major shit. If that's the case, I would head back to New Orleans and forget about the whole deal." He swallowed. "I got my ass hanging out so far right now it's unbelievable. The spooks are mounting cameras in the Fat Lady so I can snap pictures of the crooks. That should be an easy task. Maybe I could line 'em all up and ask 'em to say cheese."

Rand wanted to ask which crooks, but just nodded understanding.

"Last time I was in Managua it wasn't pretty. First they shot out my left engine and I crash-landed at Managua International. They held me for three days before the Cartel bailed me out."

"Bro?" Rand smiled. "With all due respect… what the fuck were you doing in Managua?"

"Respect this. It was a bad week. I crashed my Lodestar on takeoff out of Medellin and they gave me a spare Titan that couldn't make my normal refueling spot at Luz' farm. I had no choice but to refuel at Managua."

"Crashed…and shot down?"

"Shoot this. On the same trip… I flew through a fig tree and an oak in Mexico. Same trip." Wales grinned. "It's nothing to get a bird strike. You haven't lived until you take a squirrel strike." Rand burst into laughter. Wales joined in, finally enjoying a laugh with somebody at his unbelievable fate. "This run is about getting pictures of the cartel leaders loading cocaine onto the airplane. That should be easy," he dripped sarcasm. "Pablo probably hasn't picked up anything heavier than a pistol in the last ten years."

Rand succumbed to another gale of laughter. "What could possibly go wrong?"

At nine-fifteen they taxied up to the ramp area where the Fat Lady was parked. The cargo ramp was open and five men milled around the airplane. At nine-seventeen, Luz shot the Lear south toward Lauderdale as Rand worked the radios.

Inside the Fat Lady, Wales removed his Mexican wedding shirt and was down to his undershirt to begin a methodical review of each switch and gauge. There were a few minor changes in this cockpit set-up from the 123 at Rickenbacker.

The spooks had provided a flight engineer. Cathey introduced him as Gene but he insisted on his nickname of Fuss. A veteran of black ops with Air America and Southern Air Transport, Fuss had over a hundred covert missions under his belt.

After a familiarization flight, Cathey had ordered a team of technicians to begin the installation of the hidden cameras in the plane's cargo hold. The sneaky bastards also slipped a satellite-tracking device in the ceiling. They failed to mention this to the captain.

Wales had arranged a rendezvous with Pablo at a remote airport south of Managua for a pickup of 800 kilos of product. Camille Mouton was back to fly the co-pilot position and Fuss seemed like a regular Joe. Wales gathered the crew and briefed them for twenty minutes with Pratts groaning on the inboards. The F/E ran the checklist as the Fat Lady taxied out for takeoff.

Brophy lined the nose up on the 5000-foot concrete strip. He hit the two silver toggle switches that automatically started the outboard jets and brought them up to ninety-nine percent thrust. With the Pratts running, he could barely hear the familiar whine before popping the brakes and the plane lunged forward and moved down the runway like a milk truck with a rocket boost. As they climbed through 1,000 feet and safely clear of the trees, Wales shut off the jets. They leveled at 2,500 feet above the pastel shores of Daytona Beach on a southern course just west of the Kennedy Space Center and Lake Okeechobee, over the heart of the Everglades and directly into Key West. Wales taxied up next to several spook-driven Ryder trucks loaded with M-16s, trailblazing equipment and lagniappe.

Rand was ascending the pool ladder at eleven the next morning when the beeper on the chaise next to his bikini-clad co-pilot sounded. "Key West," Wales growled over the poolside payphone. "South ramp...fourteen oh five." The two dressed quickly and flew to the last link of Keys, where they touched down at two o'clock and taxied in slowly for the pickup. Wales stepped out of the Lincoln Town Car of Florida's future governor dot and moved quickly into the Lear. Rand restarted the left engine and had them airborne at fourteen oh-six. Wales instructed Rand to land at Tamiami. At fourteen twenty-nine, Jabba was met by Shadow in a white Ford sedan with black windows for the short trip to the Omni in downtown Miami where the DEA had rented the entire eleventh floor. Shadow had checked in the previous day to patrol the area for his boss, who was now in enemy territory. Wales noted that the $2 million earmarked for Pablo had arrived from the laundry and was stacked on the floor of the front closet of his two-bedroom suite.

As the courier exited the lobby below, Wales' DEA handler reached the eleventh floor. Shadow met him as the elevator doors opened. He pointed to the third door on the left and the tall man tapped gently on the door. Wales answered in dark pants and undershirt. "Hello Bro."

"Come on in."

"How ya feeling?" Ernest "Jake" Jacobs had growing admiration for the man that had single-handedly tripled the information the DEA had on cocaine traffic. But Jacobs was also concerned for Wales, who was clearly laying his head in the mouth of a lion. "How was training?"

"Train this. A piece of cake. Look. This Cathey guy is making me nervous."

"How so?"

"He puts a satellite tracking device on the Fat Lady and doesn't tell me. It's got an antenna on it the size of Texas… and he thinks I won't see the damn thing." He leaned forward from his chair. "I smell a rat with this bastard. I know that he and the VP and the Maestro and the Adjutant General and…"

"Easy." Jacobs paled. "Bro. Listen carefully. You have got to calm down. I've been watching these guys for a couple of years now…and you're right." He walked toward the window to see Biscayne Bay and the Rickenbacker Causeway. "But you sure don't want to challenge them. Especially from your current position."

"Position this. My current position is excellent. They know that I can make everything they want to happen, happen. My concern is after I've made it happen."

"The big boys are talking with your attorney and I hear they are close to cutting a deal… but the sheriff in Louisiana wants your ass and we need to work on him a little more."

"We will close the deal before the next mission when I bring all the bad guys to your doorstep."

"Definitely. I'm pushing as hard as I can. Do you have everything for tomorrow?"

"Cathey has me landing first in the damn jungle to unload a few things for his boys and he's got a remote control camera to snap pictures of the bad guys in Managua. If they happen to see that, I would say the mission will be a huge failure." Wales looked over to Virginia Cay. "To make 'em all feel better, I have a shopping list for your boys to load in the forward cargo area."

Jacobs took out his pen. "Go ahead."

"Two hundred boxes of Trix."

"Jacobs looked up. "Cereal?"

"Yep. It gets better. Four sets of O'Brien water skis. Three hundred pairs of panty hose, twenty VCRs, a 250- horsepower outboard Mercury and a Cuisinart toaster and food processor." Wales laughed. "Un- believable. Do you have any doubt that they want to come to the great Estados Unidos?"

Rand and Luz left the Bahia Mar at sunset after another full day of Florida therapy. They moved to Executive Airport on Lauderdale's north side via United Cab. Luz flew from the right seat for the jump over to Tamiami as he worked the radios and ran the checklists for his girl.

Wales waited in a hangar as the Lear taxied up with only the right engine turning. Rand stopped the plane for less than five seconds as Brophy, with a large Samsonite attached to his left hand and smaller duffel in his right, loaded himself on the plane. Rand flew the leg to Key West. Brophy wore his game face. "The ducks are on the pond." He watched Rand level off at 16,500 feet. "Go ahead and park the plane next to the Fat Lady. I want you to stick around until we launch in case something falls apart."

Rand felt his tension and played it straight. "Okay boss."

"Boss this. After we're gone, fly back to Lauderdale and wait. I don't have a firm plan after we are done." Brophy went to the back of the plane and prayed for Debbie and his kids. He dreamed of the day when he would be flying them around in this very jet to see the world. It was time to jettison this life. Lord, give me strength. He barely felt the plane move as Rand finessed the controls and he heard the gear come down on final. The touchdown was a greaser and Wales went forward to see two Ryder trucks backed up to the Fat Lady.

The spooks were dressed in civilian clothes and they moved at double speed while the final lawnmowers and chainsaws were loaded for the first stop at the Contra field. The captain jumped out of the Lear and waddled up the cargo ramp with the suitcase full of squeaky-clean Franklins. He placed it right behind his seat and found the nightvision goggles to place three new batteries in the holder. Landing in the mountainous jungle at night was not going to be easy with the goggles. Without them, it would be impossible. If the jungle landing were not possible for any reason, he would have to open the ramp in flight and kick out anything intended for the Contras, before proceeding into their enemy's camp for the second phase of the mission. Fuss programmed the Loran and the GNS from the charts that were not marked with a destination. The new auxiliary power unit ran well after it had been tested and re-tested.

Fuss walked Brophy through the cargo hold. A net was thrown over items for the first stop, where the net and everything under it would be unloaded. Wales could plainly see the 35mm camera lens protruding from the bulkhead as he reminded himself that he knew exactly where to look. The camera was noisy without the APU running and would shoot continuously for five minutes after the remote triggering device activated. He stepped back onto the tarmac and took a long pull of moist, warm air. He saw Rand checking out the trailblazing equipment and walked over to him. "Your tax dollars at work."

Rand shook his head with amazement. The yellow Ryder trucks pulled away and ten guys jumped in the back as the loadmaster pulled down the sliding door on the fly. "Good luck." Rand took a long look at Brophy Wales. "Say hi to everybody for me."

"Hi this. I left a bag for you and Luz in the baggage compartment. Don't spend it all in the same place." He saw Luz look out from the co-pilot's seat and blew her a kiss. Wales went serious suddenly. "If you don't see me again…" He stopped and looked into the dark sky. "Tell Debbie that I will always be watching over her and the kids. Tell her that I love her." He got the words out without his voice cracking. He soul-shook Rand's hand and marched up the ramp through the cargo. The inboard engines started, the ramp closed slowly and the Fat Lady taxied out to the runway.

Luz got out of the plane trembling. She put her arm around Rand as the odd sound of jets and pistons lumbered into the night. At about 1,000 feet, the outboards were shut off and only Pratt & Whitney groans could be heard as the Fat Lady banked to the southwest. The groan slowly dissipated and the strobes suddenly quit. The navigation lights disappeared to erase all traces of the operation.

Rand decided to wait for nearly half an hour on the ramp. "You never can tell. If they lose an engine now they will still come back here." The two felt an enormous sadness, as if El Gordo were never to be seen again. Finally, Rand read the checklist for engine start and Luz flew them back to Lauderdale where Rand pulled the satchel from the compartment behind the aft seat. In light from the Red Bird ramp, he peered into the bag and his breathing stopped. There were 20,000 pictures of Ben Franklin in there. Hole-E-Shit.

17. Pablo's Harley

"Look at us now, Mouton." Brophy Wales smiled through the hue of cockpit lights as they moved across the western Caribbean at 10,200 feet with bumps of light turbulence. "I bet Cathey is watching us right now on his satellite. I should go back and cut the fucking wires." He looked around the cockpit. "Probably got us wired for sound too."

Fuss returned to the engineer's seat after his third check of the load since takeoff. "I think it's all good." He stroked his beard and glanced at the fuel gauges for the next five hours.

The Contra camp was heavily wooded and the 3,000-foot dirt landing strip was tucked between two volcanic ridges with peaks around 4,000 feet. Wales tested his night goggles while the GNS indicated they were just twenty miles from the first stop. "Perfect." He looked out to easily see every tree and hill and turned slightly to his right to get a visual of the strip. There was a small fire burning at the camp and a flare lit to mark the threshold. "Gear down." Wales pulled the power off and banked the Fat Lady into a 45-degree bank, just a mile east of a tree-filled hill that was now above them. He made a hard turn from base to final, touched down firmly on the rough runway and stood on the brakes. The plane stopped about halfway down the runway before Wales whipped it around and taxied back to the approach end. He spun the ramp over tall grass at the corner of the strip. "Okay, Fuss, kick the shit out."

Fuss popped the cargo door open and the ramp slid down into the grass ahead of trailblazing equipment. Camille unbuckled and helped him run fifteen M-16 crates down the rollers. Forty-eight crates of ammunition followed and Fuss gave the guerrilla a quick salute before he raised the door. Wales saw the red door light disappear from the annunciator panel. He pushed the throttles up just as Camille retook his seat. "Hit 'em." Camille raised the hard plastic guards, clicked two silver toggle switches forward for the CJ-610s and the gauges began to spool up. As they reached ninety-nine percent, Wales released the brakes and the Fat Lady accelerated swiftly down the runway and launched up to 4,000 feet. "Yeeeeeeehhhhaaaaaaaa!" Wales laughed, basking in a major adrenaline rush. "Welcome to Air Bro!" The pilots pulled off their goggles.

After thirty minutes over dark jungle and rugged mountains, they descended onto a flat valley south of Managua. Fuss had programmed the 7,000-foot lighted runway into the GPS. Wales made the landing and was relieved to see the familiar face of Pablo emerge from a small building next to the lone hangar. They shut down the engines with less than an hour of fuel. Mouton's hands were soaked and he trembled with fear. Landing with a former U.S. military aircraft seemed far too obvious. "It's been nice knowing you Bro." He unbuckled his belt as Wales anxiously made his way to the ramp.

"Show time." Wales held the Franklin suitcase and as the ramp lowered he smiled his please don't kill me smile. "Buenas noches, amigo," he greeted Pablo. "What do you think of the old girl?" The smile turned to a proud grin. He handed over the suitcase. "I told you I'd find a way to beat their system."

Pablo smelled a rat. He smiled slightly under roaming eyes over churning gut. His black wiry hair and mustache were thick over his white sport shirt with dark horizontal stripes. "Where do you get such a plane?"

"Surplus from Vietnam. It took me two weeks just to clear the spider webs." Wales led him to the wingtip and pointed up to the green painted pod. "That is a jet engine. There is another on the other side." Wales led him back to the cargo ramp. "You are not going to believe this." He headed for the covered cargo and grabbed the tarp over two four-foot humps. "A present for...you." He pulled the cover to expose two new Harley Springers. The chrome sparkled from the overhead light.

Pablo flashed back to his childhood when his father had scraped up enough cash to buy him a very used bicycle. "Beautiful" he allowed. "That is very, very beautiful. Gracias." The tight feeling in his chest subsided slightly. "We do have a little problem."

Wales endured a gut sink. "Problem?" No problems.

"The fueling truck has a mechanical problem." Pablo wasn't accustomed to not getting things. "And it seems there are no spares in this part of the world."

"There is fuel on the airport?"

"Yes. In the tanks over there." He pointed to three large aboveground storage tanks.

"We will have to get buckets and load the fuel manually. It's only 2,000 gallons." He smiled. "Can we find some help?"

"That should be no problem." Pablo focused on the hangar as Fredrico emerged with four men in military fatigues.

Wales recognized the large man who had bailed him out of Somoza's bunker less than a year earlier. "Señor Fredrico. It is very good to see you, sir." Wales grabbed his hands as if they were old, dear friends. "I bring gifts from a strange land." He smiled and patted the man on the back.

"Where do you get such a big plane?" Fredrico was not in a smiley mood as Wales repeated his story. "It is very nice, Gordo." The threesome proceeded up the ramp and looked over the cargo. Pablo seemed to stare directly at the camera lens, not knowing what it was.

Wales wanted to grab him and pull him away before Pablo moved toward the water skis. "The next trip will be three times more." He pushed the remote. Close enough Cathey? He did not see the shutter move. He pushed it again. Nothing. Bastards spent too much time on the tracking device. Outwardly unfazed, Wales moved them over toward the Trix and the rest of the goodies. "Here are the items you asked for."

"It is good to see Santa Claus come so early." Fredrico smiled finally. "What is this?" He pointed at the motorcycles.

"I know Pablo likes to ride." Wales continued to smile pretty. "You name it, and I can deliver."

Fredrico waved his men over and they began to unload the cargo. "You have heard about the fuel problem?"

"Yes. We're going to need lots of men and lots of big buckets."

Fredrico spoke sternly to his lieutenant. The man ran down the ramp, started a pickup truck, and drove off into darkness. The rest of the men unloaded the goods and within fifteen minutes the aluminum hangar door slid open and the cocaine bales were exposed.

Wales needed a picture of Pablo with the contraband. He moved over to the men. "I am not sure how much product we can fit on this plane." He looked into the ramp and pointed. "Maybe we can fit some around those pumps there and add another fifty kilos to the next shipment."

"Maybe, Gordo."

"Yes, I think it is possible. Let's get a few to see if they fit." Wales went to the hangar and carried back a two-kilo package. With Pablo in trail, he ascended the ramp and tried the remote again. And again, there was no shutter movement. He ordered Mouton to start the APU. As the small turbine engine fired up loudly with his needed distraction, Wales boldly set a small ladder under the camera, reached up with a false pretense to adjust an airplane function but actually started the camera's motor that would fire a hundred shots of the ramp area in ten-second intervals. Wales had told Fuss and Camille to start a line from the hangar to hand bales to the plane. He arranged himself at the end after Fredrico and Pablo as the bales were handed down the line of five men. His boys were definitely within the focal point. John Cathey had a golden piece of evidence and Wales smiled cavalierly as he pictured his prison doors slide open.

Nine hundred and ten kilos were loaded into the plane. The fuel bucket into the wing operation was a chocolate-covered mess. With no funnel, the first ten three-gallon buckets produced around twenty as Soviet fuel spilled like rain from the high-winged American freighter. At this rate, Wales estimated another day on the ground. As dawn broke, seven exhausted men had only produced a quarter of the fuel needed. Wales came down the ramp from the cockpit fuel gauges and noticed a green and yellow truck spraying along the adjacent highway. He had an idea. He called Fredrico over. "I need that truck."

The slow moving truck sprayed into the ditch. "That truck?"

The driver was corralled, handed a thousand pesos and weed killer was pumped into an empty fuel tank with the truck's internal pump. The pump was reversed to suck fuel quickly into the truck before reversing the pump again. Soviet fuel soon filled the C-123's tanks. Two hours after sunrise, the Fat Lady was ready to sing.

Wales woke Mouton and the run for home began. Fuss plotted a course via San Pedro Sula to the Western Caribbean and the southern tip of the Yucatan, with a dogleg in the southern Gulf to west Miami and Tamiami Airport. The flight was tagged as a special military mission to circumnavigate the need for customs officials. Wales' mind clicked into overdrive. It was obvious that Cathey's boys... Click. ...the Maestro's boys... could easily form a lucrative enterprise with this unchecked pipeline under a military cover. His head swirled with an epiphany. Those... bastards.

Wales captured two hours of sleep as they had crossed the Gulf. He emerged from the plane semi-rested and made his pre-arranged call from the cleared-out hangar. In the warm Florida sun he dialed from a payphone on the outside wall of Wolf Aviation while ten DEA undercover agents milled about the general aviation field with packed heat.

"The Fat Lady is waiting." This prearranged phrase indicated that the coast was clear and the hangar was secure.

Ten minutes later, a thirty-foot Winnebago drove up the driveway to the secluded hangar on the airport's south side. Joey and Claire from Jersey looked the part of turistas on vacation in South Florida. All license tags and inspection stickers on the New Jersey-registered vehicle were current for the rendezvous at the Fat Lady's ramp. One hundred and twenty kilos were loaded into the motor home and in fifteen minutes they were out of the airport, heading east on Kendall Drive. Joey was under a straw hat, Claire behind a dramatic pair of dark sunglasses as they made their way toward the I-95 via the Palmetto. Piece o' cake.

A twenty-six-year-old blonde in a beat-up orange Camaro sat at the light that exited the Crossings subdivision onto Kendall. She took the bottle of Jack Daniels in her lap and poured half down her right thigh. A panel van across the intersection was also stopped at his light. Not so miraculously, as the Winnebago approached the intersection, the light turned from green to yellow and red for the motor home. Joey cautiously braked to a complete textbook stop. The light turned green for the Camaro and Blondie stomped the accelerator. The van also entered the intersection to the Crossings.

Joey checked his rear-view mirrors and felt his heart rate slow. He cut his eyes at Claire and whispered "one hundred...thousand...dollars," as he had for the past week. A devious smile crept up the right side of his mouth. In just thirty hours they would be at Exit 13 on the Jersey Turnpike, heavy with cash. Life is so good...and easy.

The van driver blew his horn and Joey casually looked left as it continued straight through the intersection. Instantly, the orange Camaro plowed into the panel truck with a gut-wrenching metal-to-metal thud and careened into the front of his...

"Oh shit!" Claire screamed as the van pinned the Camaro to the grill of the Winnebago. "Oh shit."

Joey jumped out to assess the damage. Uneasy panic rushed him as a gush of adrenaline thumped his heart into overdrive. Miami heat rising from the pavement was an oven. The van driver, dressed in a white tee-shirt, yelled at the woman in the Camaro, who appeared to be unconscious and bleeding from the head. Joey saw the bottle of Jack and smelled the alcohol. As his girlfriend came from the passenger side, a Dade County unit with two officers just happened to pass by and pulled in front of the scene.

Another unit pulled up as the first officers called in the accident and shook the unconscious woman. The Winnebago's radiator leaked fluid. Joey and Claire looked at each other in shock. Joey's gut dropped as the camouflaged C-123 shot past out of 800 feet into white puffy clouds. He didn't follow it long enough to see the turn toward western Arkansas.

An ambulance arrived while the officers questioned the van driver. Two tow trucks appeared within a minute of each other as the officers from the second unit directed rubbernecks around the scene into the right lane. The woman was removed from the car via the passenger door. Two paramedics put her on the gurney as she cried out in a drunken stupor. They tossed her in the ambulance and closed the double doors. The siren sounded and lights flashed the emergency eastbound down Kendall Drive.

Inside the ambulance, the woman suddenly sat up and a towel was handed to her. She gave the attendant a high five as they proceeded to their DEA vehicles parked at headquarters. She wiped the dye from her lip and nose. "That went well."

Back at the accident scene, the officer finally approached Joey. "Wrong place at the wrong time, huh?"

"Yeah."

"Can we move the vehicle?" Dark Ray-Bans hid searching eyes. A third Dade unit just happened to pull up.

"I don't think so." Joey sweated. "I can have it towed. My brother has a truck here. I'll call him." He was proud that he could think so quickly under the circumstances. So was Claire.

"You mind if I take a look in the unit?"

"Mind?" Joey thought fast. "My kids are sleeping in the back."

"Your kids?" The officer stepped toward the rear door. "You have kids in there?"

"Ahh, yeah."

"Well, let's have a look." The officer tried to open the door but it was locked. He knocked on the door. "Open up, kids!"

Joey's day just took a major dive. He thought about a sprint but quickly remembered he was always the slowest runner in the New Jersey public school system. In this battle of wits, Joey was unarmed. As the officer walked slowly toward the front passenger door, Joey finally thought of something quick to say. "Uhhhhh..."

The officer opened the door and drew his gun as he proceeded through the galley area to find that most of the unit was gutted. He spotted the familiar south Florida cargo. Joey and Claire's Florida vacation was extended to ten years.

Luz awoke at dawn. She made her way to the balcony that overlooked the harbor, halyards clanged sweetly against hundreds of masts below. The soft pastel sunrise soothed her slightly but her gut cried for El Gordo. She checked the beeper again but the screen remained blank. Rand rolled over from a deep slumber. She turned, glad to see him awake. "I hope I did not wake you."

Rand waited for the pain to crunch his temples. He stretched his arms and legs. There was no ache in his joints. He sat up and the room remained still. He turned his head, anticipating a sledgehammer to the neck. Nothing. "Hey.

Buenos días." He pieced the night together. A quiet room service meal… and twenty minutes of sweet intercourse. No bird strikes. Three consecutive nights without booze. Rand checked the clock at six a.m. He reached for the remote and turned on the television. "Look at this." He sat up and pushed the volume up.

The screen showed a large RV with contraband stacked inside. The caption below said something about the largest cocaine bust in history. The commentator parroted numbers that had been manufactured for the press. "Estimated at five hundred kilos."

"Holy shit. I think El Gordo is home." Rand listened carefully. There was no mention of who may have delivered the product. Five hundred kilos. He went to the door and opened it. The Miami Herald lay on the floor and he bent into the hall to pick it up. The front page pictured the same Winnebago and line-up of packages above the huge story of the bust. "I'm thinking that we aren't as safe as we think we are." The phone rang and Rand jumped. Getting edgy? He picked it up. "Yeeesss?"

"You've seen the papers?"

"Good to hear your voice."

"Voice this. Preflight well. Little airport in western A-R-K."

"Roger that." Rand hung up and Luz beamed relief. "Our boy is safe."

Within the hour, they'd checked out of the Bahia Mar and made it to Red Bird at Ft. Lauderdale International. Rand did a thorough preflight and filed a flight plan for Dallas Love with a watchful eye on the ramp for suspicious characters. He counted out twenty Jacksons to the Red Bird receptionist for fuel and hangar rental and moved out to the red carpet that led to the Lear.

While the tanks were being topped off, he told Luz to take the left seat. Her hair was brushed back from her forehead as she ran confidently through her cockpit setup, checking and setting each switch, eyes alert under arched eyebrows. As she slipped on her gold sunglasses, she noticed that Rand was watching her. "What is it?"

"Tell me, Luz DeSoto." He smiled slightly behind wrap-around Ray-Bans. "Is there any place in the world you'd rather be than right here, right now?" He reached over to stroke her neck. A light dose of Givenchy whacked him as she leaned over to his warm mouth for a full minute, her breast softly within his palm.

"Oh my." Rand's face was a lipsticked mess. Luz kissed him again and reached for a Kleenex. Rand laughed at the lineman standing outside the plane with his mouth agape. She wiped lipstick off and he pulled out the checklist. "Okay, captain. Parking brake."

"Set, pressure normal."

"GNS?"

"Programmed for Jet Fifty-Eight."

"Start levers."

"Cutoff"

"Antiskid."

"Checked and off."

"Penis heat?"

"Que?" She smiled over at him. Her hand wandered between his legs. "On and muy caliente."

"Altitude alerter?"

"Set at 5,000 feet."

"Before-start check complete. Let's crank 'em and get outta here." Rand raised his index finger and spun it around so the lineman knew they were ready for business. He gave thumbs-up and backed away while Luz started both engines. Rand called ground control and they were cleared to taxi to Nine Left. Luz eased the airplane smoothly as they ran the before-takeoff checklist.

An Eastern 727 flew onto the parallel runway, wheels rolled softly to the pavement as the pilot pushed nose down at the last second. "Beautiful." Luz was fully hooked on airplanes. "Is that where you would rather be?"

"Someday, my love," Rand admitted. "Not today." He brought the mike to his mouth. "The Lear One Three Sierra November is ready."

As the tri-jet cleared the runway in front of the terminal the controller responded. "Learjet One Three Sierra November, fly runway heading to 5,000. Cleared for takeoff on Nine Left."

Luz lined up the nose and moved the throttles to ninety percent as G forces pushed them against seatbacks and the jet baked down the runway. The center line markings appeared and disappeared quickly under their rear ends. Grass and cement on both sides blurred as speed increased. Luz pulled back on the yoke and the Lear smoked into the blue sky. She soaked in the power and issued commands in honey tones. "Gear to up. Flaps to zero. " She watched Rand obey as she guided the plane through puffy cumulus over aqua blue water and white sand beaches. At 5,000 feet, the controller gave them a turn west and she rolled smoothly to forty degrees of bank. "This is so perfecto." At 10,000, she lowered the nose and the airspeed galloped to 300 knots as Rand set her VOR out to the northwest course for her to track. "I love you for that," she whispered as he checked in with Miami Center.

"What's that, hon?"

"I said thank you." She set her altimeter at 29.92 passing 18,000 and flipped off the landing lights. The Everglades shrank below and the Gulf of

Mexico shone ahead. Ft. Myers went by on the left and Lake Okeechobee disappeared behind Rand's wing. Seven minutes later she leveled off at 39,000 on an offshore 283-degree course away from the Sarasota VOR.

"There's beautiful downtown Tampa, Florida." Rand could see the bay and whitewashed buildings of St. Petersburg seven miles below.

Miami Center came across the speaker. "Lear One Three Sierra November. Contact Jacksonville Center on one three two decimal four, good day, sir."

Rand switched to the new frequency and waited while a Pan Am and Eastern finished their transmissions with the new controller. There was a silence and he pushed the key button. "Jacks Center, the Learjet One Three Sierra November is checking in at Flight Level Three Niner Zero."

"Roger, sir, Three Niner Zero; I'd like to confirm your destination."

"Sierra November. Destination is Delta Alpha Lima... Dallas Love."

"Roger. Maintain Flight Level Three Nine Zero and you are cleared to Love Field via Jet Fifty Eight to Alexandria and the Kiss One Arrival to Love."

"Copy all sir."

Luz engaged the autopilot and buried her head in the GNS to recheck the coordinates on the chart against the ones Rand had programmed into the box. She could see that Rand was planning to cancel the IFR flight plan 150 miles northwest of Alexandria and fly directly to Mena under visual flight rules. The autopilot tracked the course with information from the GNS.

Rand knew they would be over the water for the next forty minutes. He unbuckled his belt and moved to the rear of the plane. "I'll be back. Set the mach at seven nine."

"Si, capitán." In deep blue of stratosphere Luz felt heat filter across her ankles. She heard Barry White's thunderous My Everything from the back speakers. Rand turned up the volume on a cassette he'd bought yesterday and White whispered a deep order: "Take it off... Take it all off." Luz recognized the song from last night and turned toward Rand. She quickly pulled off her glasses to confirm her vision.

Except for socks, Rand was naked as a jaybird. A self-massage had closed one-way check valves. He yelled over the music. "Come on back here for a second, girl."

"What...?" She couldn't believe her eyes or ears.

"Let George fly for awhile. Sometimes you just gotta trust your autopilot." He motioned her back.

"Ay...yi." Luz reluctantly left the cockpit empty.

Rand whispered with Barry. "And take off that bras-siere...my dear." He began to unbutton and unzip before moving her to the rear bench. "Clear for takeoff." Barry moved on to Honey Please as Rand watched her breasts move to the beat before a gander to her eyes. "This would be a bad time for Mach tuck."

She giggled with a thread of insanity. "Or endurance records."

"The jet is flying well."

"The jet is flying very well." Luz felt intoxicated for the next fifty miles.

Rand sang with Barry. "Dee-per and dee-per...any-time and any-place." She laughed as he entertained. Finally the song ended as the jets outside purred and pushed five hundred knots. He pulled her lower lip between his teeth and breathed in her sweetness. "I love you."

She gently pushed his head back. "What did you just say?" The newest mile-high member looked from eye to eye.

"I said I love you."

18. Miracle Number Two

Luz pulled the yoke back a tad too far on the flare. "Uh-oh." The touchdown was firm and her right hand went to the reversers and her feet pushed the brakes. "I wanted to make a perfect landing to the perfect flight."

"I personally loved it." The co-pilot smiled as he noticed that the 123 was out in the open. "The Fat Lady's here."

The Lear reversed course and taxied in. The hangar door slid open and Luz coasted in with engines shut down before the door closed behind them. Wales approached to kiss the windscreen and Luz kissed back from inside the cockpit.

"Love is in the air," Wales laughed as he opened the door.

Rand worked his way out of the right seat. "Is the mission over?"

"Mission this. I don't think so. Why?"

"The Fat Lady is out in the open." Rand pointed toward the cargo plane. "In broad daylight."

"I don't have a hangar big enough to put the old girl. And I was just getting ready to take her for a ride. Let's go."

Wales led them up the Fat Lady's ramp and pointed Rand into the left seat. Rand saw throttles the size of Texas. The enormous cockpit crunched his brain. The rudders looked like water skis and the yoke was straight out of a John Wayne movie. "Bogies at two o'clock."

The quip made Wales actually look out momentarily. "Luz, you're the co-pilot. I'll play engineer."

Rand couldn't believe his ears. "What?"

"Come on, stud, you can do it." Wales slapped him on the back. "I'm doing all the work back here."

Wales read and pointed through two checklists and before Rand could catch his breath, he found the end of the runway. He pushed the throttles forward and the Fat Lady danced onto the runway. "Holy shit."

Luz tried to adjust behind the monster window and huge iron yoke. "Do you want me to call for takeoff?"

Rand was high. "I really don't care." He saw Wales' big hand reach up and light off the outboard jets.

"Here goes nothin'." Wales laughed. "Here comes a push." He saw the gauges spin up and the CJ610s could barely be heard over the Pratts. The plane lunged forward. "Just keep it straight."

"No shit, Sherlock."

"Lock this." Wales smiled big. At eighty-five knots, Wales yelled "rotate!" over the vibrating, screaming airplane. He saw Rand pull back slightly and nothing changed.

On the second attempt, Rand pulled with the required force and the wheels lifted off the pavement. "Christ." Rand grabbed the large trim wheel. "Fat Lady all right. She's a pig." He saw Wales motion to Luz to raise the gear. The nosewheel clanged up behind them as the plane lumbered into the sky.

Wales enjoyed the ride as the flaps came up. He shut down the outboard jets, pulled the power back to about fifty percent and told Rand to level off at 500 feet. "Let's go buzz the boys at Nella." He grabbed Luz on the shoulder. "Take a heading of three zero zero."

"Okey dokey." Rand pictured himself in Vietnam as the rolling woods below shot under the huge cockpit windows. The old girl flew steadily once he got her trimmed out. He let go of the yoke and nothing changed. "Oink!"

Wales stood up to look over the instrument panel. "See that little dirt road up there?" He pointed so Rand could see his big finger.

"Yep."

"That's it."

"That's what?"

"What this. That's it. There they are." Wales could see the Titan's tail sticking out of the woods. A small shack could barely be seen from the low altitude. There were ten people out on the dirt road that served as a runway. "Buzz their ass."

"Gladly." If there was one thing Rand enjoyed.... He pulled the throttles back and checked the terrain for surprises. He didn't see any power lines or TV antennas that could ruin the day. He ducked below the tree line and brought the huge plane low enough to raise dirt from the strip as the airspeed indicator read 135. He focused on the pines on the far end of the strip and was fairly certain his wingtips wouldn't brush against the trees. "Haven't lived until you get a squirrel."

Wales' laugh was now slightly nervous. He too watched the trees at the far end. This is a crazy bastard. At the very last second, Rand pulled with damp palms on the manhole cover of a yoke and the Fat Lady missed the pine by less than ten feet as he shot her skyward.

"Yeeeehhhaaaaa!" Wales masked his slight moment of fear with his own version of insanity, thankful to have the needed laugh. Luz had ducked down so she couldn't see. "You got a wild one here, lady."

After they returned to Mena, Rand shot two landings and Luz shot three more from the right seat. Still laughing hard over the radials, the trio taxied in. The engines were shut down and the silence was deafening.

"That was fun," Rand deadpanned. "Now what?"

Wales moved into the cargo area. "It's time to hang low. The first phase of the mission is complete. I called Vilez late last night to deliver the bad news of the bust. Told him it was just a fluke. Some drunken woman ran into the motor home. It was all over the papers. With a two million deposit, there was no real grief. I told him that our part of the mission was flawless. We're shooting for the last ten days of July for the big roundup. If we get the two thousand keys on that one, we can hang low for a very long time." He looked at Rand. "We've got a few days. You have anything pressing at home?"

"Yeah. I could use a few days."

"Let's shoot to Lakefront and I'll take Luz with me to Baton Rouge. You can meet us later in the week." He saw relief move in. "What's the deal with your mom?"

"Manic-depressive." The subject was grim.

"You know there is... a cure."

"A cure?" Rand looked at him and Wales read his mind. Again. What... you know everything?

"My cousin's wife had a chronic case. Went through hell and back before he ran across this Indian guy. He gave her a dose of lithium and within a week she was her old self." Wales recognized the same helpless look he had seen on his cousin. "No-shit cured her, my friend."

"Lithium, huh?" Rand looked him in the eye and felt the damn emotion surge toward his throat. He looked away.

"It can be done, my man."

Rand's eyes welled up. "I hate to even get my hopes up. It's been a long, rough road." He gazed down at the tarmac.

"I have his name when you want it."

"Yeah sure." Why not? "Thanks."

Dan Jacobs wore a gray suit as he sat in the elegant chambers of Judge Walter Horton in downtown Ft. Lauderdale. He watched the judge's eyebrows lift as he read the updated profile. Horton finally looked up. "He is not a user?"

"No sir."

"What is driving this man?" Horton had read about the automatic camera malfunction and tried to picture Wales manually restarting it right in front of a man who would have shot him on the spot.

"My best guess, your honor, is adrenaline." Jacobs shook his head.

The judge leaned back again in his leather chair. "Obviously this man could have fled to South America or anywhere else for that matter?"

"Yes sir."

"And he didn't?"

"No sir." The DEA agent crossed his legs with ankle over knee. "In fact sir, he has risked his life beyond any agent I have ever witnessed. And now we have hard evidence against Pablo and taped evidence of the other Cartel leaders. He is the most important weapon we have in the war against drugs." Jacobs pulled pictures from his briefcase and audio tapes followed. "Through Mr. Wales, we have discovered the main source of cocaine into the country. And it is huge. He has provided us with the biggest break in the history of the DEA. And only with his help can we send them all away for life."

"This is incredible." The judge leaned forward behind the large oak desk. "We need to allow this man to continue, there is no doubt about that. What I propose is a suspended sentence and time served. We will leave him on probation and if he happens to step over the line, we have the authority to send him instantly back to prison." He folded his hands on the desk. "Would this be fair in your eyes?" He looked to Ben Richard, Wales' new attorney at ten Ben Franklins per hour.

"Yes sir. Absolutely."

"Now, we'll need to negotiate the same deal with the judge in Baton Rouge. I take it you're going to assist with that case also?" He looked to Jacobs.

"Yes sir, your honor."

Wales had waited outside. He felt instant relief when he saw the big DEA man bust a smile as he approached.

"How much slammer time?"

"None." Jake smiled even bigger.

"Excellent. I can work with that."

The three men flew to Baton Rouge the next morning to meet with the honorable Frank Valore, a law and order Italian raised in the Catholic school systems of Louisiana. Richard and Jacobs caught him on a good day.

"Do you gentlemen realize that this man has probably killed people with the import of cocaine into this country?"

Richard, comfortable in chambers, sat forward in a thick leather chair: "Your Honor, with all due respect, Mr. Wales has not been charged with murder, just as the cigarette and alcohol manufacturers have not been charged with murder." He paused, surprised that the judge didn't rebut the statement. "What my client did is reprehensible, your honor. But the expiation has already benefited the DEA and the country. I guarantee that it will cost the government at least a billion dollars to bring this Cartel to justice without Mr. Wales. This cannot be discounted." Again the judge remained silent. "We have a chance to round up eighty percent of illegal drugs that are being imported into the United States. This will come at enormous risk to the life of my client."

Finally Valore spoke. "So we should unlock the cell and let Mr. Wales fly away?"

"No, your honor. Absolutely not. No matter what the agreement is, we will continue to monitor Mr. Wales closely. If he happens to step from the straight and narrow, we will escort him back to prison for the full term."

"Agreement? What agreement do you propose?"

Richard sat forward again. "The charges are basically the same in Florida and Louisiana, your honor. We see the docket is set for Louisiana first. We just want the two presiding judges to agree that after the first sentence is issued, the second judge will not increase the sentence of the first."

"When are we set for sentencing?" Valore put on his granny glasses and flipped through the case.

"In about thirty days, your honor." Richard opened and flipped through his briefcase. "I am requesting that you review the classified material the DEA has assembled, your honor. I also request consideration of the value Mr. Wales will represent in the possible trial of a dozen traffickers." He looked toward Jacobs as he continued. "And your honor, I uh…we feel that the relationship between my client and the DEA could last for many years to come. The information he can provide is priceless."

The judge looked at Jacobs. "Priceless?"

"Your honor, Mr. Wales is a unique individual. I have come to respect him for answers that have been mysteries at the DEA for years. He has informed us of numerous leaks in our defense against smugglers. I honestly feel that he would find great satisfaction in turning state's evidence and hauling in the Cartel and others. Without him, we would now be severely handicapped."

Valore was slightly impressed. "And do you have any suspicions about his use of cocaine personally?"

"I am certain that he does not use cocaine or anything else, including alcohol."

The judge sat back. "I just can't get it out of my mind that this man defeated our borders and imported the equivalent of three billion dollars of a debilitating drug into our society. To reward him after such a lifetime of this activity rushes against every fiber of my soul." He came forward again to glare into Richard's eyes. "Mr. Richard, I will agree to your proposal, but rest assured, my sentence won't be a walk in the park with an ice cream."

"Yes, your honor." He made a quick mental note. Get a continuance in Louisiana and let the Florida judge sentence first. "I understand. Thank you."

John Cathey beamed as the VP entered the basement office. "You're going to love this, sir."

The former CIA director browsed fifty photographs. "Who is this guy?" He pointed to the Colombian with the striped shirt.

"That is the Cartel leader." Cathey wanted to jump for joy.

"And this guy?" He pointed to another large man with a gangster look.

"I think that's a low-level guy in the Interior Ministry. He can be anyone you want him to be...say, Defense Minister."

"Where was this taken?" Cathey's boss squinted at the corners of the picture.

"Close to Managua. We had a SatNav on board that quit working while they crossed the Gulf. Wales said they were deep in Sandinista country."

"And where is Wales now?" The VP moved to the table with the Miami Herald story of the enormous bust. He checked the Winnebago with a Camaro fused to the front bumper and the handcuffed Italian driver under a ridiculous straw hat.

"He's back in Arkansas."

"This story says five hundred kilos."

"That's the number we gave them." Cathey felt his career rise to the heavens. *I could be his VP.*

"What's the real number?" The taller man picked up another clipping from the Washington Post, exposing solid gold 322 cufflinks on his starched white cuffs.

"Eight hundred. But we only unloaded about one fifty in Miami."

"Where's the rest?"

"Arkansas." The ex-Marine was still uncomfortable in civilian clothes. "You don't really want to know any more than that, sir."

"Just make sure that some of it gets over to the governor's mansion. We don't need these hayseeds standing over us one day with nothing to spit into their eyes."

"We already have Governor Bubba's brother. But this bastard is slick. So far he's taken all the cash and funneled it back into the state. I'm working on him." Cathey looked away. "He does have a definite weakness."

"Like...?"

"Ladies, sir."

"I hope you can do better than that." The VP tapped his foot.

"I'll try, sir. Meanwhile, what would you like to do with these pictures? I believe they would look good on tomorrow's front page."

"Is the DEA finished with Wales?"

"They will be if we release these." Cathey smiled boldly.

"Let's wait. Their convention is coming up in the city by the bay."

"Yeah. One-way streets, two-way men and three-way women." Cathey snickered. Tellin' jokes to the VP.

The VP moaned. "Did Wales get the stuff to our boys okay?"

"Yes sir. Confirmed it this morning."

"And Wales? He has a lot to share."

"He will self-destruct, no problem. And he'll be in Valore's district." Cathey smiled again. "Credibility fades from behind bars... or six feet under."

"Good work. You are a good American." The slim man moved to the door. "I gotta go act wimpy."

Cathey watched the door close. After a cool pause, he pumped his fist. "Yesss...! Yesss...!" He gritted his teeth as his face flushed.

Rand anxiously pushed and peeked around the door to find her propped in the reading position on the bed. "Hey, how ya feeling?"

Judy Chapman was alert and her eyes focused clearly on her son. She laid her book down on the state's wooden table, and smiled warmly. "I am feeling just fine, Rand."

He kissed her. "You're looking great." He sensed that her emotional elevator was near the middle.

"I have been feeling stronger everyday." Her hands were steady. "Where have you been?"

"I have a new job."

"Really? Not on the Merlin?"

"No. The company is in financial trouble, so they laid off over half the workforce and sold the airplane. The good news is that I found a better job... flying a Learjet for a guy."

"Well!" The prayers. "A Learjet! That's exciting." She took his hand as he sat next to her on the bed. "What kind of a guy owns his personal jet?"

Where to begin? "He's an airplane broker. You know, buys and sells them." Close e-nough.

"And Reni? How is that sweet girl?" Judy had never met Reni, but she knew Rand was finally serious about someone.

Her heart sank as he quickly looked away. He did not answer. "Rand?"

He flashed to a huge fist into the side of her head, her clothes ripped, face bloodied. He looked to his mother as her eyes circled his face. "Mom." He held his breath and glanced at the ceiling. "She's dead."

"Dead! Reni is dead?" She sprang to her feet and hugged him. "Oh my God." Judy felt her son's shoulders tremble. "Oh my God, Rand." She patted him on the back and massaged his neck firmly. "Oh my God. When did this happen?"

"Last month." He finally felt relief of tears as he balanced how much her fragile state could bear. "It was in her car. An auto accident." Close e-nough.

"Oh dear God."

He also decided not to tell her that they had broken up. "It's still really hard to talk about, mom."

"God, Rand. I had no idea you were going through all this. I should have been there for you."

"I'll be okay." Rand continued to hold on to her as his face drained tears onto her shoulder.

"I'm getting out of this place soon."

"That's great news. When?"

"Next week."

"That's great. What happened? You seem so much better."

"A miracle. Just an everyday miracle." She pulled back to look in his eyes, but just as he did at age five, held on for a long silence.

Composure took a minute and he finally let go to face her. "What miracle?"

"The miracle of prayer."

Rand stared at her. "Okay."

"I've been reading the Bible that Lois Burns gave me, and I have a new counselor who showed up last week. No one knows who sent him."

"Who is he?"

"He's an Indian, you know, from India. Rashanee, something."

"Did he prescribe medication?"

"Yes."

"Lithium?"

"I think so. How did you know?"

"I've heard a few things about it." Jabba.

"Oh. I have some bad news that I should share." Judy bit her lower lip.

"Bad news?" I don't have room for bad news.

Judy sat back in the chair. "Your Great Aunt May died."

"Aunt May? The one that lives...lived...in Illinois?" Rand had only met her once. "She was sweet."

"Yes, she had a stroke." She locked her eyes on his.

"I also have some good news."

"Oh?" His eyebrows shot skyward. "I like good news."

"May was kind enough to will her nieces a nice little sum of money." Judy's eyes danced.

"Nice little sum?" Rand smiled. "How nice?"

"Three... million... dollars." Judy watched him calculate. "I just found out yesterday."

Rand sat back in disbelief. The wall behind her and his peripheral vision had blurred. "Three million dollars? To you?" His mouth gaped. "Is that right? Just to you?" He reminded himself that he was in the nut house, talking to a mental patient.

She smiled back. "Three million to me, and three million to each of the other four nieces. May didn't have any children of her own, and she had $15 million in GM stock."

"Holy maca-roni." A chill started at the lower back and pinged to the top of his head. He got a quick bad vibe. "What about dad?"

"Well let's see, Rand. I bore three children and had two miscarriages in the twenty-eight years of marriage to him. Now that I'm fifty, my professional career sacrificed for two decades of washing diapers and chasing kids around the house, he was large enough to discard me for another woman." She was stoic, suddenly in a position to make million-dollar decisions. "He was also large enough to file for divorce while I was here trying to reassemble my mind. I believe that we will keep the inheritance very quiet until my new attorney completes the divorce settlement."

Rand stared at his mother. The immediate change was striking. The dignity he remembered from the early days was reborn, from poor and insane to rich and dignified. He continued to smile at her in disbelief. "He already filed?"

She moved her head to peer through the window. A blue jay in the branch where her eyes focused suddenly took flight. "He most certainly did." She finally saw the soothing beauty of her home for the past year. "It's yet another part of the miracle."

"And this all happened in the past month?"

"It did."

The door reopened and a weighty black woman gave Judy a stern look. Rand felt major vibes as if a drug dealer were present. The woman spoke. "In the yard in five." The door closed.

Rand looked back at his mom. "Who was that?"

"The Miracle." Judy moved toward the sink and checked her hair in the mirror. She looked twenty years younger than when she had arrived.

Rand wondered if he were dreaming. He followed a silent Judy past the nurses' station through metal doors to a manicured St. Augustine acre beneath tall pines. The sky seemed to be bluer than ever before. The Miracle waited beneath the lone live oak as moss draped each branch. She took Judy by each hand and hugged her. "This must be your boy." The woman hugged Rand and refused to let go until he felt her power through massive bosom. Rand felt his tense muscles suddenly relax and the woman put her hand to the back of his head. "Oh, what a beautiful son."

Rand nearly choked up. He saw her look past him and he followed her eyes to eight women making their way to the oak. There were hugs all around. Judy looked at a puzzled son. "We do this every Sunday at noon."

They all stepped into the open grass and formed a circle. The big woman took Rand's hand as did a younger black female. His mother was directly across from him with a visible air of serenity. This must be a dream. Rand felt an incredible pulse of ten humans flow through him and miraculous warmth at his heart. They all stood still and closed their eyes, smiling. A great peace quieted the rampage that had flowed through the bonded group for the longest and shortest minute of his life. Slowly, a clear, strong voice began to sing. It was The Miracle. Rand had to open one eye to confirm that is wasn't a recording.

A-mazing grace
How sweet
the sound
that saved
a wretch
li-ike me
I once was lost
but now am found
Was blind
but now
I see....

Tears flowed down twenty-two cheeks as they all looked to the blue sky.

19. Come on Bitch

The national broadcasts by the three major networks beamed the convention into forty percent of all the homes in the United States from the Cow Palace in San Francisco. During the event, directed and choreographed by the opposition party leadership, the polls began to move left. This was happening despite the right's best effort to institute a new national expletive: Liberals. Bleeding heart liberals. The warrior for muted blacks was battered by hatred from the right. The Reverend T.D. Watts was scheduled to speak in prime time.

Through a series of dots the VP now held, in his hands, the text of the speech the Rev was set to deliver in the next twenty-four hours. Time to act.

The Fat Lady arrived in the midnight skies of New Smyrna Beach, Florida. Brophy Wales dismounted, encouraged by news of a possible circumnavigation around the steely bars of federal prison. He completed a series of phone calls to Medellin and confirmed that 2,000 kilos of powder awaited his arrival. His DEA handlers were cautiously optimistic that the sting would lead to the arrest of all three leaders, and that other divisions of the agency would wait in line for a chance to tap the wealth of information Wales possessed.

Luz and Rand crossed the Gulf at midnight deep within the stratosphere. They would begin a descent into Ft. Lauderdale just past the line of weather that ended in one hundred miles. Luz noticed a positive change in her captain's demeanor after his trip to New Orleans and Mandeville. She had made a quick trip to Mexico City for a series of cash deposits and was glad to be back with her man. Shadow snoozed in the back as Rand pointed the radar ahead on the

160-mile range and back to the eighty-mile range. There was a definite line of thunderstorms at about seventy miles, nine minutes ahead. Distant bursts of light confirmed radar echoes.

"That's a pretty big one there." Rand pointed to a bright red return on the screen. "The good thing about Learjets is that thunderstorms are for entertainment purposes only. In the Merlin days, we either picked our way through or we would have to go around the entire line." Again the sky lit up ahead as it had in Hiroshima. One of the red returns took up a thirty-mile increment as Rand pointed the radar's tilt to the zero-degree mark. There were ten monster cells ahead that were mature and the remaining green returns on the screen were either monsters raining themselves out or intensifying into new monsters. Few thunderstorms reach to 40,000 feet, but as evidenced by two cells ahead, some do. One was directly on Jet Fifty-Eight. "Let's get a deviation to the south about twenty degrees."

"Okay my captain." Luz keyed the mike. "Jacksonville Center, Lear One Three Sierra November requests twenty degrees right for weather." She put the mike down and expertly adjusted the tilt to just below the zero-degree mark, which brought a green return at about sixty miles. At five degrees down, the color turned to red, heavy precipitation. As with tilts below the zero mark, the weather was below them.

Rand leaned forward to shield his eyes from the instrument lights and peered into starlit sky. Huge flashes illuminated ahead in a solid line of weather. As the Lear approached the line, Rand saw Mr. Airspeed jump momentarily up ten knots. Lightning shot from cloud to cloud below. "It's a beautiful thing, being so high." He smiled over to Luz. Both felt safe although there was only air between them and the dark Gulf, eight miles below.

Tranquility vanished from Rand's face with another bump, followed by a quick jolt of turbulence and a flameout of the right engine. And just like that, the beauty of flying a Learjet inverted to a nightmare.

Rand immediately threw the igniters to re-light but the engine unwound swiftly toward zero and he knew instantly that the situation was grave. His head flooded with adrenaline and his recall was that the manual called for a descent to 20,000 feet for a restart. Rand moved the tilt on the radar ten degrees down. "Shit." Lightning outside and red returns on the radar screen screamed that they were headed for hairy arms of the biggest monster he'd ever seen. They plunged into a cell that painted for thirty miles and caught a downdraft that sucked them to a nose-down dive. He thought about turning around but knew it would be the same sad story. "Get the engine restart checklist off the quick reference list, Luz."

Luz fumbled with the list with trembling hands. She kept looking for Rand's easy-going no problema face, but it had been replaced with frantic searching eyes.

Without an engine to crunch thin air into the cabin for thick, breathable air, the pressure began to leak. The altitude warning horn sounded loudly as cabin pressure rose to over 10,000 feet. "Put your mask on." Rand quickly switched his mike control to his oxygen mask. "Jacks...the Learjet Three Sierra November is in an emergency descent to 20,000 feet...uhh...flight level two-zero-zero. We have an engine flameout and are attempting a restart." He pulled his mask up to speak to Luz. "Keep the list out and hold on."

A violent jolt welcomed them into a 50-degree right bank as the monster exhaled cold air from 40,000 feet to the surface in a hundred-foot wide shaft at minus fifty Fahrenheit. Rand wrestled the wings level until a breath rose from the warm Gulf waters with a force that knocked the sleeping Shadow onto the floor via the ceiling. Luz was sure the airplane had come apart. Just behind that shaft, another cold shaft moving downward at a 150 miles per convinced Rand that this was not a survivable flight. "Engine heat on!" He hit two silver toggles behind his left thigh but didn't have time to see that the left engine heat switch had failed. Crunching slaps of hail sounded like gravel on the windscreen. His head hit the instrument panel in front of him as the Lear flipped to a 110-degree right bank. Rand's gut commanded a barrel roll with a hard kick of right rudder but the Lear had lost obedience. He saw Mr. Attitude with blue side down. Mr. Airspeed was a corpse. Rand had lost his friends and realized that he was in an inverted, flat spin. He saw Mr. Altitude unwind through streaks of instrument lights as glasses broke in the cabin. His face smashed into the glareshield and his oxygen mask jammed into the bridge of his nose. Luz was an unconscious rag doll over her yoke. He wanted to reach for her, but extreme turbulence only allowed him to hold on for dear life. Gravel pounded the windscreen. A shotgun blast to the face was a lightning strike. Thunder rolled as adrenaline snaked his brain and he caught a glance at the radar: All red. He flashed to A-toney. What goes around...comes around. Rand kicked the rudder again. Nothing. This absurd dream is finally ending. He eyed the landing gear handle, but couldn't reach it. You're gonna pay. Another deafening blast of gravel. Never amounted to shit. Shadow's 300 pounds again went to the ceiling before landing flat on his back with a thud. Rand saw his mother's smiling face, young and happy. He kicked left rudder. Nothing.

Rand finally lunged at the gear handle and lowered it. He gave a hard push on the right rudder and full aileron. Mr. Attitude rolled blue side up at 18,000 feet. Rand pushed the nose down to revive Mr. Airspeed. They were out of the cell and into light precip through 12,000. Rand finally got his right hand off the yoke, grabbed Luz by the hair and jerked off her oxygen mask and pulled her head by her hair away from the yoke. Blood streamed steadily from a cut on the bridge of her nose.

He saw a definite end to red returns that were scattered on his screen and he attempted to pick his way around. He pushed the left engine throttle forward and banked hard to the south to avoid a large cell. Accumulated hail on the left engine inlet suffocated the life from his remaining engine that also powered his last generator. "You...motherfucker." Rand Chapman held a straight wing glider as his main flight instruments died in darkness. The battery supplied only enough to power the gyro for a standby attitude indicator, its internal light and one VHF radio as he sank swiftly toward dark, shark infested water.

Mr. Altimeter was not his friend through 2,000 feet. Rand banked around a cloud that shot lightning horizontally. In between rain showers, silence screamed that this was the end. He looked quickly to the right engine RPM gauge that windmilled at fifteen percent. Mr. Airspeed barely breathed at 200 knots as he silently rehearsed a ditching. He would break the descent at a hundred feet, stall out just above the water and hope the sharks wouldn't eat them. Great plan. He looked at Luz one final time. At 700 feet, he freed his hand from the yoke to push the start switch to high ignition. The right engine spun up slowly as ice began to melt from the inlet. He needed to push the nose down to help the start process but Mr. Altitude would not allow it. He pulled back on the yoke for the impact on the waves and faint optimism shoved the right engine throttle to the firewall. "Come on bitch." The jet lunged forward with a burst of redeeming thrust and the sweetest engine whine... ever. The airplane held altitude at fifty feet and began to accelerate and climb away from sharks under power of a cold right engine at maximum thrust. Rand raised the gear and she climbed better. At 1,000 feet, he popped the right generator back on line; the radar and radio lights were reborn. He could see just one small green return of light rain as he restarted the left engine. The plane popped from the eastern edge of the line into a clear night sky. The lights of Tampa-St. Pete shone gloriously, just forty miles ahead. Rand felt, with great relief, a strong pulse on the co-pilot's neck.

Shadow crawled groggily toward the cockpit. "Goddamn. I hope you're finished," he whispered.

Rand turned. "Are you okay?"

"Fuck no. I think my ribs are broken."

The gravity of total responsibility hit the captain's seat like a ton of bricks. What did I do wrong? Could I have avoided that? His heart sank with one of two possible answers.

Rand turned to Shadow. "Can you pull Luz out of here?"

He crawled up to the cockpit again as Rand engaged the autopilot and unbuckled her seatbelt. Through pain, Shadow pulled Luz by the underarms to the cabin floor. The passenger oxygen masks had released from the ceiling and dangled from the rubber cords. Shadow strapped a mask around her face and her eyes came open momentarily.

Luz regained consciousness. "What happened?" Her eyes focused on Shadow. "Oh my God." She knew they had been at war. She saw blood on her hand after touching her busted mouth. There was a knot on the right side of her forehead and she felt faint. She got to her knees and leaned up to Rand. "Are we okay?"

Rand flipped through the Jeppeson manual for Tampa and found an approach control frequency. "Yes. How are you?" The right side of Rand's face hid the blood stream onto his shirt and manuals.

"I'm okay." She moved back into the right seat. "Where are we?"

"That's Tampa right there." He looked ahead to the sea of lights below. He held up his hand to Luz and gave the new frequency a try. "Tampa Approach, Learjet One Three Sierra November at 5,000 feet."

The speaker answered. "Lear One Three Sierra November, this is Tampa Approach. How do you hear, sir?"

"Loud and clear."

"Roger, sir. We've been trying to contact you. Say your conditions."

Rand pulled the mike to his bloody lower lip. "We're okay, sir. Had an engine failure and we dropped into the business end of a thunderstorm."

"Are you declaring an emergency?"

Thoughts of lights and sirens, a vision of the FAA poking around to ask lots of questions made up his mind. "Negative." He looked at his wounded co-pilot and grabbed her chin. "You okay?"

"I think that I am okay." She saw the blood on Rand's face. "Oh, your face is bleeding."

"Yes, baby. Let's shoot over to Lauderdale. We need to be in position in the morning."

"Of course, my captain. Her lip was swollen and her eye was going to be black.

"The plane is flying well."

The landing was at Ft. Lauderdale's Executive Airport. All three visited the emergency room at the hospital downtown before checking into the Bahia Mar. Shadow had four broken ribs and Rand received stitches on his left forehead. Luz took stitches under her front lips. Her bottom teeth seemed loose.

As they emerged from the emergency room, Luz found strength. "What happened out there Rand?"

He put his arm around her. "Well, while you were sleeping..."

John Cathey finally got the word from the upper portion of the building that he occupied on Pennsylvania Avenue. It was time to expose the Nicaraguan government for the lying drug-smuggling villains that they were. Although the polls continued to show the thespian with a commanding lead over a bland challenger, it was high time to divert attention away from the convention of bleeding heart speeches. Cathey deposited glossy prints of the shots taken from the aft bulkhead of the Fat Lady into a large manila envelope. He positively identified the Cartel leader and took a SWAG, sophisticated wild ass guess, as to the identity of the remaining figures in the picture. In plain view was the image of one Brophy Wales. He called his contact at the Washington Times and arranged a rendezvous to transfer the shots and text, with a spin, of the events that had led to the photographs.

Brophy Wales came down the elevator at the downtown Miami Omni. As the sun defeated the horizon to the east, pastel colors of Florida began to illuminate the day. Shadow sat in the lobby and, as the elevator opened, Wales gave him a quick eye contact. Camille Mouton waited outside the lobby in the airporter, a 1975 Chevelle. Wales kept airporters at six different small airports in Florida. They were parked in the FBO or long-term lots with the ignition key just lying on the front right tire. Each car had the look of a beat-up wreck, but under each hood was a perfectly tuned engine. With the constant possibility of a tail, he had another path to invisibility.

Mouton wheeled north and checked his rear-view for tags. "Mornin', boss."

"Boss this. I've got the ducks on the pond." Wales smiled big. "Just got off the horn with Vilez. He'll be flying back on the Fat Lady with us."

"You got to be shitting me." Mouton swerved. "How the hell did you do that?"

"What's the second most powerful thing in the world, Mouton?"

"Pussy."

"You are correct. You win the prize." Wales patted him on the back. "I painted the most beautiful picture for my boy Carlos. We're having a big party in a place he's always wanted to go: New York City."

"He's flying back with 2,000 keys of cocaine so he can get his ass run over by a taxicab? I'm sure Pablo would kill him if he knew."

"Kill this. You're not listening, Mouton. I know a comedian in Greenwich Village, an Aussie sheila, does a great impression of Olivia Newton-John."

"You are a true genius." Mouton recalled that Vilez had every album, every film of the Australian actress. He laughed.

"Genius this. She told him how bloody horny she was before whispering that it was coke that made her pussy itch with passion. That she had a private gig in the village Sunday night and she would love to meet him at her new place on Tenth Street." Wales reached over and patted Mouton on the back. "There's gonna be a fuckin' goin' on, but it's gonna be Uncle supplying the stiff one."

"And he fell for it?"

"Fall for this, Mouton. When you want something to happen so badly, you do crazy, stupid things. Hook, line, sinker, the entire boat. He took it all." Wales looked ahead as a Florida state trooper passed in a dark Mustang. "I just hope we can trust our boys."

"Jacobs?" He gunned onto the I-95.

"Damn Mouton, I wonder about you sometimes. Jacobs is about the only guy I trust that works for Uncle."

Mouton exited at Commercial Boulevard in Lauderdale to the beach and wheeled next to the black sedan of Agent Jacobs in the empty parking lot of the Seawatch Restaurant. Wales switched cars and Mouton departed with dreams of his future Andean palace stocked with half-naked babes.

Wales caught his breath. "It's all set, Jake. Señor Vilez will be accompanying me on my return to the Estados Unidos."

"You must be kidding!"

"He will be flying in to LaGuardia on Eastern 825 from Ft. Lauderdale on Sunday. He will proceed to 27 Tenth Street in the Village to meet a contact that will not be there. You should make something happen before he gets there. But please, don't mention my name."

"This is great."

"I gotta ask, Jake, how much do you know about this Maestro goomba?"

"Who?"

"That's what I thought."

"Outside my domain, Bro. I've been told many times to stay away from political theories."

"Theory this. Cathey's suddenly all over the place and he thinks he's invisible." Wales leaned against his door to face the agent. "I have eyes and ears all over Central America."

"Do I need to hear this?"

"I don't know. Do you want to bury your head in the sand?"

"I've got a family...four kids." Jake paled with reluctance. "Tell me what you've heard."

"This might take a while." Wales scanned the parking lot and considered a bug in the car. "Let's take a walk."

"Where?" Jake watched Wales open his door.

"Leave your jacket in the car."

The agent followed the Jabba waddle behind the restaurant to the beach. They took seats on a bench under a palm. Atlantic air pushed leaves gently while Wales told of an M-16 manufacturer and a flight school. "Hear this. Our boy Cathey is running some kind of money scheme with the General in Panama to ship arms to the Iranians."

"Whoa. This is far-fetched." Jake smiled. "Okay, where did you hear that?"

"Let me finish. I don't think you want to know yet."

"Okay."

"There is cash stirring with the load we brought in from Nick. You know we only dropped a hundred keys at Tamiami."

"Only?"

"That was only a tenth of what we brought in."

"Where's the rest?"

"It continued to Mena."

"Mena?"

"In a southern-as-they-come state. The boys have me running and funding quite an operation... a flight school for the Nick rebels, a production line of unmarked M-16s."

"What about law enforcement?"

"It's all taken care of by the governor and his brother."

"Shit." Jake watched waves hit the beach ahead. "He's taking the powder?"

"Hell no. He's too slick to fall for that. He's cashing in on politics. Thinks he's gonna be president one day." Wales shook his head with incredibility.

"This is complicated. Who's coordinating this?"

"It's coming from real high. Cathey's the face."

"Where?"

"You know where the Permian Basin is?"

"In Texas?"

"Bingo." Wales smiled. "You don't have to answer this."

"Okay."

"I know that you have a plant set in Pablo's group." Jacobs flinched backward. "It's okay, she's still safe." Wales read his mind: Goddamn. "Evidently, you all had some video taken of a transfer in Ft. Meyers last month." Wales looked to the agent as he stared to the sand below. "Your partner had me trace the airplane's tail number." Jacobs finally looked up for information. "It's a corporate asset from a drilling company in Odessa, Texas. The company is run by close ties to the... our...VP."

"You must be shitting."

"Shit this. Your boys have a videotape of his sons taking delivery of at least two kilos."

"Holy shit."

"I don't know what you want to do with that info, but I would get the girl out of Colombia."

"Today." Jacobs conceded.

"And I would be eternally grateful if you could get me a copy of the tape of Ft. Meyers. It would be my get out of jail free card."

"That...won't be easy."

The reporter from the Washington Times laid the pictures down on the desk of his editor. "Look at this."

On top of the stack was the shot of Brophy Wales, Pablo and a man that Cathey said was a defense minister in the Sandinista Government. The editor whistled. "This will look nice on the front page."

20. Uranus

The right reverend peered to his speechwriter in San Francisco. "This is beautiful." He imagined how he would use his booming voice to deliver each portion as a distinct sadness hovered above him. He knew that the American experience was a beautiful thing for the European herd that had voyaged across the Atlantic to be welcomed by the sight of the Statue of Liberty and the promise of equality and prosperity. Or the South American herd that came with their families intact for their children's education. Or the Asian herd that came for space, education and unchecked liberty. But the herd the reverend led was different. His herd looked, talked, and walked different. His herd was bewildered, confused and angry.

They had been ripped from their homes four generations earlier, severing family trees, cutting their roots and replanting them on a desert of hate and mistrust. No one ever said to them: Welcome to America! They slaved stifling cotton fields and were paid nothing. Yet it was they that were called thieves when attempting to provide for their families. In the land of equality, they were not allowed in the same bathroom as the other herds or allowed to drink from the same water fountain.

In 1968, the leader of the African herd was strong. He began to call the white man's bluff. He eloquently pointed out specific words of the Constitution. He pointed to hate. He pointed to great injustices done. He preached peace. And he was shot to death.

As the leader bled to death, another man, not as strong, not as stirring, not as eloquent, stood over the dying man and promised to carry on the fight for justice. Throughout the years, as he listened to enormous atrocities from his people, he remained calm and focused. Yet when he spoke on his people's behalf, the descendents of the framers of freedom and liberty would call him nigger. And they would call all of his people niggers. White life was a beautiful picture while the ghettos rang with gunfire and role models gulped Mad Dog on the corner.

The reverend knew that in this America, ears were deafened with a trembling fear disguised as prejudice and hate. Despite all the denials to the contrary, he knew the truth. Yet, the tall black man had a faith that held him strong against slander and ridicule. He was assured from above that he was no more and no less than any person who walked the soil from the Atlantic to the shaky ground on which he now stood. God had graced him with ability to read, although he knew that for a century it was a crime in this land to educate people of his color. This atrocity was overcome and his generation was the first to read the U.S. Constitution. He loved the first sentence of his speech:

Tonight we come together bound by our faith in an almighty God, with genuine respect and love for our country and inheriting the legacy of a great party, which is the best hope for redirecting our nation on a more humane, just and peaceful course.

He smiled at his editor. "Beautiful."

It is not a perfect party. We are not a perfect people. Yet we are called to a perfect mission: To feed the hungry; clothe the naked; to house the homeless; to teach the illiterate and to choose the human race over the nuclear race.

He flipped forward to the economic heart of his message:

The President says the nation is in recovery. Those 90,000 corporations that made a profit last year but paid no Federal taxes are recovering. The 37,000 military contractors who have benefited from the President's more than doubling of the military budget in peacetime are surely recovering. The big corporations and rich individuals who received the bulk of a three-year, multi-billion dollar tax cut are recovering. But no such recovery is under way for the least of these. Rising tides don't lift all boats, particularly those stuck at the bottom.

The reverend nodded as he scanned the conclusion:

I have a message for our youth. I challenge them to put hope in their heart and not dope in their veins.

In every slum there are two sides. When I see a broken window...that's the slummy side. Train some youth to become a glazier; that is the sunny side. When I see a missing brick...that is the slummy side. Let that child in the union to become a brick mason and build; that is the sunny side. When I see a missing door...that is the slummy side. Train some youth to become a carpenter; that is the sunny side. When I see the vulgar words and hieroglyphics of destitution on the walls...that is the slummy side. Train some youth to be a painter and artist; that is the sunny side.

We come from disgrace to amazing grace. Our time has come. Give me your tired, give me your poor, your huddled masses who yearn to breathe free and come November, there will be a change because our time has come. Thank you and God bless you.

The reverend got on his knees. He asked a just God to let the speech be heard without hatred. Yet he knew... he knew... that millions would hear the speech and call him nigger. And he was right.

While cameras rolled on the convention floor in San Francisco, a newspaper was delivered by the thousands on the streets of Washington D.C. The front page carried a photograph and article that masked a political agenda: to keep those in power, in power. The target audience was the mainstream American herd, which had few resources to watchdog the commercial press. The propaganda tossed out by the acta non verba group to a story-hungry media would soon network itself across the country. Timing was everything. As a result of the story, the chance to halt nearly three-quarters of the world's cocaine trade would die. As a result, millions would self-inflict themselves with a fortune-killing, family-killing, future-killing drug. All done to divert the nation's short attention span away from the bleeding hearts in San Francisco.

Rand's beeper sang. The line on the pager read 09-6879888-5. He made the call to a payphone where Wales waited, in the hotel lobby at Pier 66 at the Intracoastal in Ft. Lauderdale. "Yes?"

"Yes this. Pink and round on the water...in the café in twenty." Wales whispered in the phone.

"Oh-tay." Rand called the valet and looked at Luz, who was checking her busted lip in the mirror. "Gotta run, mi amor. Bro wants to talk." Rand slid his trunks down and grabbed a pair of shorts and sandals. "The ocean will have to wait."

"I think that I will stay in the hotel, at the pool." Luz brushed her hair out.

"Good idea. I think things are gonna start happening. Stay at the pool or in the room until I get back." He planted a kiss on her neck from behind. The rented Thunderbird waited outside the lobby with engine running. Rand fingered the windows down to allow an ocean breeze through. Alabama sang the anthem for him and he turned it up loud when asked. He found a spot in the lot at Pier 66 and headed toward a corner table in the lobby café. Wales sat with Mouton and Fuss, his back to the wall to check every creature that entered; most were rich raisins from the northeast.

"We have gathered here today." Wales smiled. "What the hell happened to you?"

"Wasn't pretty, boss." Rand touched the butterfly bandage on his left eyebrow. "Your airplane tried to kill me."

"Kill this. What happened?"

Rand gave him the full account of the near-ditch, near-deather.

"How many thunderstorms have you flown through?"

"One too many."

"One two this. We need to check that engine. That sucker shouldn't flame out with a gust of wind." He cut his eyes to check Shadow, who gave no sign of trouble.

"I was just glad the bitch decided to re-light. I'd be a shark turd by now." Rand grinned. "I might divert to Toronto next time I paint a big cell."

A waitress landed four glasses of water and Wales spotted a tiny black dot floating in his. As she turned he stopped her. "Darlin'. Would you bring me a new glass without ice in it please?" As he watched her move to the bus table, he took a serious tone. His Mexican wedding shirt was pajama comfortable. No comfort would be possible if he knew that his picture was all over the streets of Washington, D.C.

Wales continued to scan the crowd casually while Shadow smoked a cigarette within view, in the lobby. "Okay boys. We're gonna fly after lunch to the Fat Lady." He looked quickly back to Rand. "I want you to come back here and stand by for the duration. If something blows up, I want to know you can scoop us in a matter of minutes. Keep a good eye out for Colombians and stay within fifteen minutes of the Lear tomorrow and the next day."

"Oh-tay."

"If you hear anything... anything... I should know or you think I might want to know, beep me." The brown eyes looked for understanding and got it. "If we are not back in three days, by Saturday, get your ass out of here via Palm Beach. I'm talking commercial. Leave the Lear here and skedaddle." He looked intently at Rand. "And have a nice life."

Rand felt his gut churn. "A nice life...?"

"If we're not back by Saturday, surely we have all died of lead-poison."

"Can I keep the jet?" Rand managed to make the other two laugh.

Wales continued to smile through his adrenaline orgy. "Jet this. You can fight Uncle Sugar for it." He patted Rand on the back. "How's your mom?"

Rand jumped slightly at the surprise question. "My mom? She's doin' good. Much better, in fact."

"Good." He grabbed Rand's shoulder lightly. "Now go have lunch with your co-pilot and save enough strength to fly for an hour or so." Wales could not hide his good feeling toward Rand. "Life is good?"

Rand stood. "Couldn't be much better."

"Better this."

Rand hand-flew the Lear up to 15,000 before he made a power-off descent into New Smyrna Beach, where the Fat Lady hid behind an aluminum hangar. Wales and his two crew members moved quickly to the bigger plane and within a minute the Lear streaked down the runway. Just for grins, Rand let Luz fly back to Lauderdale at 1,000 feet along the beach, scaring the hell out of the bored, banner-towing pilots that hug the beach with advertisements of dollar beers and happy hours. "We're fifteen minutes from the Bahamas." Rand pointed to the radar, which painted Andros off to the left. "One day girl."

"I would like that." Luz held the jet softly in her hands as she kept the airspeed at 250 for the short hop back into Ft. Lauderdale-Hollywood. Rand shut down the engines in front of Red Bird Aviation and kissed her on the mouth. "Beautiful." He ordered the fuel to be topped off and waited for them to finish before he paid in cash from the satchel of Franklins. It was good to have 10,000 walking-around dollars in his pocket. He had opened twenty-eight more accounts around the Pontchartrain on his last visit.

Red Bird's young receptionist drove them to the terminal car rental. She didn't notice two dark-skinned South Americans following in the white sedan. Neither did Rand, as he drove the rented Thunderbird to the Bahia Mar. Back in the room, he clicked on the TV while he and Luz undressed for a swim.

CBS News ran a promo for its coverage of the convention in San Francisco before the anchor appeared for the five-thirty report. "The convention is in full swing tonight with a full slate of leaders scheduled to address the delegates. But first... Breaking news on Nicaragua. The Washington Times reported today that top ministers in the Sandinista government have been directly involved with cocaine trafficking into the United States. In pictures released with the story, a government official is seen loading bales of cocaine into an airplane bound for Florida."

Rand's jaw dislodged with video footage of the Fat Lady on the ground at New Smyrna. A reporter was on the scene. "The sting was set up by the Drug Enforcement Agency and proves Sandinista government involvement in illegal importation of cocaine, confirming the administration's accusations that the regime is corrupt and that the U.S.-supported Contras should be allowed to arm."

"Hole-E-Shit." Rand saw Luz tremble with the image of the Fat Lady beaming out to the entire nation. "We need to get the fuck out of here." The phone rang and his beeper went off simultaneously. He glanced down: 09-7889886-1. His adrenaline spiked as he picked up the phone. "Yes?"

"Get home. Now."

"No shit. I saw it." The line was already dead. Rand put the phone down and missed the receiver. He reset it with shaking hands. He called the valet to bring around the T-Bird. In the lobby he noticed a Latino with a thin frame and steely eyes. Oh boy. He saw another one watching him as he came out into the drive when the rental arrived. They both just happened to move out into the driveway as Rand pushed the accelerator wishing for about ten times the engine he now had.

Luz looked at Rand. "Did you see them?"

"Matter of fact...I did." He glanced over. "Whaddaya think?"

"They are Colombians. No doubt."

"And how do you know that?" He checked the rear-view.

"I can just tell." She saw a gold Mercedes parked in the lot at the Sheraton as they passed. "And there are two more."

"Two more?" Rand looked around and back into the mirror. "Where?"

"In the gold Mercedes behind you." She leaned to look out of the side mirror.

Rand saw the car get out on the road behind them, maintaining a good fifty-yard tail. His heart began to process another adrenaline rush. "You know Luz, life used to be so simple. I would just teach flying to total incompetents and go to Lafitte's and order a dozen or so birds and pass out in my bed. I'd wake up with a major headache everyday. But nobody ever... and I mean ever... wanted to kill me." Rand figured he'd have a better chance of flying to Uranus on a skateboard than outrunning the German sedan. "I miss Lakefront. I had some good friends there. Everybody seemed to like me there." He checked the mirror as they passed Pier 66. The bridge was down with no sign of going up, and the Pacific Princess was docked below and to the left. "Hey! There's the damn Loveboat. Nobody ever tried to kill me at Lakefront... on purpose."

Luz slumped slightly in her seat as they turned off Seventeenth Street toward the airport. "They are still there?"

Rand glanced back. "Oh yeah." He blinkered to the far right lane. "Hungry? Want a donut or somethin'?"

"No, thank you." She cut her eyes at her crazy man.

"Dave Morgan tried to kill me once. Spun a Cougar out over the swamp one fine day." Again he glanced, hoping he would wake up very soon in a relieving cold sweat.

The radio remained on. "And here's a little tune from Willie Nelson."

"You've...got to be shitting me." Rand pushed the button and picked up another station from Miami. It was Buffett. "Sing it Jimmy." He sang along loudly to Son of a Sailor, glancing back before turning down the street and into the FBO. "I have a plan, girl." He parked in the small lot and walked through the empty lobby and into the hangar. He tried to whistle but nothing came out except dry air. "Get in the right seat and get us a clearance."

"To where?"

"West Palm." Rand winked.

"Yes, my captain." Luz moved normally to the Lear, which was parked in the corner of the hangar. She opened the door and squeezed into the right seat as the two Colombians headed for a Cessna 182. They did not have a key to the plane and set down a leather bag just larger than a Mac 10 sub-machinegun under the wing. One of the men pointed at the pitot tube and said something before glancing in Rand's direction. He figured correctly that these men knew very little about the airplane they were discussing. Rand was very glad to see a lineman fueling a Beech Baron near the Cessna. He casually walked up to him.

"How about pulling the Lear out for us? We'll be leaving here in about twenty minutes, when Mr. Wales shows up." He was loud enough for the boys to hear.

The lineman looked over across the wing. "Would you like it out now?"

"Now would be nice." Or ten seconds ago. He eased over to the Lear and stuck his head through the open door. "How ya doing, darlin'?"

Luz kept her head down as she programmed the GNS. "You see our friends over there?"

"Si, Señorita," he whispered. The lineman was there with the tug and attached the tow bar to the nose gear. Rand looked up at him. "Ya got a red carpet?"

"Yessir."

"It would be a nice touch." Rand smiled.

"No problem." The young guy pulled the plane into the ready position in front of the lobby and laid a traditional red carpet by the entry door on the tarmac.

The Colombians remained unnoticed by the FBO staff. A young female receptionist returned to the office after dropping customers at the terminal building. A cooler breeze blew off the ocean as the sun began to sink to the west behind afternoon cumulus. Rand's hair moved slightly.

"Luz? Would you please put the tower on the number one radio?" As he watched her dial in the frequency, Rand spotted the tail number of the Piper Navajo next to the two Colombians. N82PM. He leaned into the cockpit with one foot on the entry door, cupped his left hand around the mike and pressed it to his lips. "Tower! This is Navajo Eight Two Poppa Mike. We are on fire!!"

"Calling Lauderdale Tower... Say again."

Rand pushed the key button again, his voice in panic, "I say again...Navajo Eight Two Poppa Mike at Red Bird Aviation facing south on the tie-down area...We are on fire, sir! Please send the trucks!" He put the mike down and glanced at Luz. "Crank the right motor, girl."

"Roger Poppa Mike. Will do." The controller pushed his red fire station button and within thirty seconds the first of two screaming, flashing, firetrucks rushed to the surprised ramp area.

The Colombians suddenly lost interest in the 182 and began a nonchalant move toward the hangar as the truck screeched to a stop. In the confusion, Rand quickly boarded and closed the door behind him, clambering into the left seat. "Call for taxi." He fired up the left engine and taxied toward Nine Left, blowing the red carpet up against the hangar door. He looked over to Luz. "Nicely done." As the two Colombians explained that they knew nothing about a fire, the Lear barreled down the runway and shot into the skies of South Florida, safer with each foot of altitude. They hugged the coast to West Palm Beach while Luz filed a flight plan across the Gulf to Baton Rouge. As she called Miami Center for clearance, Rand pushed the throttles for a climb to 39,000 feet.

Luz cancelled IFR though 17,000 feet on the descent into Baton Rouge as Rand began an eastward descending spiral to 1,000 feet. He tree-topped it into the familiar rectangular Abita Springs Airport within the dark pine forest. He asked ol' Harvey to bury the jet in the hangar. The old man whistled between his front teeth at the sight of a Learjet on his ramp as Rand slipped him two Franklins. Nothin' unusual bout seein' somethin' unusual round here. Rand asked for and received the keys for a Warrior that slept on the ramp. Twenty minutes later, he landed the loaner on One-Eight Right at Lakefront Airport and taxied over to Aero. Dawn was working the nightshift. She looked at Rand like he was a leper when he asked her to call a taxi for him and his Latin companion. He had changed. His hair was long and scraggly; his skin was a dark tan. It seemed decades had passed.

The cab delivered the pilots to St. Philip Street and the wrought iron gate of Lafayette Place. Rand introduced Luz to his apartment before he fell into restless sleep. The phone rang at seven the next morning. "Yes?"

"Yes this. Beignets and coffee in fifteen."

"Oh-tay." Rand hung up and looked in wonder at Luz.

"I can't believe it. He's here in New Orleans."

"What?" She jumped out of bed. "Where?"

"Just around the corner."

Rand and Luz took the table for four in the back corner of the outside patio of Café DuMonde. Wales slipped in off Decatur and joined them. "Morning, kids."

Rand looked around the cafe. "News flash Bro: There're some folks out there that are not diggin' you."

"You are very observant. Good move getting back here." Wales' air of confidence was clearly thinner.

"How'd you get here?" Luz asked.

"Parked the Fat Lady at Mena and Camille and I flew the Seneca into Lakefront. Been up all night." Wales scanned the crowd.

"Bro...What de fuck is going on?"

"I've been doublecrossed. There are some dangerous people in Washington right now with deep, dark secrets. They would like to find a permanent silencer for me."

"It's been nice knowing you, Bro." Rand smiled at the dead man sitting. "You know Harvey at Abita?"

"Of course."

"He's got your jet. I told him to fill the tanks." Rand tried to guess his first response. Tank this... Fill this... Jet this.

But it was just: "Okay, thanks. I'll be in touch." Wales smiled at Luz. "Hang very low for awhile." He looked to Rand, stood before the beignets arrived, kissed Luz, gave Rand a soul shake, waddled across Decatur and disappeared into the Quarter.

21. Acta non Verba

Judge Valore opened the door from his chambers and walked into the courtroom as the defendant slowly got to his feet. Wales felt confident, knowing that the judge in Lauderdale had thrown away the book with glowing phrases: "Rarely do I waive incarceration for such a serious offence, but when a man risks his life for the good of our system, it goes beyond anything I have ever witnessed. Mr. Wales, I sentence you to probation and timed served."

As Valore read over that very sentence, his face began to flush. His feelings as a devoted Catholic, sworn to find forgiveness and love in his heart for all of God's creatures, were overcome by sheer hatred for the smuggler. He could barely look at Wales. He could only see him delivering tons of vile white powder to the society that Valore was hired to protect. He could only see the ruined families and the open wound that drugs had inflicted on the nation. He read over the letter from Wales' attorney, which reminded him of the plea agreement they had made. And his face flushed redder. He looked up from the signed plea bargain and rage rushed him. He looked back down. Finally, he was controlled enough to speak, but the strict law-and-order judge could not hide outrage.

"If I had the remotest idea, the slightest idea, that Mr. Wales would not receive a jail sentence in Florida, under no circumstances would I have accepted this plea agreement." He flashed eyes of scorn through his wire glasses under thick black hair. He wanted to rip his impotent robe off. In the church, he was a trustee, commentator and senator. In this court... his own court... he had been railroaded.

As Wales and his attorney sat back in their chairs, the defendant wondered what was for lunch. He knew that his former friends in Colombia had put a huge price on his head, so he had increased his shadows from one to five. Three of them blended just outside the courthouse now. They had also been there while he testified and watched fifteen former colleagues hauled off to prison as a result. He felt his contribution to the drug war had begun to pay off for everyone as he waited patiently for the government to round up more cartel members. He was bigger than Lafitte. Wales saw the overhead lights reflect off the glasses of the man in the black robe.

"As far as I'm concerned, drug dealers like Mr. Wales are the lowest, most despicable type of people. In my own opinion, people like you, Mr. Wales, should be in a Federal penitentiary. You all ought to be there working at hard labor. Working in the hottest sun or the coldest day wouldn't be good enough for drug dealers like you."

Labor this.

"Your probation is going to be strict. No bodyguards."

Wales watched his attorney jump to his feet. "Your honor! My client has a million-dollar price on his head."

Valore stared him down. "Take your chances, Mr. Wales. Take your chances. Have bodyguards with guns, and take your chances." He swallowed. "And if you leave Louisiana, I don't care if it's the CIA, I don't care if it's the State Department, I don't care if it's the U.S. Attorney, I don't care who it is, you don't go any place, any place, without my personal written approval in advance."

Richard peered up to the judge. "Do you want them all to notify you? Mr. Wales happens to speak with all those agencies."

Valore continued turning his scorn toward the defense table. "We only have one government, sir."

"In this case," the lawyer responded, "I have found that not to be exactly true."

The Federal judge, on the bench for a dozen years, reached into his legal arsenal and found a grenade. And he lobbed it at the table that faced him. "As a further condition of your probation, Mr. Wales, you will reside at the Salvation Army Community Treatment Center at 7361 Airline Highway, Baton Rouge, Louisiana for a period of..." He looked up as the attorney stood. "...six months."

Richard spoke loudly. "That's a double-cross by the government!"

Now it was Valore's eyes that narrowed. "It is not a double-cross."

"Yes, sir, it is."

"Read the plea agreement."

"I have read the agreement, your honor; I am very familiar with it. I hammered it out. It says no incarceration." The lawyer fumed.

Wales sat stoically and realized that this was the way they would shut him up. No bodyguards at an unprotected facility in a sentence handed down swiftly from the Federal judge. He pictured himself the clay pigeon. They won. He admired the subtlety of the sentence. Acta non verba.

The judge continued. "This is not incarceration." He stared at the defense table. "Mr. Wales, would you like to withdraw your plea?"

Wales did not answer. Plea this.

"Let me tell you what." Valore pointed his finger at the most important drug informant in the history of the United States. "I would love for this plea agreement to be broken. I'd love for it to be broken right now."

22. Luz Means Light

Rand lay awake once more. Six months had passed since the last flight with Brophy Wales. The Voodoo economic plan of the White House was based on a trickle-down theory that American voters had sucked up with unprecedented gullibility. The gulf between rich and poor was widening and the New Orleans economy had not been trickled upon. Rand had landed the only new job at Lakefront Airport, flying boxes, single-pilot to Louisville every weeknight for UPS in an early-model Swearingen Metroliner. There was no autopilot, so he handflew seven hours each night around thunderstorms, through ice and rain, but mostly through smooth night air. It gave him an over-abundance of time to ponder the complications of the spinning rock below. He loved the peace of flying at night, and occasionally brought Luz along to keep him company. But the night flying also collected its toll. His circadian rhythm was a disaster as he checked the clock at 2 p.m. on this Saturday afternoon. The phone rang and he pulled the receiver.

"Lakefront statue at 1630."

"Okay."

"Okay this." Dial tone.

Rand took a dive into the pool before he dressed and found his machine parked in the courtyard. The SS had been augmented with a Harley Road King. Rand shifted up the I-10 to West End and cruised Lakeshore Drive along the Pontchartrain to the airport entrance and a stop in front of the granite ménage a trois. Under the adjacent oak was a shape of Jabba. A Mexican wedding shirt gave Rand a positive ID. He dismounted and made his way to his former employer. "Hey Bro." They high-fived, Afro style.

"You look like a ghost."

"Thanks. I haven't seen the sun in four months."

"Never thought I'd see you as a freight dog."

"It's the only job that's come up so far. It ain't so bad."

"Remember the guy who gave you the rating ride on the Lear?"

"Tack Marshall. Of course."

"Course this. He's now on the hiring committee at Eastern."

Rand stared blankly. "Really?"

"He called me to get his nephew rated in the Lear." Wales laughed.

"My application is in at Eastern."

"I know. I asked him to pull it."

"Really?"

"You are on your way to the bigs."

"Hole-E..." Rand looked at him. "Thanks Bro. Thanks."

"You'll be hearing from them soon."

Rand looked to the towering cumulus above. "Wow."

"I told you that you're blessed." Wales popped him on the back. "Where's Luz?"

"Mexico." Rand's thoughts were atomic. "Her dad has cancer."

"I know. I want to make it down there but I got a Federal judge up my rear end."

"Yeah, you've been all over the papers. Why don't you haul ass?"

"Haul this. I have a plan." He looked to Rand. "Have you connected any dots?"

"Just the part about the press. That's all I can see."

"And that's only because you're looking for it." The night's first cool breeze swirled in the oak above as the sun faded into haze. "I have connected some serious dots... perhaps too many."

"Good, we'll have a nice picture to present at your wake." Rand scanned for Shadow. "What's the plan?"

"I've been working with a TV reporter in Baton Rouge."

"Now you're talkin'."

"I've got to go public."

"Definitely. But...Can you get any higher, like a big network guy or 60 Minutes?"

"I've tried. They're not interested. It's not surprising." Brophy's eyes moved constantly toward the road and to the terminal building. "But we are going to start shooting a couple of documentaries. I'm going to ruffle some serious feathers."

"This should be good."

"I'll start slow and hope they will start backing off."

"And if they don't?"

"This fat boy has much to share. We will begin a gander into the Boys running this Contra operation to the oligarchy that seems..."

"Oligarchy?"

"Check a dictionary. A few well-placed dots... say Federal judges, CIA directors, a governor here and there; a few in Congress... can create an oligarchy beyond your wildest imagination. They can loot and bankrupt huge corporations, steal elections, start wars, assassinate anyone..."

"It's this bad?"

"Yes."

"Sounds far-fetched."

"Fetch this. You have seen some of it yourself. You should see all the crooks that have surfaced in the Contra operation and the Mena and Cartel operations. Hell, they have been running all this from the basement of the White House. There's nothing they won't compromise in lining pockets with cash."

"They...? Who is they?"

"A surging group of Ivy League white breads. The VP represents the political front."

"The VP?"

"I'm absolutely positive of it. His people led the entire Nick operation. The press kept asking what the President knew about the money and arms transfers but never focused on what the VP knew. The President didn't know jack, as usual." Wales shook his head. "Then this S&L thing comes up and half his family is pigging out at the trough. I saw a video of his two sons, loading a King Air up with powder. That tape has mysteriously vanished from the face of the earth. Now I find out that these Boys have controlled the CIA since the inception. Hell, the VP was the director. They are becoming unstoppable, invincible."

"So what can we do?"

"Remember the test and the game we talked about out west?"

"Of course."

"Truth is the answer. Tell the truth and the rest will take care of itself."

"Sounds easy enough."

"And the truth remains... that you are blessed." He handed Rand a FAA form.

"What's this?" Rand noticed his name written in the transfer of ownership line. "What is this?"

"I'm giving you the jet."

"The Lear? What the... why?" Rand's face blushed red.

"Because you know how to fly her and... the IRS has already taken the Seneca and the Mercedes and the house and everything they can get their grimy hands on."

"No shit."

"The transfer was done two months ago and I buried her in a hangar at a faraway airport."

"Where?"

"Don't worry about it now. Let her sit for at least two years. Luz knows where it is."

"Luz?"

"Have you ever read Genesis?"

"Negative."

"In the first chapter, there is mention of light. She is your light. Luz translates to light in Spanish. Don't mess it up." He smiled. "And she is the only child of the richest man in Mexico."

"Luz?"

"Her mother died of Lupus ten years ago and the ranch and jewelry store and a half-billion in cash will all go to her."

"Jewelry store...?"

"But it's not her money and it won't be yours."

Rand had gone numb. "Uhh...why?"

"Because it's God's money." Wales had Rand up against the ropes. "He is giving you all this because He knows that you will handle it."

"Bro, I ain't a Christian."

"Ain't this. I don't want to be lumped into that title either. Just read the Bible and do what it says."

"Sounds easy." Rand smiled. "What does it say?"

"Have you read any of the scripture?"

"Uh, negative...just the stuff that was read to me at church."

"Follow Christ. That's all He ever asked. Just to follow Him. It will come naturally after you make the change." Wales touched Rand's arm. "I ask you again: What have you done to get here... to get light from that sky?" He motioned upward.

"Nothin'."

"Will you pray with me?"

"Uhhh. Sure."

Wales had no idea what he was about to say. "Dear Lord, open these eyes to the truth, let them read the written word and lead him to the light. The book of Luke is a starting point for the unsure." Wales opened his eyes. Nothing more came to him. He looked down. "In your name, we give the glory. Amen."

Rand looked over to Jabba. "Do you really believe that someone is watching over you?"

"Yes." Wales pulled an index card that was ripped in half from his shirt pocket and handed it to Rand.

The Truth will set you free. "What's this?"

"A line for the tombstone."

"Whose?"

"Mine."

From a payphone two blocks from his White House basement, John Cathey realized that the Cartel just weren't paying close enough attention to the legal proceedings to their north. His call was received in the mountaintop palace overlooking the smaller hills of Medellin. "For your information, Mr. Brophy "El Gordo" Wales is residing in Baton Rouge, Louisiana. He has been ordered to be there every night at six p.m. by a U.S. Federal judge. Would you like the address?"

"Indeed I would." Mr. Vilez found an ink pen in the holder next to the gorilla's hand ashtray. He smiled wryly as he took down the address on Airline Highway.

23. Silver Wing

The Eastern Airlines logo on his blue-and-white ticket envelope was an artist's adaptation of a flying falcon. Rand Chapman sat at gate C7 at Moisant as the silver 727 turned toward the gate. The whine of jet engines died soon after the plane came to a smooth stop. He could only imagine what it would be like to fly such a jet around the world for the next thirty-five years.

He looked over his application again. Nearly 4,000 hours logged, a type rating in the Lear. He had the highest rating the FAA could issue, the Airline Transport Rating. His hands sweated slightly when he looked over the education section of the application. This, he knew, would be the tricky part. Rand formulated his answer to the obvious question. Turn the train around. He would talk about the rough days on the oil rigs, the endless nights of pulling five miles of drilling pipe out of the earth and the thousands of problems they encountered as a crew. He would elaborate on the fact that failure was not an option. That even if the pipe broke in half two miles below the ocean floor, they had to find a way to retrieve and repair it, while anticipating the next inevitable problem. As for the social sciences, he would talk about the hundreds of people he came to know. Rand Chapman has an education. He let out a sigh.

A red-headed stewardess pointed Rand to his seat at 1A. He stowed his carry-on in the overhead and returned the smile as he sat down. Her glow announced that she was one of the many new hires, obviously happy to be employed by one of the world's greatest airlines. As the economy passengers filed by to the rear seats, she made her way over to Rand. "I see you're going for an interview."

"Yes ma'am." Rand wondered if the interviewers would ask her anything about what she might see in him. He quickly discarded the thought as absurd.

"Well, good luck." She touched his arm lightly. "This is a great time to get hired. I hear there will be at least 400 more pilots added to the seniority list this year. And you could be one of the first." She glanced toward the cockpit. "We were just talking about that coming over from Atlanta."

Rand's heart pumped. "Yeah, it would be great if they hire me." Dimmed overhead lights were shaded behind a panel. Rand inhaled the beauty of the world's most successful jetliner. Dean Martin sang More over constant hiss of overhead eyeball vents. Rand looked around at the large leather seats. He and a business suit were the only ones in this section. "So this is First Class."

"Yes sir. Well, what can I get you?" She studied the young face, happy to see new blood enter the older pilot group.

"How 'bout a Coke?"

"Hey, I'm serving a nice dinner on the way to Miami. I'm talking about a drink-drink. Not sodie...pop." She touched his arm again.

But... "Yeah, but I have a physical in the morning."

She looked him up and down. "I can tell you right now, you aren't going to have a problem with the physical." She squeezed his bicep.

"Not today." He smiled convincingly. "A coke is all I need."

"You got it, my man." She turned toward the galley and Rand checked her trailer. He took a long draw through his nose and pushed his head against the seat of comfort. This… wouldn't be hard to take. He felt like he'd been here a thousand years before.

The plane pushed back and taxied out to Runway One before the captain set the throttles to the takeoff setting. The Boeing roared down the runway and completed a slow rotation as three Pratt and Whitneys launched the classic jet into the darkening skies over the Big Easy. Rand turned his head to watch Kenner whisk beneath and looked west as they ascended over the Pontchartrain. His eyes locked onto the setting sun toward Baton Rouge and as the plane began to bank south, the pine forest of the north shore became visible. He recognized the Tchefuncte and the field at Abita carved within the trees. He spotted the state hospital. Through haze over the lake, he saw the south shore return to the forward section of his oval-shaped window.

Rand felt the captain lower the nose at 10,000 feet and heard the jet accelerate. Through his window he saw, in the dim twilight, Lakefront Airport slide beneath. He pictured faces of all the people he had come to know and love there. They were all with him. The silver swept-wing slowly covered the field behind him. Good bye, old friend.

Epilogue

The Answer

On a dark Louisiana night, before flight simulators were widely used, a four-engine Delta DC-8 was practicing approaches and landings at Moisant field in Kenner with the number one and two engines at idle to simulate a dual engine failure. The captain under training had pulled the remaining engines on the right wing to idle as he found himself high on the VASI lights. The plane descended faster than expected and he was forced to apply nearly maximum power to three and four. The nose began to rise as yaw overcame the self-inflicted jet. As the airspeed disappeared, the nose fell and didn't stop until it reached the third floor of the Moisant Hilton. Fire engulfed each of the hotel's rooms, filled with overnight guests. The accident dramatically marked the need for simulators in the airline industry.

Twenty years later, a Southwest 737 from Houston safely landed on Runway One with fifty passengers, including Rafael Salazar and Bernardo Vasquez. The men crossed Airline Highway with duffle bags over shoulders and checked into the sparkling lobby of the rebuilt Airport Hilton. They had flown Mexicana from Medellin to Mexico City to Matamoros, where they had crossed the border on foot and hitchhiked to the Harlingen, Texas airport. There, they had found their way to the Southwest ticket counter.

Vasquez paid cash for a room. An hour later, the men entered the hotel's restaurant to meet Jaime Cruz, who had arrived a day earlier from Miami. Cruz gave them the keys to a Buick Skylark parked in the lot. In the trunk was an Ingram Mac-10 machine gun that fired .45 caliber bullets at a rate of fifteen rounds per second. Cruz had test-fired the weapon a week earlier out on Alligator Alley over the Everglades before packing it tightly with the ammo and driving across Florida, Alabama, Mississippi and into Louisiana on I-10. He had waited patiently for the remaining accomplices to arrive. Now, with his mission complete, he jumped the 7 p.m. Whisperjet to Miami.

The next day, Vasquez and Salazar drove over to Baton Rouge, where they checked into the luxurious Jay Motel. They paid $31.92 in cash for two rooms. Before leaving Kenner they had visited Anthony's, a small clothing store. Vasquez bought two identical raincoats and used them to cover the goods in the trunk before heading over to Baton Rouge.

The Jay offered few amenities. But it did have a fabulous view of industrial Airline Highway. It also had a spectacular view of the parking lot at the Salvation Army halfway house just a few hundred yards south. Salazar and Vasquez watched from their room as a white Cadillac backed into a spot at 6 p.m. sharp. A big dark-haired man hurried to the side door and the Fleetwood remained in the lot all night. Salazar set an alarm for five a.m. to confirm that his target departed, on schedule, at sunrise.

Their target was already under fierce attack. Immediately after Valore's sentencing, bureaucrats began to barrage Brophy Wales with an infinite supply of legal weapons. The Internal Revenue Service led the charge. The IRS used Wales's own sworn testimony to slap a lien on his property of $29,487,000. Wales had spent half of the last six months fighting for the government with testimony that closed three streams of smuggling and convicted seven major traffickers. The other half was spent fighting the faceless junkyard dogs of the IRS. Ernest Jacobs had been told in no uncertain terms that his career was over if he spoke to Wales again.

The confiscation of his property was in full motion. The Fat Lady was gone, along with the helicopter, two boats and two Senecas. The IRS had taken all the family's furniture, except for the kitchen table and the beds. Inside their empty house, Debbie Wales studied the latest court order from the Feds.

After another fruitless day attempting to prove that some of his wealth was legally earned, Brophy Wales left the echoes of his bare hardwood floors at five-thirty p.m. With his Mercedes confiscated, he headed for the Salvation Army in the white Fleetwood he had borrowed from his father.

At five-fifty, Vasquez backed the Buick three feet from the donation drop box in the parking lot of the Salvation Army. His donation was wrapped in two black raincoats. He laid them just inside the red doors of the box and moseyed around the corner as Salazar casually strolled across from the Jay into the parking lot. He fished for a Marlboro and lit it as he watched the Cadillac enter the lot.

Brophy Wales eased the Fleetwood past a gray Buick and backed into a spot thirty feet from the door of the Salvation Army, ten feet from the donation drop boxes. He spotted a skinny man standing alone next to the boxes smoking a cigarette, but he was empty-handed. The man did not seem to notice him until Wales shut down his engine. Wales knew that his goose was cooked when he saw the man retrieve and open a package from the box. It was now obvious that the man was Colombian. Wales smiled grimly with the realization that the insurmountable fight was over. Ironically, he admired his assassin's technique. The Colombian dropped the raincoats quickly to the ground, exposing the lethal Mac 10. Wales pictured Valore. As a further condition to your sentence, Mr. Wales... Salazar leveled the barrel with a silencer screwed to the end as Wales held his smile.

His natural reaction was to hold hands up to his head for the onslaught. The first six rounds blew out the driver's-side window and pierced the heavy door before exiting the car without touching Wales. Two bullets lodged in a portable sign over a hundred feet away. The next entered Wales's head just behind the ear lobe, making a one-centimeter oval on the surface before penetrating the cerebrum, severing the brain stem and exiting into dusk air. The remaining rounds were overkill. Two more hit and shattered his left arm and two ribs. The fifteenth bullet ripped through his chest as glass from the first bullet still bounced on the asphalt below. Except for crisp snick-snick sounds that emitted from the silenced Mac 10, the assassination was relatively peaceful.

Salazar walked quickly to the Buick and wheeled onto Airline Highway where he picked up Vasquez at the next corner. They proceeded back to Moisant while darkness blanketed this side of the planet. The assassins laughed at their apparent success until they were miraculously caught by the FBI boarding the 7 p.m. Whisperjet to Miami.

Brophy Wales slumped over and lay bleeding on the front seat of his father's car. Three holes blasted clean through his head left red furrows in his scalp. The photographic mind, quick wit, sharp tongue and perpetual smile of confidence had been vanquished in an instant. His soul lifted from the bubble into bright light. Tomorrow, the engraver would begin on his tombstone with the phrase in the pocket of the bloody Mexican wedding shirt.

Believe this... Yes. He answered.